# TROLLOPE CENTENARY ESSAYS

*Also by John Halperin*

The Language of Meditation
Egoism and Self-Discovery in the Victorian Novel
Trollope and Politics
Gissing: A Life in Books
The Theory of the Novel *(editor)*
Jane Austen: Bicentenary Essays *(editor)*
Henry James: *The Golden Bowl (editor)*
George Gissing: *Denzil Quarrier (editor)*
Anthony Trollope: *Sir Harry Hotspur of
Humblethwaite (editor)*
Anthony Trollope: *Lord Palmerston (editor)*

# TROLLOPE
# CENTENARY ESSAYS

Edited by
## John Halperin

St. Martin's Press    New York

Printed in Hong Kong
First published in the United States of America in 1982

ISBN 0–312–81894–7

---

**Library of Congress Cataloging in Publication Data**

Main entry under title:

Trollope centenary essays.

Includes bibliographical references and index.
1. Trollope, Anthony, 1815–1882 – Addresses,
essays, lectures.    2. Novelists, English – 19th
century – Biography – Addresses, essays, lectures.
I. Halperin, John, 1941–
PR5686.T7          1982    823'.8 [B]        81–21326
ISBN 0–312–81894–7                            AACR2

---

In memoriam

**Charles Percy Snow**
1905 – 1980

# Contents

*Notes on the Contributors*                                        viii
*Introduction*   John Halperin                                        x

*Lana Medicata Fuco:* Trollope's Classicism   *Robert Tracy*         1

Trollope the Traveller   *Asa Briggs*                               24

Trollope and Ireland   *Janet Egleson Dunleavy*                     53

Trollope's Country Estates   *Juliet McMaster*                      70

Trollope's Idea of the Gentleman   *Arthur Pollard*                 86

Trollope's Dialogue   *Robert M. Polhemus*                          95

Trollope Revises Trollop   *Andrew Wright*                         109

Trollope's *Autobiography*   *A. L. Rowse*                         134

Trollope the Person   *N. John Hall*                              146

*Index*                                                            182

# Notes on the Contributors

**Asa Briggs** (Lord Briggs) is Provost of Worcester College, Oxford, and Chancellor of the Open University. His many previous publications include *Victorian Cities*, *The Nineteenth Century* (editor), *The History of Broadcasting in the United Kingdom* and *Iron Bridge to Crystal Palace: Impact and Images of the Industrial Revolution*.

**Janet Egleson Dunleavy** is Professor of English at the University of Wisconsin, Milwaukee. Her publications include *George Moore: The Artist's Vision, The Storyteller's Art* and (with her husband, Gareth W. Dunleavy) *The O'Conor Papers*. From 1971 to 1979 she edited the *American Committee for Irish Studies Newsletter*. She is currently working on a study of Trollope's Irish novels, a study of the manuscript revisions of Mary Lavin, and (with her husband) a biography of Douglas Hyde.

**N. John Hall** is Professor of English at Bronx Community College and the Graduate Center, City University of New York. His many publications include an edition of Trollope's *The New Zealander*; *Salmagundi: Byron, Allegra, and the Trollope Family*; *Trollope and His Illustrators*; *The Trollope Critics* (editor); and *The Letters of Anthony Trollope* (editor). He is at present writing a biography of Trollope.

**John Halperin** is Professor of English at the University of Southern California. He has been a Fellow of Wolfson College, Oxford, of the Rockefeller Foundation, and of the American Philosophical Society. In 1978–9 he was a Guggenheim Fellow. Among his many publications are two books on the Victorian novel; the highly acclaimed *Trollope and Politics*; and, most recently, *Gissing: A Life in Books*, a critical biography. He has edited volumes of essays on novel theory and on Jane Austen, and works by Trollope, Gissing and Henry James. He is currently writing a life of Jane Austen.

**Juliet McMaster** is Professor of English at the University of Alberta, and a Fellow of the Royal Society of Canada. She is the author of *Thackeray: The Major Novels, Jane Austen on Love, Trollope's Palliser Novels* and (with R. D. McMaster) *The Novel from Sterne to James*.

**Robert M. Polhemus** is Professor of English at Stanford University. He is the author of the influential book *The Changing World of Anthony Trollope* and also *Comic Faith: The Great Tradition from Austen to Joyce*. The recipient of a Guggenheim Fellowship (1980/81), he is currently working on a study of love in nineteenth-century British fiction.

**Arthur Pollard** is Professor of English at the University of Hull. He has written on several Victorian novelists, including full-length studies of Mrs Gaskell and of Trollope, and has edited the letters of the former (with J. A. V. Chapple) and a literary history of the period. He is particularly interested in the literary representation of social and cultural values in the nineteenth century.

**A. L. Rowse** is an Emeritus Fellow of All Souls College, Oxford, and a Fellow of the British Academy. He has spent most of his working life at Oxford, teaching and researching the Tudor period, in particular the Elizabethan age. He has published his collected poems, several volumes of essays and autobiography as well as many historical works.

**Robert Tracy** is Professor of English at the University of California, Berkeley. He was a Guggenheim Fellow (1981/82) and recently he spent a year as Kathryn W. Davis Professor of Slavic Studies at Wellesley College. He has edited Trollope's *The Way We Live Now* and is the author of the widely praised *Trollope's Later Novels*. He has translated *Kamen'* (*Stone*) by Osip Mandelstam.

**Andrew Wright** is Professor of English at the University of California, San Diego. Presently he is serving for two years as Director of the University of California Study Center for the United Kingdom and Ireland, based in London. He has published full-length studies of Fielding, of Blake, of Jane Austen, of Trollope and of Joyce Cary.

# Introduction

## JOHN HALPERIN

Anthony Trollope ceased to be read for thirty years because he confessed that he wrote at regular hours and took care to get the best price he could for his work.

Somerset Maugham, *The Summing Up*

In 1958 Bradford A. Booth, in a summary discussion, referred to 'the chaos of criticism' in Trollope studies in these terms: 'I know nothing in literary history to match the divided opinions on Trollope's novels . . . among [the] forty-seven novels there are only a handful that someone has not called his best . . . On the other hand, there is the widest possible divergence of opinion on a single title. If there is someone to declare that a given novel is certainly Trollope's best, there is someone to retort that it is without the slightest doubt his worst.'[1]

A quarter-century later there is little more that we can be certain of as far as Trollope's many books are concerned – except for one important, one over-riding thing. Gordon Ray has said it: 'Trollope was a great, truthful, varied artist . . . who left behind him more novels of lasting value than any other writer in English.'[2] While readers may disagree about their favourite or least admired novels among Trollope's productions, on one thing at least it would seem there is no disagreement at all: Trollope's indisputably major status on the roll of the great, the pre-eminent, English novelists.

Evidence of academic interest does not make this so, for academic interest, like other kinds, is fickle. But a continuing readership is something else, something transcending the sort of disputation to which Booth refers. Trollope's works have attracted an ever-widening audience as the years (especially the last fifty) have passed. Just now the critical interest is there as well.

More has been published during the past few years on Trollope than on Dickens or George Eliot or Thackeray. In terms of scholarly output alone, only Hardy among the Victorian novelists has kept pace with Trollope.

A perusal of Trollope-related volumes published during the years 1977–83 renders up the following list (I omit articles):

*1977*
John Halperin, *Trollope and Politics: A Study of the Pallisers and Others*
James R. Kincaid, *The Novels of Anthony Trollope*

*1978*
P. D. Edwards, *Anthony Trollope: His Art and Scope*
Johanna Johnston, *The Life, Manners, and Travels of Fanny Trollope*
John Charles Olmsted and Jeffrey Welch (eds), *The Reputation of Trollope: An Annotated Bibliography 1925–1975*
Arthur Pollard, *Anthony Trollope*
R. C. Terry, *Anthony Trollope: The Artist in Hiding*
Robert Tracy, *Trollope's Later Novels*

*1979*
Betty Jane Breyer (ed.), *Anthony Trollope: The Christmas Stories*
Helen Heineman, *Mrs Trollope: The Triumphant Feminine in the Ninteenth Century*
Juliet McMaster, *Trollope's Palliser Novels: Theme and Pattern*

*1980*
Tony Bareham (ed.), *Anthony Trollope* (new essays)
N. John Hall, *Trollope and his Illustrators*
Geoffrey Harvey, *The Art of Anthony Trollope*
Walter C. Kendrick, *The Novel-Machine: The Theory and Fiction of Anthony Trollope*

*1981*
N. John Hall (ed.), *The Trollope Critics* (reprinted series)
Coral Lansbury, *The Reasonable Man: Trollope's Legal Fictions*
B. J. S. Breyer (ed.), *Anthony Trollope: The Complete Short Stories* (forty-two stories to be published in five volumes; three volumes in print through 1981)
N. John Hall (General Editor), *Selected Works of Anthony Trollope* (thirty-six titles in sixty-two volumes: a facsimile edition)
R. H. Super, *Trollope in the Post Office*

*1982*
Andrew Wright, *Anthony Trollope: Dream and Art*
*Anthony Trollope: The Complete Short Stories* (remaining two volumes; see above)
John Halperin (ed.), *Trollope Centenary Essays* (new essays)
Another collection of new essays on Trollope edited by Arthur Mizener
Shirley Letwin, *The Gentleman in Trollope: Individuality and Moral Conduct*

*1983*
N. John Hall (ed.), *The Letters of Anthony Trollope*, two volumes

The total is ninety volumes – an astounding figure for a six-year period.

Trollope has become the favourite English novelist of a great many people. His literary reputation, however, has had a chequered history. His first novel, *The Macdermots of Ballycloran*, written in 1845 when he was in his thirtieth year, was published in 1847. The reviewer in the *Critic* assumed the new author was a young lad: 'if he have already reached maturity of years, his case is hopeless'.[3] After *The Macdermots* came *The Kellys and the O'Kellys* (1848) and *La Vendée* (1850). All were failures with the public, though *The O'Kellys* is a passable novel. In 1852 Trollope began to write *The Warden*; it came out in 1855. Now forty, he commenced at last to enjoy some critical success. But it was not *The Warden* and its successor *Barchester Towers* (1857) that established his reputation, though this is the popular idea. The appearance of *Framley Parsonage* in the widely read *Cornhill* (under Thackeray's editorship) in 1860–1 made Trollope an instant public favourite – he was by then closer to fifty than forty.

His greatest years of popularity were those from the early 1860s to the early 1870s. By 1863 the *National Review* could declare, truthfully, that Trollope had become 'almost a national institution'[4] (between *The Warden* in 1855 and *Framley Parsonage* in 1860–1 Trollope had published *Barchester Towers*, *The Three Clerks*, *Doctor Thorne*, *The Bertrams*, *The West Indies and the Spanish Main* and *Castle Richmond*). The *National Review* article went on:

So great is [Trollope's] popularity; so familiar are his chief characters to his countrymen, so wide-spread is the interest felt about his tales, that they . . . form part of the common stock-in-trade with which the social commerce of the day is carried on . . . [There are] imaginary personages on Mr Trollope's canvas with whom every well-informed member of the community is expected to have at least a speaking acquaintance.[5]

Between 1862 and 1874 Trollope's annual income averaged £4500 – high indeed. Towards the end of his career his income diminished, but he continued to be widely read. His popularity extended to America, France and Germany, among other places.

In the two decades following his death in 1882 and the publication of his *Autobiography* in 1883 (it was written in 1875–6), demand for his books virtually disappeared. This has often been attributed to Trollope's admission in the *Autobiography* that he wrote for money and thought of himself as just another tradesman providing a product at a price for public consumption. The general public tends to know little about art; it is often thought of as being produced in a highly rarefied atmosphere – in a garret, amidst starving infants and a wife who coughs. To those who believe this sort of thing, the *Autobiography* would be shocking. It hurt Trollope's immediate posterity; there is little doubt about that. But even without its publication, as Donald Smalley has pointed out, it is more than likely that Trollope's work would have suffered neglect: 'A new generation with new predilections found the scenes and characters of Trollope too remote for the impact of immediacy and too near for possessing the charm of the remote.'[6] We should know by now that every generation puts back upon the shelf the books its fathers and grandfathers venerated – it is the way of all flesh. And when one had written as much as Trollope and been as popular, the reaction is likely to be more violent when it comes – as indeed it had come earlier in the century against the works of Byron, Scott, Tennyson and Dickens. And there is another factor. The 1890s witnessed a romantic revival of sorts, with renewed public interest in plot and escapist adventure (this was the age of Haggard, Stevenson and Kipling) and considerably less in character, in psychological realism. The nineties marked the nadir of George Eliot's reputation – and the resurrection of Disraeli's. These were Henry James's 'treacherous years'. George Gissing watched in despair as Hall Caine's novels outsold his.

The rest of the Trollope story is better known. After the anti-Victorianism of the war-weary Edwardians and Georgians had gone its way and the builders of the Empire had been dead a while, Trollope's world seemed sufficiently remote to be fascinating once again. Interest in him revived. Several studies appeared in the 1920s. With the publication of Michael Sadleir's *Trollope: A Commentary* in 1927 and his bibliography of Trollope the following year, the race was on. During the Second World War Trollope suddenly became the favourite reading of an English population badly in need of a quieter world to contemplate and into which to disappear, if only for a few hours. Full-length studies of the novelist began to proliferate after the war. In the 1950s and 1960s the revival burgeoned – until, in the 1970s, as I have indicated, the stream became a flood. In a time of moral chaos, the sure, fixed values of an earlier, more self-sufficient age seem soothing, reassuring.

I shall not attempt to say why Trollope speaks to us today with a voice so powerful and unique. Different readers will always hear different voices. Trollope buffs know how compulsively readable he is, how real his people seem, how engaging their predicaments are. For us, as for Trollope himself, the fictional personages are often more interesting than the people we actually meet – more 'real' in the sense in which great art is always more 'realistic' than 'real' life. This is what James meant when he said that Trollope's genius lay in his complete appreciation of the usual. Most readers of fiction want to believe the truth of what they read, and Trollope convinces us of this truth more effectively perhaps than anyone else who has ever written novels (Jane Austen may be the one exception). Trollope's mimetic genius makes a mockery of all the formalist arguments about 'showing' and 'telling': if you want to know what the texture of life was like in the third quarter of the nineteenth century, go to Trollope.

Readers of novels, like spectators at a play, often wish to be able to suspend their disbelief and enter body and soul into the human dramas unfolded before them. It takes a master to make this spiritual exchange possible. If anything is clear now, a hundred years after Trollope's death, it is that he is a master. Posterity is especially lucky that a man with so great a gift was so compulsive a writer: one need never stop reading him.

NOTES

1   Bradford A. Booth, *Anthony Trollope: Aspects of His Life and Art* (Bloomington, Ind. and London, 1958) p. 229.
2   Gordon N. Ray, 'Trollope at Full Length', *Huntington Library Quarterly*, XXXI (1968) 334.
3   See *The Critic* for 1 May 1847, vol. 344.
4   *Anthony Trollope: The Critical Heritage*, ed. Donald Smalley (London and Boston, Mass., 1969). Introduction, p. 4.
5   *National Review*, XVI (Jan. 1863) 28–9.
6   *Critical Heritage*, Introduction, p. 6.

# Lana Medicata Fuco: Trollope's Classicism

## ROBERT TRACY

'. . . They were putting up the hatchment . . . and Master Fred saw that the undertakers had put at the bottom "Resurgam". You know what that means?'

'Oh, yes,' said Frank.

'"I'll come back again"', said the Honourable John, construing the Latin for the benefit of his cousin. '"No", said Fred Hatherly, looking up at the hatchment; "I'm blessed if you do, old gentleman . . . I'll take care of that." So he got up at night, and he got some fellows with him, and they . . . painted out "Resurgam", and they painted into its place, "Requiescat in pace"; which means, you know, "you'd a great deal better stay where you are". Now I call that good . . .'

Frank could not help laughing at the story, especially at his cousin's mode of translating the undertaker's mottoes. . . .

*Doctor Thorne*, ch. 4

Trollope's acquaintance with Latin and Greek began early, with his father as his teacher. 'From my very babyhood . . . I had had to take my place alongside of him as he shaved at six o'clock in the morning,' the novelist tells us in *An Autobiography*, 'and say my early rules from the Latin Grammar, or repeat the Greek alphabet; and was obliged at these early lessons to hold my head inclined towards him, so that in the event of guilty fault, he might be able to pull my hair without stopping his razor or dropping his shaving-brush.[1] Thomas Adolphus Trollope, Anthony's elder brother, recalls a similar early introduction to the *Eton Latin Grammar*, a confusing and badly arranged work originally compiled by the Tudor schoolmaster William Lily, and in general use until the middle of the nineteenth century. Tom was about six when their father began his teaching, and describes how the elder Trollope 'used during the detested Latin lessons to sit . . . so that his hand might be ready to inflict an instantaneous pull of the hair as the *poena* (by no means *pede claudo*) for every blundered concord or false quantity'.[2]

This kind of paternal instruction was not uncommon, as the boyhoods of John Stuart Mill and Tennyson indicate. Thomas Trollope, the father of Anthony and Tom, was a graduate of Winchester College and of New College, Oxford, both founded by William of Wykeham, Bishop of Winchester in the fourteenth century, with the intention that Winchester College would act as a preparatory school for New College. The elder Trollope was eager that his sons should follow in his footsteps, not because he particularly admired classical learning but because he knew that such a course – the acquisition of Latin and Greek – certified a man's status as a gentleman, a necessary prerequisite of a professional career. The ability to quote Latin or Greek, and to understand them when someone else quoted them, was one of the outward signs of a gentleman, implying an education at one of the great public schools and perhaps also at one of the universities, the early gathering places of those who were to rule. The reforms of Thomas Arnold, who became headmaster at Rugby in 1828, assumed that the study of Latin and Greek could be given a moral as well as a social function.

In an essay 'Public Schools', written for the *Fortnightly Review* in 1865, Anthony Trollope quotes with approval from Howard Staunton's *The Great Schools of England* (1865); Staunton concedes the scholarly and educational inadequacies of the public schools, but argues that 'these schools have to be regarded less in themselves, perhaps, than in their relation to a particular fashion of society . . . The great endowed schools are less to be considered as educational agencies, in the intellectual sense, than as social agencies.' And Trollope himself, in words that are somewhat at odds with his account of his own school-days in *An Autobiography*, extends the argument by claiming that the schools enable 'the sons of those among our gentry who are rich, and of those who are comparatively poor, to be educated together, and thus to be welded into one whole, which is the backbone of English public and social life'. Thomas Trollope and his son would have agreed that the public schools educated their students for life by allowing those who were to govern the nation to recognise each other early.

'Whilst there we made our friendships', Anthony writes;

> There we learned to be honest, true, and brave. There we were trained to disregard the softnesses of luxury, and to love the hardihood and dangers of violent exercise. There we became men; and we became men after such a fashion that we are feared or loved, as may be, but always respected, – even though it be in spite of our ignorance . . . few among us do not feel that it has more than compensated for that lack of real instruction of which we all complain.[3]

The passage echoes Squire Brown's meditations in *Tom Brown's School Days* (1857) as he sees Tom off to Rugby: 'Shall I tell him to mind his work, and say he's sent to school to make himself a good scholar? Well, he isn't sent to school for that – at any rate, not for that mainly. I don't care a straw for Greek particles, or the digamma; no more does his mother. What is he sent to school for? . . . If he'll only turn out a brave, helpful, truth-telling Englishman, and a gentleman, and a Christian, that's all I want.'

The elder Trollope's ambitions, combined with his financial problems, led him to propose an unconventional *cursus studiorum* for his sons. Each was destined to be a Foundation Scholar at Winchester, one of the seventy pupils supported by an endowment created by the school's founder. To become a Scholar it was necessary to be nominated by one of the trustees, who filled up vacancies in rotation, a system adopted for Hiram's Hospital in *The Warden*. Thomas Trollope solicited a presentation for each of his sons as each was born. Once promised, however, the place would only be available when the potential Scholar was of age *and* when one of the seventy already in residence departed for one reason or another. To obtain for his sons the benefit of a public school education while they awaited preferment, Thomas Trollope moved his family to Harrow, 'as he had friends among the masters at Harrow, and as the school offered an education almost gratuitous to children living in the parish'.[4] To do so, he rented a local farm at a very high rent – high, Anthony suggests in 'Public Schools', because those who owned land in the parish of Harrow were well aware that they could charge a tenant for the educational benefits his sons would receive.

At Winchester, when the Trollope brothers were there, the school consisted of the seventy Scholars plus 130 fee-paying

'Commoners'. The number of Scholars and their traditional status meant that there was no invidious distinction in favour of the fee-paying boys. Both Trollope brothers attest that all students at Winchester considered themselves equals, and were so treated. But Harrow was different. There fee-paying boys – 'foreigners' – were very much in the majority; their number fluctuated between about 280 and 115 in Anthony Trollope's day, while only a few local boys claimed their free tuition: ten in 1818, seventeen in 1825. The inhabitants of the parish had brought suit in 1809 over what they considered a subversion of the school founder's original intent – again there is an anticipation of *The Warden*. A succession of eighteenth-century headmasters had increased the number of fee-paying pupils from outside the parish, who gradually crowded out the local boys. But the courts upheld the school's right to admit 'foreigners'. Although boys from the parish retained their rights, they were despised by the foreigners, 'received', Anthony writes, 'not on equal terms, because a day-boarder at Harrow in those days was never so received'. His brother confirms this account of miserable exclusion: 'What a Pariah I was . . . a . . . "village boy" . . . one of the very few, who by the term of the founder's will, had any right to be there at all; and was in consequence an object of scorn and contumely on the part of all the *paying* pupils. I was a charity boy.'[5]

Each Trollope son duly entered Harrow as a 'village boy' at the age of seven, Anthony in 1822, but his subsequent academic career was erratic. At the end of three years his tutor, Henry Drury – Thomas Trollope's friend and Byron's Harrow tutor – apparently 'expressed an opinion that' Anthony's 'juvenile career was not proceeding in a satisfactory manner at Harrow', and he was sent 'to a private school at Sunbury' near London 'kept by Arthur Drury', Henry's brother. There, despite his poverty, he 'lived more nearly on terms of equality with other boys than at any other period during my very prolonged school-days'. But at Sunbury he was also accused, with three others, of perpetrating 'some nameless horror', probably an experiment with sex. Trollope was considered the leader 'because I, having come from a public school, might be supposed to be the leader of wickedness!' The incident throws a not unexpected light on the contemporary reputation of Harrow.

In 1827, in accordance with his father's plan, Anthony received his place at Winchester, and spent the next three years there. His brother Tom had preceded him, in 1820, and left in 1828. 'In accordance with the practice of the college, which submits, or did then submit, much of the tuition of the younger boys to the elder', Tom became Anthony's tutor, which made him responsible for such instruction as his younger brother received, emphasised by daily thrashings 'with a big stick'. In 1830, Anthony became a day-boy at Harrow once again, since his chances of a scholarship to New College seemed remote. He remained at Harrow until April 1834, when he ended his formal education. In the summer of 1834 he spent six weeks as a classics teacher at a Brussels school kept by another of the ubiquitous Drurys.

Latin and Greek comprised the entire course of study at Harrow and Winchester – and the other public schools – in Trollope's day. He tells us that he had 'never learned the multiplication table, and had no more idea of the rule of three than of Conic Sections'.[6] At Harrow, Mathematics did not become a compulsory subject until 1837, nor Modern Languages until 1851, and even then not very much time was allotted for these subjects. The exclusive attention given to Latin and Greek did not, however, mean that they were well learned, or well taught; they were not, in fact, taught at all in our sense. The masters' responsibility was not to instruct but to hear recitations and punish failure. Each student was supposed to work through a set passage of Latin or Greek for each recitation period, and to be able first to translate the passage word by word in the word order of the original, occasionally parsing or answering questions about constructions, and then to offer an idiomatic English translation.

Students prepared for recitation periods by studying the assigned passage together, or, as at Winchester, with an older student acting as tutor; at Harrow the masters acted privately as tutors, being directly feed by each pupil's guardian, but not feed for their work with village boys. Students were also expected to write from two to six lines of Latin verse each day, on a theme set by a master, and to recite these verses, which were required to be grammatically and metrically correct. Since masters tended to repeat themselves, the boys knew that themes recurred. Darwin, a year older than Tom Trollope, was at Winchester with him, and recalled that, while the better students wrote their own verses, many depended on 'small, but bulky quartos, the accretions of I know not how many generations of boys; in which almost every possible subject had been made the theme of a verse-task'.[7] The

*Gradus ad Parnassum*, which indicated the metrical quantity of words and phrases and contained synonyms, epithets, and the like, was also used. In *An Autobiography* Trollope suggests that this exercise helped him develop a necessary 'harmony' in his prose style:

> The boy, for instance, who learns with accuracy the prosody of a Sapphic stanza, and has received through his intelligence a knowledge of its parts, will soon tell by his ear whether a Sapphic stanza be or be not correct. Take a girl, endowed with gifts of music, well instructed in her art, with perfect ear, and read to her such a stanza with two words transposed, as, for instance –
>
> *Mercuri, nam te docilis magistro*
> *Movit Amphion* canendo lapides,
> *Tuque, testudo, resonare septem*
> *Callida nervis* –
>
> and she will find no halt in the rhythm. But a schoolboy with none of her musical acquirements or capacities, who has, however, become familiar with the metres of the poet, will at once discover the fault. And so will the writer become familiar with what is harmonious in prose. But, in order that familiarity may serve him in his business, he must so train his ear that he shall be able to weigh the rhythm of every word as it falls from his pen. This, when it has been done for a time . . . will become so habitual to him that he will have appreciated the metrical duration of every syllable before it shall have dared to show itself upon paper.[8]

Finally, students were expected to commit to memory the Latin and Greek texts they read; a passage construed one day was to be recited in the original language on the next. A boy could gradually memorise all of Homer, Virgil and Horace, but he usually forgot one passage while memorising the next. At Harrow, Trollope's friend Charles Merivale recited Virgil's *Eclogues* and *Georgics*, and all of Catullus, Juvenal and Lucan to his tutor in 1824. In 'Public Schools' Trollope lists the *Aeneid*, the Odes of Horace, and four books each of the *Iliad* and the *Odyssey* as items memorised, adding that 'this learning by heart of verses was the great literary feat' at

Winchester; 'Alas me, how easy it is to forget an "Aeneid", and how hard to learn one!' The task was somewhat lightened by repetition – at Winchester, Virgil, Horace and Homer were read through twice during the twelve-year course. Trollope's facility in introducing apposite Latin quotations, especially from Horace, into his fiction undoubtedly stems from this memorisation, as do the frequent classical references of other Victorian writers and orators. Even a careless student retained something – 'Neque amissos colores / lana refert medicata fuco.'[9]

In both 'Public Schools' and *An Autobiography*, Trollope is scornful of the education he received. 'During all the years at Winchester,' he tells us in 'Public Schools', 'I never once underwent any attempt at instruction from any master, either in Latin or Greek, or on any other subject!' At Harrow, 'There was no teaching, – nor was there any possibility that the masters should teach.' He goes on to explain the makeshift tutorial methods at both schools, and the masters' responsibility for 'hearing, and not . . . teaching'. In *An Autobiography* he is more scathing:

> When I left Harrow I was all but nineteen, and I had at first gone there at seven. During the whole of those twelve years no attempt had been made to teach me anything but Latin and Greek, and very little attempt to teach me those languages. I do not remember any lessons either in writing or arithmetic . . . when I think how little I knew of Latin or Greek on leaving Harrow at nineteen, I am astonished at the possibility of such waste of time.

'As much classics as either school gave him he might have acquired in his father's study,' Escott comments, 'if the teacher and the scholar had not come to open war before the course was over.'[10]

Trollope's views about the inadequacies of public school education are borne out by other contemporary critics. 'Boys of average ability and application learnt very little,' wrote Matthew James Higgins ('Jacob Omnium') in 1860, 'and dull or idle boys learnt positively nothing at all.'[11] But the system did not always work as badly as Trollope says it did. We know he was neglected by his school-fellows and resented as a charity pupil by his masters. He admits his own 'resolute idleness and fixed

determination to make no use whatever of the books . . . thrust
upon me, or of the hours' as he sat 'with Lexicon and Gradus
before me'.[12] Charles Merivale, the historian of Rome, and
Cardinal Manning were among Trollope's Harrow contemporaries, and both clearly learned a good deal, though of
course they both later attended universities. But Tom Trollope
remembers that when he went to Oxford from Winchester he had
little work to do: 'the classical lectures were such as I had left a
long way behind me . . . as for a "pass" degree, I was just as
capable of taking it when I left Winchester (with the exception of
logic, and what was called "divinity") as when I did take it'.[13]
Though the pages of *What I Remember* are much more liberally
sprinkled with Latin tags than Anthony's novels, and so suggest a
greater store of classical learning, the two brothers' education was
similar enough to make us sceptical that Anthony learned as little
as he says he did, especially when Tom hints that Anthony's
picture of their childhood circumstances is generally too dark.
Anthony's *Autobiography* is a carefully drawn picture of a self-
made man who triumphed over a neglected and impoverished
childhood to become successful as a civil servant, as a novelist,
and even as a classical scholar, thus winning the right to be the
companion of those who had shunned him in his boyhood. The
book's theme inevitably shapes its treatment of material,
especially in the early chapters.

In keeping with this theme, Trollope announces that in the late
1830s, as a Post Office clerk in London, he 'did learn to read
French and Latin. I made myself very familiar with Horace, and
became acquainted with the works of our own greatest poets.' He
also claims that 'I am now' – 1875–6, when he wrote *An
Autobiography* – 'a fair Latin scholar, – that is to say, I read and
enjoy the Latin classics, and could probably make myself
understood in Latin prose. But the knowledge which I have, I
have acquired since I left school, – no doubt aided much by that
groundwork of the language which will in the process of years
make its way slowly, even through the skin' – a grudging but
probably accurate admission.[14]

As a writer, Trollope's initial attempt at a classical subject came
in 1851, when he wrote his first magazine article, a long review of
volumes I and II of Merivale's *History of the Romans under the Empire*;
the review appeared in the *Dublin University Magazine* in May 1851.
Trollope disagreed with Merivale's views about Julius Caesar:

'Hence arose in my mind a tendency to investigate the character of probably the greatest man who ever lived . . . and also a taste generally for Latin literature, which has been one of the chief delights of my later life.'[15]

This review was followed by a second, also in the *Dublin University Magazine* (July 1856), officially dealing with the next three volumes of Merivale's *History* but in fact a summary of Augustus's career as Merivale recounts it in volumes III and IV. Trollope subsequently turned to classical subjects at intervals, as in his fiction he returned to Irish themes from time to time. In 1870 he prepared a retelling of Caesar's *Commentaries (De Bello Gallico* and *De Bello Civili)* for inclusion in a series called 'Ancient Classics for English Readers':

I began by reading through the Commentaries twice, which I did without any assistance either by translation or English notes. Latin was not so familiar to me then as it has since become, – for from that date I have almost daily spent an hour with some Latin author, and on many days many hours. After the reading of what my author had left behind him, I fell into the reading of what others had written about him, in Latin, in English, and even in French . . . I was most anxious, in thus soaring out of my own peculiar line, not to disgrace myself. I do not think that I did disgrace myself. Perhaps I was anxious for something more. . . .

The book I think to be a good little book. It is readable by all, old or young, and it gives, I believe accurately, both an account of Caesar's Commentaries . . . and the chief circumstances of the great Roman's life. A well-educated girl who had read it and remembered it would perhaps know as much about Caesar and his writings as she need know.

Trollope was disappointed that no one praised his efforts, and that a friend referred to it as his 'comic Caesar'. 'Mr Trollope's *Caesar* I cannot read without laughing,' wrote Mrs Oliphant in 1874, 'it is so like Johnny Eames' – a recollection, perhaps, of Johnny's plan, in *The Last Chronicle of Barset*, to solace his disappointed love with the study of Greek. Trollope suggests that he was resented because of his amateur standing, and ironically quotes Pliny's 'Ne sutor ultra crepidam.'[16]

Trollope became interested in Cicero during his investigations of Caesar's career. He came to admire the great orator as one who had combined public service and literature, as he himself had done, and as an honest man who had done his best to defend the republic he was pledged to serve against a series of noble but dishonest opportunists: Catiline, Caesar, Antony, Augustus. In 1877 he published two essays in the *Fortnightly Review*, 'Cicero as a Politician' (1 Apr.) and 'Cicero as a Man of Letters' (1 Sep.) – preliminary studies for his two-volume *Life of Cicero* (1880).

These four essays and two books represent Trollope's formal contribution to classical scholarship and his effort to prove to himself and to his contemporaries – especially those who had known him as incapable of learning his lessons or winning prizes at Harrow and Winchester – that he could succeed and even excel intellectually as well as economically and socially. They are part of his campaign to justify, and at the same time escape from, his younger self.

Trollope's formal scholarship is historical rather than literary, though the *Commentaries* and Cicero's speeches and philosophical essays have been accepted as literature, at least by teachers of Latin. Trollope's initial interest was in the careers of Julius Caesar, Augustus and Cicero, in their writings as evidence for their lives, especially their political lives, and in their ideas about how one should live – about behaviour, especially political and social behaviour, the chief concern of his novels.

The two reviews of Merivale's *History* spend a good deal of time retelling the careers of Caesar, Pompey and Augustus, but Trollope's own attitude emerges clearly. Caesar was 'probably the greatest man who ever lived', but hardly a good man. He was rather an instrument of Providence for destroying the Roman Republic and initiating the Empire, a necessary stage in 'the gradual amelioration of the human race'. British and all European civilisation derives from Rome's Imperial achievement, which made the Empire 'the common parent of modern nations'. Caesar's career was permitted to bring this about:

> The human mind cannot conceive that the Creator would allow the career of an Alexander or a Caesar, a Frederick or a Napoleon, if the aggrandisement of a man, or a nation, were to be the sole result of such violence and bloodshed; but when history shows us that the civilisation of nations can be traced to the ambition of individuals, she teaches us her most useful

lesson, explains to us why heaven permits the horrors of war, and vindicates the ways of God to man.[17]

Trollope's theory of history is both progressive and providential, and emphasises his sense that his own civilisation is a continuation of classical civilisation. When he wrote, classical and Biblical scholars were beginning to question the assumption that the ancient world could be understood and evaluated by projecting contemporary values back upon its men and events and that classical writings offered valid patterns of heroic or honourable behaviour. But Trollope spurned revisionist theories. In his introduction to Caesar's *Commentaries*, he briefly summarises the 'facts' that everyone knows about Caesar – that he said, 'Veni, vidi, vici', that he crossed the Rubicon, and adds that 'in the following . . . memoir . . . no effort shall be made, – as has been so frequently and so painfully done for us in late years, – to upset the teachings of our youth, and to prove that the old lessons were wrong. They were all fairly accurate . . .'[18]

In all his writings on classical topics, Trollope consistently suggests analogies between the Roman world and his own. Caesar's activities are as important to nineteenth-century Englishmen as the activities of Napoleon or Bismarck. But Trollope distinguished between Caesar's importance as the creator of modern Europe and the dangerous tendency to take him as a model and as a justification for dictatorship, a tendency found in Carlyle's *On Heroes, Hero-Worship, and the Heroic in History* (1841) and in 'that most futile book' *Histoire de Jules César* (1865–9) by Napoleon III – a work which defended Caesar's, and by implication Napoleon I's and Napoleon III's, overthrow of governments they were pledged to defend, and hinted at parallels between Napoleon III and Augustus. Trollope criticised Merivale for being 'too prone to have a hero . . . The history of the Romans is a higher theme than the life of Caesar.'[19] Trollope would have agreed with Mill, who in *On Liberty* (1859) condemned 'the sort of "hero-worship" which applauds the strong man of genius for forcibly seizing on the government of the world and making it do his bidding'. His treatment of Melmotte, that 'financial Napoleon' of *The Way We Live Now*, is Trollope's fullest treatment of Caesarism and the specious arguments used to justify it; it develops directly out of his comments on Merivale's *History*, while characteristically treating Caesarism as a nineteenth-century problem.[20]

Trollope admired Cicero because he was unlike such ruthless opportunists as Julius Caesar and Augustus, who felt

> none of those inward, flutterings of the heart, doubtful aspirations, human longings, sharp sympathies, dreams of something better than this world, fears of something worse, which make Cicero so like a well-bred polished gentleman of the present day. It is because he was so little like a Roman that he is of all the Romans the most attractive.[21]

Though Trollope defends Pompey against Merivale's strictures, he was not really interested in any other Roman statesman, for only Caesar and Augustus still affected modern life, as much so as Pitt or Mirabeau or Danton. But Cicero alone was humanly accessible. Trollope became fascinated by Cicero when he reviewed Merivale's *History*, but had had to remove 'an apology for the character of Cicero which was found to be too long as an episode' from his review. During the next thirty years, Trollope became less sure that Caesar's importance made him great. 'There are some of us who think that such a man, let him be ever so great – let him be ever so just . . . will in the end do more harm than good.'[22] Cicero became Trollope's hero, partly because his letters made his personality more intimately known than was possible with other Greek and Roman statesmen, and consequently made him seem contemporary; and partly because Trollope projected aspects of his own personality – and the social popularity he had always wanted – onto Cicero. 'What a man he would have been for London life!' Trollope exclaims.

> How he would have enjoyed his club, picking up the news of the day from all lips, while he seemed to give it to all ears. How popular he would have been at the Carlton, and how men would have listened to him while every great or little crisis was discussed! How supreme he would have sat on the Treasury bench. . . . How crowded would have been his rack with invitations to dinner! . . . How the pages of the magazines would have run over with little essays from his pen![23]

But there are objective reasons for Trollope's fellow-feeling. He describes *De Officiis* as 'the most perfect of' Cicero's works, 'an essay in which he instructs his son as to the way in which a man should endeavour to live so as to be a gentleman'. Trollope's novels offer the same course of instruction. *De Officiis* presents a practical philosophy for getting on honourably in the world, a system of practical ethics which is echoed and explored in Trollope's novels. Cicero recognises the inevitable complexity of moral choice, and the necessity of weighing relative benefits and evils.[24] And Cicero's *Pro Archia* defends literature in terms that Trollope repeats in his various defences of novels and novel-reading – that moral writers celebrate virtuous men, and by doing so instruct their readers and offer them patterns to emulate.

Trollope never learned or relearned Greek in adulthood, as he had relearned Latin, and his interest in Greek history and literature is comparatively slight; his library contained works of Caesar, Cicero and Horace, and nineteen volumes of 'Ancient Classics for English Readers', but apparently no Greek texts. He did, however, consider himself competent to advise Blackwood about the advisability of publishing Du Cane's translation of the *Odyssey*.[25] He considered Greek culture and Greek history less important than their Latin equivalents because they were less clearly connected with his own world, less clearly still affecting modern life. 'Interested as the scholar, or the reader of general literature, may be in the great deeds of the heroes of Greece, and in the burning words of Greek orators, it is almost impossible . . . to connect by any intimate and thoroughly-trusted link the fortunes of Athens, or Sparta, or Macedonia, with our own times and our own position', Trollope declares in his introduction to Caesar's *Commentaries*: '. . . Herodotus is so mythic that what delight we have in his writings comes in a very slight degree from any desire on our part to form a continuous chain from the days of which he wrote down to our own.'

Reviewing Trollope's *Clergymen of the Church of England*, Henry Alford, Dean of Canterbury, a Greek New Testament scholar and editor of the *Contemporary Review*, surmised that 'Mr Trollope's acquaintance with Greek is of the very slightest.' Trollope records the charge in *An Autobiography* without quite denying it: 'That charge has been made not unfrequently by those who have felt themselves strong in that pride-producing language. It is much to read Greek with ease, but it is not disgraceful to be unable to do so. To pretend to be able to read it without being able, – that is disgraceful.'[26] Later a *Spectator* review of *Cicero* took Trollope to task for mistranscribing the Greek of a passage from Dio Cassius's *Roman History*, and calling the passage 'so foul-mouthed that it can be only inserted under the veil of its own language'.[27] In fact, Trollope's transcription of the Greek is correct save for two letters in a single word, and since Dio accuses Cicero of pandering for his own wife and committing incest with his own daughter, Trollope's decision seems valid by Victorian standards.

There are no Greek tags, as far as I can remember, in Trollope's novels, and Mr Crawley and his two daughters are the only characters whose knowledge of Greek is important, in contrast to all those who can recognise or translate a quotation in Latin. Crawley's Greek, like his Hebrew, is one more thing that sets him apart from other men, even other clergymen, and tempts him into pride. But he shares Trollope's sense that classical literature, like ancient history, can offer a commentary on modern life. If history comments on public life, literature comments on private life, as when Crawley compares himself to the blinded Polyphemus and to Milton's Samson. 'The same story is always coming up', he tells his daughter. 'We have it in various versions, because it is so true to life.' His daughters have learned Greek because there is nothing else for them to do at home, and because their father shares Thomas Trollope's eagerness to instruct his children. There is a subtle touch – Crawley urges the girls to compete with one another in learning the *Antigone* by heart, and tells them their motto should be 'Always to be best; – always to be in advance of others.' Hippolochos gave his son Glaukos the same advice (*Iliad* VI. 208); it is just the kind of Homeric echo Crawley would invoke. The reference to the *Antigone* recalls the two sisters of that play, affected by their father's disgrace, and Antigone's role as her father's guide and support in *Oedipus at Colonus*. And, when Mrs Proudie sends Mr Thumble to take over Crawley's parish, Crawley refers to him as 'one of the angels of the church', aware that Thumble is too ignorant to know that *angelos* in Greek means 'messenger'. As Thumble retires in defeat, Crawley turns to Aeschylus's *Seven against Thebes*, a play about repelling an invading usurper, 'reading out, or rather saying by rote . . . great passages from some chorus . . . with great energy'.[28]

In his fiction, Trollope usually alludes to or quotes from classical poetry rather than from Caesar or Cicero. In his early novels allusions are more frequent than quotations, and are often intended to be facetious. In *The Warden*, Eleanor Harding is called an Iphigenia, to be sacrificed for her father's sake, and there is some heavy-footed fun with Tom Towers of the 'Jupiter', his thunderbolts and his Olympus (this sort of thing died slowly – Meredith repeats it thirty years later in *Diana of the Crossways*, with his Mr Tonans). Mr Quiverful is a 'clerical Priam' and John Bold is the 'Barchester Brutus'. In *Barchester Towers*, the Archdeacon and Bishop Proudie are compared to Venus and Juno competing for the apple (the diocese). Mrs Proudie is Achilles, armed for battle, and Medea, ready to eat Mr Slope as 'they did with their captives in her country'. The Signora invokes Dido. Most of these references are in the spirit of mock heroic, as in the mock-epic simile used when Mrs Proudie's gown is ripped:

So, when a granite battery is raised, excellent to the eyes of warfaring men, is its strength and symmetry admired. . . . But, anon, a small spark is applied to the treacherous fusee – a cloud of dust arises to the heavens. . . . As Juno may have looked at Paris on Mount Ida, so did Mrs Proudie look on Ethelbert Stanhope when he pushed the leg of the sofa into her lace train.

The tone is reminiscent of *The Rape of the Lock* – which is itself recalled, in a kind of double parody, when the Archdeacon plays whist at the Warden's tea party: 'at the fourth assault he pins to the earth a prostrate king, laying low his crown and sceptre, bushy beard, and lowering brow, with a poor deuce. "As David did Goliath", says the archdeacon. . . .'[29] Robert W. Daniel, introducing the Signet edition of *Barchester Towers* (1963), suggest that an elaborate, if inconsistent, parody of the *Iliad* is in progress, with Barchester as Troy, the Proudie camp as the Greeks, and Archdeacon Grantly's partisans as Trojans, with each group divided against itself, as in Homer. This catches the tone, but forces too much consistency on Trollope's sprinkling of allusions.

He continued to make such allusions throughout his career. In *Can You Forgive Her?* Alice Vavasor has Horace's fault – 'that when at Rome she longed for Tibur, and when at Tibur she regretted Rome' (*Epodes*, i.8). Jeffrey Palliser reflects that Lady Glencora 'might yet have as many sons as Hecuba'. In *Phineas Redux*, Phineas finds Dublin 'his Tibur, and the fickle one found that he could not be happy unless he were back again at Rome'. Mr Boffin shows his ignorance, and probably his lack of a public school education, when he remarks, in *The Prime Minister*, that 'We all

know what bread and the games came to in Rome . . . To a man
burning Rome . . . for his amusement, dressed in a satin petticoat
and a wreath of roses.'[30] In *The Way We Live Now* the American
Mrs Hurtle, more violent than an Englishwoman, compares
herself to the savage Medea; Melmotte is also compared to Medea
for his alleged ability to 'boil the cauldron' until 'ruined fortunes'
are 'so cooked that they shall come out of the pot fresh and new
and unembarrassed'. The disgraced Felix Carbury thinks of
suicide, 'But as this idea presented itself to him he simply gathered
the [bed] clothes around him and tried to sleep. The death of Cato
would hardly have for him persuasive charms.' Cato, as Trollope
knew from Plutarch and from Merivale's account, 'threw himself
on his bed, as if about to take his rest for the night; but when all
was quiet, he seized his sword and thrust it into his stomach'.
Melmotte, who commits suicide, 'wrapped his toga around him
before his death' with a display of bravado. Caesar, Trollope was
to write in the *Life of Cicero*, 'is supposed to have gathered his toga
over his face so that he might fall with dignity' when he was
stabbed; the phrase reminds us that we are to see Melmotte as a
modern Caesar, unscrupulous and lawless[31] (the public anarchy
portrayed in *The Way We Live Now* causes Trollope to make more
allusions to ancient history than he usually does in his fiction).
Nor is there any insuperable obstacle to seeing John Caldigate's
voyage to Australia, his entanglement with the Circean Mrs
Smith, and his return home as a kind of modern *Odyssey*.

Like many other Victorian writers, Trollope likes to quote from
Latin literature, sometimes translating, sometimes citing the
original Latin. He occasionally quotes from Juvenal, Ovid or
Virgil; but Horace occurs far more frequently and in fact is the
source of most of Trollope's classical quotations. These are always
apposite, whether used by Trollope himself to define a situation or
character, or put into the mouth of a character to help reveal his
personality and social status. The reader always knows that a man
who quotes in Latin has been educated as a gentleman. Since
women rarely learned Latin, Trollope's female readers sometimes
had to be satisfied simply to contemplate this secret language,
though he often assists them with a translation or some kind of
paraphrase. ' "Carpe diem" ', says Colonel Stubbs to Ayala in
*Ayala's Angel*. ' "Do you know what 'carpe diem' means?" "It is
Latin perhaps." "Yes; and therefore you are not suffered to
understand it. This is what it means. As an hour for joy has come,

do not let any trouble interfere with it." '[32] Latin tags identify some of Trollope's characters and define the world in which they move, and into which the reader is admitted, with a reminder that admission is a privilege rather than a right.

Such passages are so common that it is only possible to glance at a few of them. 'The "Ruat coelum, fiat justitia", was said, no doubt, from an outside balcony to a crowd, and the speaker knew that he was talking buncombe', Trollope remarks in *The Last Chronicle of Barset*. 'The "Rem, si possis recte, si non, quocunque modo", was whispered into the ear in a club smoking room, and the whisperer intended that his words should prevail.'[33] 'There are so many men by whom the tenuis ratio saporum has not been achieved . . . that goblets of Gladstone may pass current', is his comment in *Phineas Redux*, as Phineas suffers through a bad meal at Mr Kennedy's house, washed down with 'Gladstone' claret.[34] In *The Way We Live Now*, Mr Alf writes an enigmatic article about Melmotte's railway project that is 'In utrumque paratus', and Melmotte, meditating on his own strange destiny, 'assured himself that a great part of him would escape Oblivion. "Non omnis moriar", in some language of his own, was chanted by him within his own breast.'[35]

Trollope's characters are sometimes as apt with Latin tags as their creator. Ned Spooner urges his cousin to propose again to Adelaide Palliser by quoting Horace: ' "Ludit exultim metuitque tangi." For Ned Spooner had himself preserved some few tattered shreds of learning from his school days. "You don't remember about the filly?" "Yes I do; very well", said the Squire. "Nuptiarum expers. That's what it is, I suppose. Try it again . . . Horace's filly kicked a few, no doubt." '[36] Roger Carbury reminds a friend that 'In Rome they were worshipping just such men as this Melmotte' in Horace's day. 'Do you remember the man who sat upon the seats of the knights and scoured the Via Sacra with his toga, though he had been scourged from pillar to post for his villainies? I always think of that man when I hear Melmotte's name mentioned. Hoc, hoc tribuno militum! Is this the man to be Conservative member for Westminster?'[37] The old Duke of St Bungay pleads his unfitness for office on account of age in a conversation with Plantagenet Palliser in *The Prime Minister*: 'The old horse should be left to graze out his last days. Ne peccet ad extremum ridendus'; in *The Duke's Children* the same man writes to Palliser on the same subject, citing the same Horatian poem: 'I am bound at last to put in the old plea with a determination that it shall be respected. "Solve senescentem." It is now, if I calculate rightly, exactly fifty years since I first entered public life.'[38] Palliser quotes Horace and Virgil when expostulating with his sons in *The Duke's Children*. Money, he tells them, ' "ought to have no power of conferring happiness, and certainly cannot drive away sorrow. Not though you build palaces out into the deep, can that help you. You read your Horace, I hope. 'Scandunt eodum quo dominus minae.' " "I recollect that", said Gerald. "Black care sits behind the horseman" '. Gerald has remembered the passage, and caps his father's quotation by an English version of the next line but one: 'post equitem sedet atra Cura'. And Palliser does not get the phrase quite right: 'minae / scandunt eodem quo dominus' is what Horace wrote.[39] Later, in another interview, Palliser quotes Virgil:

> 'Facilis descensus Averni!' said the Duke, shaking his head. 'Noctes atque dies patet atri janua Ditis.' No doubt, he thought, that as his son was at Oxford, admonitions in Latin would serve him better than in his native tongue. But Gerald, when he heard the grand hexameter rolled out in his father's grandest tone, entertained a comfortable feeling that the worst of the interview was over.[40]

Trollope's most sustained use of Horace occurs in *An Old Man's Love*, his last completed novel. His hero, Mr Whittlestaff, falls in love with Mary Lawrie, his young ward, but loses her to a younger and more dashing rival. Whittlestaff is a man who turns to literature for consolation when things go wrong. Disappointed in an earlier love affair,

> He took to his classics for consolation, and read the philosophy of Cicero, and the history of Livy, and the war chronicles of Caesar. They did him good, – in the same way that the making of many shoes would have done him good had he been a shoemaker . . . Cicero's de Natura Deorum was . . . effectual. Gradually he returned to a gentle cheerfulness of life.

Whittlestaff's particular favourite is Horace, read in surroundings that recall the Sabine Farm, on the grass in a beech-grove:

Here he was wont to sit and read his Horace, and think of the affairs of the world as Horace depicted them. Many a morsel of wisdom he had here made his own, and had then endeavoured to think whether the wisdom had in truth been taken home by the poet to his own bosom, or had only been a glitter of the intellect . . . 'Gemmas, marmor, ebur', he had said. 'Sunt qui non habeant; est qui non curat habere.' I suppose he did care for jewels, marble, and ivory, as much as any one. 'Me lentus Glycerae torret amor meae.' I don't suppose he ever loved her really, or any other girl. Thus he would think over his Horace, always having the volume in his pocket.[41]

'Percontatorem fugito nam garrulus idem est', he tells Mary, when they discuss a gossipy neighbour. 'I've taught you Latin enough to understand that.' And Horace helps him to realise that he ought to give Mary up:

'Intermissa, Venus, diu rursus bella moves? Parce, precor, precor.' This was the passage to which he turned at the present moment; and very little was the consolation which he found in it. What was so crafty, he said to himself, or so vain as that an old man should hark back to the pleasures of a time of life which was past and gone! 'Non sum qualis eram', he said. . . .[42]

Throughout the story, Mr Whittlestaff is continually contrasted – or contrasts himself – with his rival, who is a man of action, just as Horace often deprecates his own placidity, his avoidance of great deeds and great affairs.

Trollope quotes Horace so frequently in his novels that the works of the Roman poet become a kind of running commentary on them, an urbane ironic voice in counterpoint to the narrative. And Horace is perhaps important in another way. He often reminds us of his *imbellis lyra*, his inability to celebrate wars and triumphs, his self-imposed restriction to trivial subjects: the pleasures of a quiet country life, wine, women. 'Mecum Dionaeo sub antro / quaere modos leviore plectro.'[43] And in *Ars poetica* (*Epistles*, II.3), Horace urges a kind of literary realism, an avoidance of bombast, extravagance, the fantastic or grotesque. Trollope's usual choice of subject, and his methods, are similar, allowing for the great changes between his time and Horace's. Trollope writes of the ordinary, the usual, as Henry James pointed out. He does not portray spectacular heroism or the crash of empires. Even his Prime Minister is shown in private life rather than in political action, and, when Mr Gresham and the Duke of St Bungay discuss a high office for Mr Bonteen, Trollope quotes Horace – in Theodore Martin's translation – to tell us he cannot attempt to depict 'a conversation so lofty':

> But whither would'st thou, Muse? Unmeet
> For jocund lyre are themes like these.
> Shalt thou the talk of Gods repeat,
> Debasing by thy strains effete
> Such lofty mysteries?[44]

Trollope avoids both melodrama and the Imperial theme, and follows Horace's prescriptions for literary plausibility. 'Nos convivia,' he could say with Horace, in a phrase that might serve as a general epigraph for his novels, 'nos proelia virginum / sectis in iuvenes unguibus acrium / cantamus.'[45]

NOTES

1 Anthony Trollope, *An Autobiography*, World's Classics edn (London: Oxford University Press, 1950) p. 14 (ch. 1). I wish also to acknowledge a general debt to Frank Pierce Jones, 'Anthony Trollope and the Classics', *Classical Weekly*, XXXVII (15 May 1944) 227–31; and to John W. Clark, *The Language and Style of Anthony Trollope* (London: André Deutsch, 1975).
2 Thomas Adolphus Trollope, *What I Remember* (London: Richard Bentley and Son, 1887) I.3, 58. For the *Eton Latin Grammar*, see M. L. Clarke, *Classical Education in Britain, 1500–1900* (Cambridge: Cambridge University Press, 1959) pp. 6, 7, 50.
3 Anthony Trollope , 'Public Schools', *Fortnightly Review*, I (1 Oct 1865) 479–80, 486.
4 *Autobiography*, p. 2 (ch. 1).
5 *Autobiography*, p. 4 (ch. 1); *What I Remember*, I.77. See also Howard Staunton, *The Great Schools of England*, rev. edn (London: Strahan, 1869); E. D. Laborde, *Harrow School Yesterday and Today* (London: Winchester Publications, 1948).
6 *Autobiography*, pp. 5, 6, 8 (ch. 1); 36 (ch. 3).
7 Clarke, *Classical Education in Britain*, p. 59. See also Staunton, *Great Schools of England*; Laborde, *Harrow School Yesterday and Today*.
8 *Autobiography*, pp. 236–7 (ch. 12). The quoted passage is from Horace, *Odes*, III .xi.1–4.
9 Clarke, *Classical Education in Britain*, pp. 53, 55; Trollope, in the *Fortnightly Review*, I.479. The quoted passage is from Horace, *Odes*, III.v.27–8: 'wool steeped in purple dye never regains its original colour'. St Jerome and others

use this image as a way of expressing the ineradicable nature of a classical education (thus my title: 'Wool Steeped in Purple Dye').

10   Trollope, in the *Fortnightly Review*, I.478–9, 483; *Autobiography*, pp. 17–18 (ch. 1); T. H. S. Escott, *Anthony Trollope: His Public Services, Private Friends, and Literary Originals* (1913; repr. Port Washington, NY: Kennikat Press, 1967) p. 19.

11   M. J. Higgins, 'Paterfamilias to the Editor of the *Cornhill Magazine*', *Cornhill Magazine*, I (May 1860) 609.

12   *Autobiography*, p. 15 (ch. 1).

13   *What I Remember*, I.196, 215. In his mid-sixties, Tom's continued enthusiasm for Horace sent him pony-trekking in the Sabine hills in search of Horace's farm, the *fons Bandusiae*, and other Horatian sites. See *What I Remember*, III.385.

14   *Autobiography*, pp. 53 (ch. 3); 18 (ch. 1).

15   Ibid., p. 101 (ch. 6).

16   Ibid., pp. 338–9 (ch. 18); Michael Sadleir, *Trollope: A Commentary* (London: Oxford University Press, 1961) p. 124 (1st edn 1927; rev. edn 1945). The quotation from Pliny may be translated, 'let the cobbler stick to his last'.

17   See Trollope's 'Merivale's History of the Romans', *Dublin University Magazine*, XXXVII (May 1851) 611–12.

18   Anthony Trollope, *The Commentaries of Caesar* (New York: John B. Alden, 1883) p. 4.

19   *Autobiography*, pp. 101 (ch. 6); 338 (ch. 18); *Dublin University Magazine*, XXXVII.613.

20   J. S. Mill, *On Liberty* (1859) ch. 3. For Melmotte and Napoleon, see Robert Tracy, *Trollope's Later Novels* (Berkeley and Los Angeles, Calif.: University of California Press, 1978) pp. 170–1.

21   Anthony Trollope, *The Life of Cicero* (London: Chapman & Hall, 1880) I. 20.

22   See Trollope's 'Merivale's History of the Romans', *Dublin University Magazine*, XLVIII (July 1856) 32; and his *Life of Cicero*, I. 1–2; II. 139.

23   Ibid., I. 37–8.

24   Ibid., I.117. For a full discussion of Trollope and Cicero, see William A. West, 'Trollope's Cicero', *Mosaic*, IV (1971) 143–52. For Trollope's ethical relativism and its source in Cicero, see Ruth apRoberts, *The Moral Trollope* (Athens, Ohio: Ohio University Press, 1971).

25   Lance O. Tingay, 'Trollope's Library', *Notes and Queries*, CXCV (28 Oct. 1950) 476–8; *The Letters of Anthony Trollope*, ed. Bradford Allen Booth (London: Oxford University Press, 1951) p. 399 (Trollope to George Eliot, 13 Aug 1878).

26   *Autobiography*, p. 201 (ch. 11). Alford's review appeared in the *Contemporary Review* (June 1866).

27   *Life of Cicero*, I.14; *Spectator*, LIV (12 Mar. 1881) 353–4.

28   Anthony Trollope, *The Last Chronicle of Barset*, ed. Arthur Mizener (Boston, Mass.: Houghton Mifflin, 1964) pp. 517 (ch. 62), 323 (ch. 41), 107 (ch. 13).

29   Anthony Trollope, *Barchester Towers and The Warden* (New York: Modern Library, 1950): *The Warden*, pp. 98 (ch. 11), 185 (ch. 20), 56–7 (ch. 6); *Barchester Towers*, pp. 234 (ch. 5), 547 (ch. 33), 296–7 (ch. 11); *Warden*, p. 59 (ch. 6).

30   Anthony Trollope, *The Palliser Novels* (London: Oxford University Press,

1973) 6 vols: *Can You Forgive Her?*, I.pp. 149 (ch. 14), 261 (ch. 25); *Phineas Redux*, I.p. 7 (ch. 1); *The Prime Minister*, I.p. 100 (ch. 11).

31 Anthony Trollope, *The Way We Live Now*, ed. Robert Tracy (Indianapolis: Bobbs-Merrill, 1974) pp. 224 (ch. 27), 100 (ch. 13), 418 (ch. 52); Charles Merivale, *History of the Romans under the Empire* (London: Longmans, Green, 1870–3) II.362; *The Way We Live Now*, p. 676 (ch. 83); *The Life of Cicero*, II. 211.

32 Anthony Trollope, *Ayala's Angel*, World's Classics edn (London: Oxford University Press, 1929) p. 248 (ch. 26).

33 Anthony Trollope, *The Last Chronicle of Barset*, pp. 461–2 (ch. 56). 'Ruat coelum . . .' is a common proverb; 'Rem, si possis recte . . .' is Horace, *Epistles*, I.i.65–6. The Latin phrase may be translated thus: 'Make money, honourably if you can, if not, however you can.'

34 *Phineas Redux*, I.86 (ch. 10). The Latin is Horace, *Satires*, II.iv.36: 'tenui ratione saporum'. Trollope has, quite properly, altered the first two words to their nominative form. The Latin phrase may be translated, 'the subtle theory of flavours'.

35 *The Way We Live Now*, pp. 238 (ch. 30; quoting Virgil, *Aeneid*, II. 61) and 503 (ch. 62; quoting Horace, *Odes*, III.xxx.6). The first phrase may be translated thus: 'prepared for any event'; and the second: 'I will not entirely die'.

36 *Phineas Redux*, I.257 (ch. 29; quoting Horace, *Odes*, III.xi.10–11). Horace describes here a three-year-old filly who 'gambols and is skittish at a touch, not broken in for marriage'.

37 *The Way We Live Now*, p. 448 (ch. 55; quoting Horace, *Epodes*, iv.20). Horace describes a rich upstart who promenades the Sacred Way with an ostentatious toga three yards wide (about half a yard was proper), and takes a theatre seat for which his low birth disqualifies him. The Latin phrase may be translated, 'when *this* sort of fellow is a military tribune'.

38 *The Prime Minister*, II.349–50 (ch. 76); *The Duke's Children*, p. 169 (ch. 22). The Latin is Horace, *Epistles* I.i.8–9. Trollope applies the lines to himself in the *Autobiography*, p. 232 (ch. 12): 'Solve senescentem mature sanus equum, ne / peccet ad extremum ridendus [et ilia ducat].' The Latin may be translated thus: 'Be wise in time; turn out the old horse, lest / His broken wind and gait make watchers jest.'

39 *The Duke's Children*, pp. 195–6 (ch. 25; quoting Horace, *Odes*, III.i.37–40). The ode endorses the man who desires only *satis* – enough to satisfy his needs. *Eodum* is a misprint for *eodem*. The untranslated phrase means, 'menaces climb to the same spot the master climbs to'.

40 *The Duke's Children*, pp. 515–16 (ch. 65; quoting Virgil, *Aeneid*, VI.126–7). Modern texts prefer *Averno*, but *Averni* occurs in some Victorian editions, and in some manuscripts. The Latin may be translated thus: 'The road down to Hell is easy. Night and day the gates of dark Pluto stand open.'

41 Anthony Trollope, *An Old Man's Love*, World's Classics edn (London: Oxford University Press, 1936) pp. 15 (ch. 2; quoting Horace, *Epistles*, II.ii.180–2: 'Gemmas, marmor, ebur, Tyrrhena sigilla, tabellas, / argentum, vestes Gaetulo murice tinctas, / sunt qui non habeant, est qui non curat habere') and 177–8 (ch. 16; quoting Horace, *Odes*, III.xix.28). The two quoted phrases may be translated as follows: 'jewels, marble, ivory . . . he who does not have these things does not need to have them'; and 'steady love

for my Glycera burns me'.

42  *An Old Man's Love*, pp. 155 (ch. 14; quoting Horace, *Epistles*, I.xviii.69: 'Percontatorem ... idem est') and 181 (ch. 17; quoting Horace, *Odes*, IV.i.1–3). The two quoted phrases may be translated as follows: 'I flee the questioner, for he is talkative'; and 'Would you have me try again the long-suspended contests of love, O Venus? Give over, I pray, give over. I am no longer such a man as once I was'.

43  The two passages (Horace, *Odes*, I.vi.10, and II,i,39–40) may be translated as follows: 'unwarlike lyre'; and 'seek with me modes played on a lighter string in Dione's grotto.'

44  *Phineas Redux*, I.359 (ch. 40; quoting Martin's translation of *Odes*, III,iii.70–2).

45  The quotation is from Horace, *Odes*, I.vi.17–19, and may be translated thus: 'I sing of dinner parties, of the struggles of maidens with trimmed fingernails fiercely fighting off young men.'

# Trollope the Traveller

## ASA BRIGGS

Trollope's *Travelling Sketches*, published in 1866, is not mentioned in his *Autobiography* (1883): it consisted of short pieces which first appeared in the *Pall Mall Gazette*, none of which attracted much attention from contemporaries. Trollope did discuss in his *Autobiography*, however, with comments of unequal length and interest, how and why he had come to write his one-volume *The West Indies and the Spanish Main* (1859), his two-volume *North America* (1862), his two-volume *Australia and New Zealand* (1876), and, not least, his *South Africa* (1878).

Trollope was characteristically self-critical, greatly as he savoured each of his travels. The first of the four specialised travel studies he regarded as the best book that had come from his pen, 'short, amusing, useful and true'[1]: it included large parts of central America and ended not in the West Indies, but in Canada, which figured in *North America* too. The second, more ambitious, he thought of as 'not a good book', 'tedious and confused' and 'hardly likely to be of future value to those who wish to make themselves acquainted with the United States'.[2] The third was put quietly in its place as 'a thoroughly honest book . . . the result of unflagging labour for a period of fifteen months'.[3] The fourth was written too late in his life for him to attempt a judgement: all he stated in his *Autobiography* was the amount of money he received for it, £850, less than half of the amount he received in the same year for *Is He Popenjoy?*[4]

As always, Trollope attached supreme importance to 'truth', but, since he wanted to entertain as well as to inform, he was concerned in his four major travel books to extend his readers' imagination as well as their knowledge.[5] He knew that his readers, increasingly drawn to travel books, were ready. 'That men and women should leave their homes at the end of summer and go somewhere – though only to Margate', he wrote in the first of the

*Travelling Sketches*, 'has become a thing so fixed that incomes are made to stretch themselves to fit the rule.'[6] Trollope stretched *his* travels to include Kingston, 'of all the towns that I ever saw . . . perhaps, on the whole, the least alluring'; Cincinnati, 'slow, dingy and uninteresting, but with an air of substantial civic dignity'; Ballaarat [*sic*], 'very pleasant to the sight, which is, perhaps, more than can be said for any other "provincial" town in the Australian colonies'; Wellington, about which he said little except that it was 'built only of wood' and reminded him of St. Thomas in the Virgin Islands, 'but in appearance only';[7] and Bloemfontein, about which he said much — 'not peculiarly beautiful' but 'complete and neat', with an air of 'contentment and general prosperity which is apt to make a dweller in busy cities think that though it might not quite suit himself it would be very good for everybody else'.[8]

After rereading Trollope's travel books and studying in retrospect the immediate reactions to them, it is possible to qualify both some of his judgements on their relative merits and some of the judgements of his contemporaries. *The West Indies* does not stand out so prominently either in content or in organisation, and is riddled with what often seems like prejudice. *South Africa* has similar qualities. *Australia and New Zealand*, while packed with 'much valuable information', is neither more nor less perceptive than *North America*, although it lacks colour.[9] As for *North America*, for all its weaknesses, including those recognised by Trollope and his contemporaries, it has a special significance in relation to his life and work. Because it was intended by Trollope to make late amends for his mother's 'somewhat unjust' book about 'our cousins over the water',[10] it is a necessary element in his biography. Because, as he put it in his first chapter, it had been the ambition of my literary life to write a book about the United States',[11] it is inevitable that its claims and weaknesses should be subject to independent critical tests. It was, moreover, one out of more than two hundred somewhat similar books on North America produced by fellow Englishmen during the previous forty-five years.[12] 'For a dozen years we have been surfeited with descriptions of rambles by Englishmen through the United States,' wrote one reviewer, 'and it must be confessed that, so far as mere narrative description is concerned, we have read more instructive books than Mr Trollope's.' The itinerary of their 'tours' was often more interesting, and when the itineraries converged 'not even he' could 'give charm to the *crambe repetita* of so many predecessors'.[13]


I


There is one basic point about which there can be no doubt. Trollope enjoyed travel. It was also a necessary part of his youth and of his work.[14] After his first spell in Ireland he was called upon to explore 'a considerable portion of Great Britain' on horseback with 'a minuteness which few have enjoyed'.[15] His rural (and urban) rides were writing as well as seeing trips, for, as Frederick Page remarked, 'from the mere number of his books one might have thought that Trollope must have been writing all the time, at home, in railway carriages, on board ship'.[16] He had made three visits to Italy by the end of 1857, visited Egypt in the following year, where he finished the very English *Dr Thorne*, went on to the Holy Land and returned via Spain. The West Indies and central America followed in 1858. Once again Trollope wrote as he travelled: 'the descriptions come hot on the paper from their causes'.[17] Not surprisingly, he thought of himself as belonging to 'the travellers' guild'.[18]

His American trip in 1861 was different in two respects – first, in that he obtained leave from the Post Office to undertake it, and, second, in that he intended from the start to write a book about it. 'No observer', he said of his mother, 'was ever less qualified to judge of the prospects or even of the happiness of a young people. No one could have been worse adapted by nature for the task of learning whether a nation was in a way to thrive.'[19] It was for this reason that he was determined to make amends. It mattered little to him that his visit coincided with the American 'War of Secession', though he was interested in it, and he did not visit the South. 'A man might as well be in Westminster Abbey during the Coronation of her Majesty', *Fraser's Magazine* complained, 'and not look at the ceremony.'[20]

The popularity of travel books during the 1850s and 1860s was perfectly compatible with 'Podsnappery'. *Travelling Sketches* pandered to the public. It described types rather than characters, characters with common names like Smith, Robinson and Miss Thompson, the kind of names Trollope had spurned in his early novels. It also introduced classes of characters, like 'unprotected female tourists' or 'the united Englishmen who travel for fun'. It is neither better nor worse than the many travel articles in *Punch*, like an article of 1858 with the title 'Why Englishmen Are So Beloved upon the Continent'. 'Because they never foster the delusion,' the *Punch* writer explained, 'that by letting their moustache grow they may succeed in passing themselves off as natives of the Continent.' And referring to Trollope's hero, Palmerston, who died one year before *Travelling Sketches* appeared in book form, the writer added, 'Because whatever grievance they may fancy they have sustained, they never more than twenty times *per diem* swear Lord Palmerston shall hear of it.'[21]

Trollope went on a second visit to the United States, this time a 'mission', in 1868.[22] While welcoming the private hospitality and saluting the grand public efforts 'made by private munificence to relieve the sufferings of humanity',[23] he none the less dwelt as he had done – and as he was to dwell in some of his later novels – on the fact that 'at the top of everything ... the very men who are the least fit ... occupy high places'.[24] Yet the novel he finished in Washington, *He Knew He Was Right*, scarcely reflects this preoccupation.[25]

*Australia and New Zealand* was the record of travels originally intended by his wife and himself to see their 'shepherd son'.[26] Yet, before going, he signed on with a newspaper to write a series of articles. 'If the travelling author can pay his travelling bills,' he told his readers, 'he must be a good manager on the road.'[27] He had also ensured equally prudently that if the *Great Britain*, the ship in which he travelled to Australia, sank, 'there would be new novels ready to come out under my name for some years to come'.[28] He was writing all the time on the journey, which he found very tiring,[29] returning, none the less, via America from San Francisco to New York through Salt Lake City, where he met Brigham Young. Both Australasia and America were to figure in his later work,[30] although it is doubtful whether he would have needed to travel there to write *Harry Heathcote of Gangoil*, the Christmas number of the *Graphic* in 1873, or *The American Senator* (1877), which, as a reviewer in the *Athenaeum* said, 'might just as well have been called "The Chronicle of a Writer at Dillsborough" ... The Senator might have been cut out of the book almost without affecting the story.'[31]

Trollope travelled to the last – he made a long trip to Italy in the late winter and spring of 1881 – and returned to the source,

Ireland, twice in 1882. It was Ireland more than any other place on his itineraries which brought together the 'real world' of fact and the world of fiction which he created, and, if he never wrote a travel book about it, he felt deeply about all its problems. Trollope's Irish novels, according to T. H. S. Escott, an early and knowledgeable critic, presented 'a true picture of the country, a true insight into its people';[32] and the last of these novels, *The Landleaguers*, unfinished when Trollope died, has been described as 'the closest he ever came to writing documentary fiction'.[33]

In Trollope's travel books we get only rare glimpses of his 'inner life', carefully kept out of his *Autobiography*. In *Travelling Sketches* he dwelt more on nature than on society: 'to be able to be happy at rest among the mountains is better than a capacity for talking French in saloons'.[34] Likewise, in *Australia and New Zealand*, he compared eighteenth-century 'grand tours' with nineteenth-century expeditions: 'in the last century Englishmen travelled to see cities, and to see men, and to study the world – but in those days mountains were troublesome, and dark valleys were savage, and glaciers were horrible'.[35] He admired the members of the Alpine Club, who went on very different journeys from his own.[36]

Sometimes these glimpses are related to a broader perspective. He begins one chapter of *The West Indies*, for example, with the words 'How best to get about this world which God has given us is certainly one of the most interesting subjects which men have to consider, and one of the most interesting works on which men can employ themselves.' Comparing the development of transport to the development of a child, he claims that men have so far reached only the learning-to-use-a-knife-and-fork stage, 'though we hardly yet understand the science of carving'. 'We know that the world must be traversed by certain routes, prepared for us originally not by ourselves, but by the hand of God.'[37] Given such an interesting perspective, the chapter is curiously uninteresting, although it hints at the futuristic concerns which were to be expressed in *The Fixed Period* (1882). Trollope criticised the French way not only of promoting transport ventures but of discussing such issues.

> When has truly mighty work been heralded by magnilo-
> quence? . . . If words ever convey to my ears a positive contra-
> diction of the assertion which they affect to make, it is when they
> are grandly antithetical and magnificently verbose. If in

addition to this, they promise to mankind 'new epochs, new views, and unlimited horizons', surely no further proof can be needed that they are vain, empty and untrue.[38]

It is partly because of such a desire to deflate that it is not this chapter out of Trollope's three important travel books which lingers in the mind, but chapter 14 of *North America*, where he deals not with canals or railways but with hotels. 'I consider myself as qualified', he exclaimed with feeling, 'to write a chapter on hotels – not only on the hotels of America but on hotels generally. I have myself been much too frequently a sojourner at hotels. I think I know what an hotel should be, and what it should not be; and am almost inclined to believe, in my pride, that I could myself fill the position of a landlord with some chance of social success, though probably with none of satisfactory pecuniary results.'[39]

Trollope did not like American hotels – either their methods of management or the services they offered – but he did recognise that American hotels of the future would create a new demand. 'The hotel itself will create a population – as the railways do. With us railways run to the town; but in the states the towns run to the railways. It is the same thing with the hotels.'[40] By contrast, English hotels – or inns – looked to the past. 'The worst about them is that they deteriorate from year to year instead of becoming better.' There was only the slightest touch of nostalgia in his statement that 'since the old days are gone, there are wanting the landlord's bow, and the kindly smile of his stout wife'. The new railway hotels, he added, were 'frequently gloomy, desolate, comfortless and almost suicidal'.[41]

While praising Swiss hotels as the best in the world, Trollope reserved special criticism for those he thought the dearest – the French. Running through his travel books, despite his professed cosmopolitanism,[42] there is a strong anti-French note, which applies to things as well as to people. 'Cotton-velvet sofas and ormolu clocks stand in the place of convenient furniture, and logs of wood at a franc a log fail to impart to you the heat which the freezing cold of a Paris winter demands.'[43] One of Trollope's main complaints against New York hotels was that they were full of French furniture. 'I could not write at a marble table whose outside rim was curved into fantastic shapes' or sit on 'papier mâché chairs with small velvety seats'. When he complained to the landlord, he was told that his house had been 'furnished not in accordance with the taste of England, but with that of France'.[44]

Passing from descriptions of things (to which Trollope was always sensitive) to the framing of ambitious generalisation was always rather too easy for Trollope the traveller, as it is, perhaps, to most intelligent travellers, and rather more of Trollope the deflating self-critic might have been salutary. 'All America', he went on, 'is now furnishing itself by the rules which guided that hotel-keeper. I do not merely allude to actual household furniture – to chairs, tables and detestable gilt clocks. The taste of America is becoming French in its conversation, French in its comforts and French in its discomforts. French in its eating, and French in its dress, French in its manners and French in its art.'[45]

## II

Some generalisations in the important travel studies went deeper, and some of them have been subjected to sharp criticism. Two, in particular, deserve further examination. The first related to the West Indies, the second to the United States.

Throughout *The West Indies*, which, as we have seen, Trollope considered his 'best book', there is an open distrust of the negro, even of his religion: 'I think', Trollope wrote of the negro in chapter 4, 'Jamaica-Black Men', 'that he seldom understands the purpose of industry, the object of truth, or the results of honesty'.[46] It was not that Trollope dwelt for long on 'the black skin and the thick lip' – those, he said, the visitor got quickly used to: he lingered rather on psychological qualities which he held that negroes shared with children or dogs. 'They best love him who is most unlike themselves'; 'the more they fear their masters, the more they will respect him.'[47]

The generalisations multiply, although Trollope was aware of the differences between the islanders.[48] 'They have no care for tomorrow, but they delight in being gaudy for today.' 'They are greedy of food, but generally indifferent to its quality.' They would be 'altogether retrograde if left to themselves'. 'These people are a servile race, fitted by nature for the hardest physical work, and apparently at present fitted for little else.' Yet they had little inclination to work. 'Without a desire for property, man could make no progress. But the negro has no such desire; no desire strong enough to induce him to labour for that which he wants.'[49]

Trollope did not condemn the emancipation of slaves, but he held that 'we expected far too great and far too quick a result from emancipation'.[50] 'The negro's idea of emancipation was and is emancipation not from slavery but from work.'[51] Trollope strongly criticised 'philanthropists' of the Exeter Hall variety[52] who objected to the importation of 'coolie labour' into the West Indies, believing that this importation would force negroes to work in order to compete. Trinidad was judged favourably in comparison with Jamaica because it had imported ten or twelve thousand immigrants from Madras and Calcutta during the previous eight years and had in consequence reached a far higher level of work and prosperity. 'There is at present in Port of Spain a degree of commercial enterprise quite unlike the sleepiness of Jamaica or the apathy of the smaller islands.'[53]

It is fitting, perhaps, that Trollope's most persistent West Indian critic this century has been the late Prime Minister of Trinidad, Eric Williams. Curiously, however, he said little of Trollope's relatively favourable views of Trinidad and concentrated on his unfavourable views of Jamaica.[54] He noted how Trollope in drawing a contrast between Jamaica's 'past glory' in the eighteenth century and its economic decline, following the abolition of slavery, had nothing to say about export of new crops or of 20,000 freeholders owning less than ten acres. Trollope's gloomy picture was certainly unrelieved – for it embraced both economics and politics. 'Are Englishmen in general aware', he asked, 'that half the sugar estates in Jamaica, and I believe more than half the coffee plantations, have gone back into a state of bush . . . that chaos and darkness have swallowed so vast an extent of the most bountiful land that civilisation had ever matured?'[55] And, he went on, the continued existence of 'Queen, Lords and Commons' in Jamaica (thought not in Trinidad, where legislative power was entirely in the hands of the Crown[56]) made a mockery of representative institutions.

The House of Assembly is not respected. It does not contain men of most weight and condition in the island, and is contemptuously spoken of even in Jamaica itself, and even by its own members . . . Let any man fancy what England would be if the House of Commons were ludicrous in the eyes of all Englishmen. . . . In truth, there is not room for machinery so complicated in this island. The handful of white men can no

longer have it all their own way; and as for the negroes – let any
warmest advocate of the 'man and brother' position say
whether he has come across three or four of the class who are fit
to enact laws for their own guidance and the guidance of
others.[57]

Trollope wanted Jamaica to adopt the British nineteenth-century
gospel of work, therefore, but to dispense with its seventeenth-
century British-type constitution. He was more sensitive than
some visitors to the role of coloured (as distinct from black) people
in the West Indies,[58] but very insensitive to the long-run effects of
importing Indian (or Chinese) labour. 'The blood of Asia will be
mixed with that of Africa', he prophesied, 'and the necessary
compound will, by God's infinite wisdom and power, be formed for
these latitudes, as it has been formed for the colder regions in
which the Anglo-Saxon preserves his energy, and his works.'[59]

God was not left out of this prophecy. 'Providence has sent
white men and black men to these regions in order that from them
may spring a race fitted by intellect for civilisation: and fitted also
by physical organisation for tropical labour.'[60] Trollope spoke too,
in what was to become familiar late-nineteenth-century language, both about Britain's 'noble mission' and 'the welfare of the
coming world' being in the hands of 'the Anglo-Saxon race'.[61] Yet
the mission for him was not Imperial. If it were 'fated' that the
West Indies should pass into the hands of 'another people', this
would not worry him.[62] He said nothing of their becoming
genuinely 'independent',[63] but he welcomed American independence and viewed with 'composure' 'the inevitable, happily
inevitable, day when Australia shall follow in the same path'.[64]
'The mother country in regarding her colonies', he stressed,
'should think altogether of this welfare, and as little as possible of
her own power and glory . . . If we keep them, we should keep them
– not because they add prestige to the name of Great Britain, not
because they are gems in our diadem, not in order that we may
boast that the sun never sets on our dependencies, but because by
keeping them we may best assist in developing their resources.'[65]

Trollope disliked Disraeli, whose version of 'Imperialism'
seemed to him as dangerous as his political opportunism in
Britain itself. The tone of his writings, therefore, was very different
from that of J. A. Froude, who later in the century was to cover
much of the same ground.[66] He objected, too, to the vacillations of

the Colonial Office, which reflected 'the idiosyncracies of the individual ministers who have held the office of Secretary of State rather than a settled course of British action'.[67]

None the less, Eric Williams was right to describe *The West Indies* as 'merely an expurgated version' of Thomas Carlyle's *Occasional Discourse upon the Nigger Question*, published in 1849 and for Williams 'the most offensive document in the entire world literature on slavery and the West Indies'.[68] It is easy to trace the parallels, despite Trollope's distaste for the writings of Carlyle, which Williams does not note;[69] and it was certainly Carlyle who told Trollope 'that a man when travelling should not read, but "sit still and label his thoughts"'.[70] There is one reference to Carlyle in the chapter on New Granada, and it bears out Williams's assessment.

As far as I am able to judge, a negro has not generally those gifts of God which enable one man to exercise rule and master-ship over his fellow-men. I myself should object strongly to be represented, say in the city of London, by any black man that I ever saw. 'The unfortunate nigger gone masterless', whom Carlyle so tenderly commiserates, has no strong ideas of the duties even of a self-government, much less of the government of others. Universal suffrage in such hands can hardly lead to good results.[71]

In referring to the city of London Trollope was moving his imagination homewards, and it is important to remember, of course, first that there was no universal suffrage in Britain in 1859, and second that Trollope was not in favour of introducing it. When he arrived in San José, Costa Rica, he felt as 'if he were riding into a sleepy little borough town in Wiltshire'.[72] There were hard-working Germans there as well as Spaniards and Indians, but the images of home returned again when before climbing Mount Irazu he recalled 'clambering to the top of Scafell-Pike'.[73]

Trollope was not usually, however, the kind of traveller who referred everything back to the places he knew best or to the kind of people he knew at home. If the latter had been his bent, he would have preferred white society in Jamaica, where the planter has 'so many of the characteristics of an English country gentleman that he does not strike an Englishman as a strange being'. There was scope there, also, for a country gentleman, Trollope argued. 'They have their counties and their parishes. . . . They have county society, local balls, and local race meetings. They have local politics, local quarrels, and strong old-fashioned local friendships. In all these things one feels oneself to be much nearer to England in Jamaica than in any other of the West Indian islands.'[74]

It was because this society was under threat that Trollope did not care to linger there. 'Not only coloured men get into office, but black men also.' 'If we could, we would fain forget Jamaica altogether', he wrote. 'But there it is; a spot on the earth not to be lost sight of or forgotten altogether, let us wish it ever so much. It belongs to us, and must in some sort be thought of and managed and if possible governed.'[75]

The warning was necessary, for six years later insurrection in Jamaica disturbed the peace which Trollope had identified with torpor; and on this occasion British intellectuals divided dramatically on the issue of whether or not to support Governor Eyre (ex-explorer of Australia), who had ruthlessly put down a negro rebellion.[76] Carlyle and Ruskin were on one side; Mill and most 'intellectuals' on the other. Between 1859 and 1865 the Jamaican sugar economy had prospered, but between 1866 and 1876 in the aftermath of the crushed rebellion elected assemblies disappeared not only in Jamaica but also in several other West Indian islands. Trollope would doubtless have approved of the outcome, including a statement in the report of a Royal Commission which visited the Windward Islands in 1884 and praised non-representative government for 'new endeavours . . . to supply the benefits and appliances of civilisation'.[77]

In 1859 Trollope looked with hope rather than with fear at the conclusion of his journey not to the West Indies – or to Costa Rica – but to the United States. It was there, he felt, that contemporaries could discover 'the best means of prophesying . . . what the world will next be, and what men will next do'.[78]

## III

'I have ever admired the United States as a nation', Trollope wrote in *North America*. 'I have loved their liberty, their prowess, their intelligence, and their progress. . . . I have felt confidence in them, and have known, as it were, that their industry must enable them to succeed as a people, while their freedom would insure to their success as a nation.'[79]

Trollope's attitude to the United States, therefore, was radically different from his attitude to the West Indies before he visited either place; and if he ended *The West Indies* with a reference to the United States, he could not complete *North America* without making a few cross-references to the West Indies. In particular, in one disturbing passage he looked forward to the gradual extinction of negro members in the United States and their possible replacement by 'coolies from India and China' as in Guiana and the West Indies.[80] He also reiterated his belief in 'the intellectual inferiority of the Negro', emphasising that he restricted his belief to 'those of pure Negro descent'. He saw a difference between the intellectual and social status of the 'coloured', stating that, whereas he had never met 'in American society any man or woman in whose veins there can have been presumed to be any taint of African blood', in Jamaica they were 'daily to be found in society'. Trollope was no de Tocqueville, as he admitted, and he presumably meant Society with a capital S.[81]

There were the same references to 'the Creator' in *North America* as there had been in *The West Indies*. He was the real author of 'Development' in which Trollope put his trust. There was an old story, 'told over and over again through every century since commerce has flourished in the world; the tropics can produce – but the men from the North shall sow and reap and garner and enjoy'. The 'cosmopolitan' Trollope could be very non-parochial in his generalisations.

> If we look to Europe, we see that this has been so in Greece, Italy, Spain, France and the Netherlands; in England and Scotland; in Prussia and in Russia; and the Western world tells us the same story. Where is now the glory of the Antilles? Where the riches of Mexico and the power of Peru? They still produce sugar, guano, gold, cotton, coffee . . . but where are their men, where are their books, where are their learning, their art, their enterprise?[82]

Trollope immediately pitted New York, Boston, Philadelphia, Chicago, Pittsburgh and (his mother's) Cincinnati against New Orleans, Charleston, Savannah, Mobile, Richmond and Memphis.

The same attitude towards 'development' dominates *South*

*Africa*. 'The progress to be most desired is that which will quickest induce the Kafir to put off his savagery and live after the manner of his white brother.'[83] In the diamond fields of Kimberley, where blacks outnumbered whites, higher wages were doing more to raise black fortunes than religion – 'the spasmodic energy of missionaries' – philanthropy or even educational – 'the unalluring attraction of schools'. 'Who can doubt but that work is the great civiliser of the world – work and the growing desire for those good things which work only will bring?'[84] Trollope was 'realistic' enough to note that the great black majority was sceptical about such civilising forces. 'Were it to be put to the vote tomorrow among the Kafirs whether the white man should be driven into the sea or retained in the country, the entire race would certainly vote for the white man's extermination.'[85]

Unlike the United States, divided South Africa offered few hopes of long-term political unity. Yet if Trollope saw South Africa after the annexation of the Transvaal – and this gave political point to his book – the fact that he saw the United States during the Civil War forced him to consider at least the relationship between 'development' and political aspiration.[86] In *South Africa* he criticised the 'political confusion' in the South following the victory of the North, adding that 'we are all convinced that in one way or another a minority of white men will get the better of a majority of coloured men'.[87] The problem of South Africa could not be settled by leaving a small pocket of independent black power. 'Of what real service can it be to leave to the unchecked dominion of Kafir habits a tract of 1,600 square miles when we have absorbed from the Natives a territory larger than all British India . . . Whether we have done well or ill by occupying South Africa . . . we can hardly salve our consciences by that little corner.'[88]

Trollope had not foreseen a war between the States of the American Union in 1859 or, as he called it, a 'disruption'.[89] Nor, as we have seen, was it his main theme in his two travel volumes. He could not avoid it, however, and the war weaves its way through the book.[90] He had four points to make, and they all involved considerable generalisation. First, 'I do not see how the North, treated as it was and had been, could have submitted to secession without resistance.'[91] Second, 'The North and the South must ever be dissimilar.'[92] 'The Southern States of America have not been able to keep pace with their Northern brethren . . . they have fallen behind in the race'.[93] Trollope's sympathies, unlike those of many (though not all of) his fellow-countrymen, were with the North. Third, 'the preaching of abolition [of slavery] during the war is to me either the deadliest of sins or the vainest of follies': 'it is the banner of defiance opposed to secession'.[94] None the less, 'every Englishman probably looks forward to the accomplishment of abolition of slavery at some future day. I feel sure of it as I do of the final judgement. When or how it will come I cannot tell.'[95] Fourth, secession would be 'successful'; 'I cannot believe that the really Southern States will ever again be joined in amicable union with those of the North.'[96] 'I think that there will be secession, but that the terms of secession will be dictated by the North, not by the South.'[97]

There was an element of irony in the fact that while Trollope had long wanted to write a book about the United States, unlike his mother's, or so he felt, to 'add to the good feeling which should exist between two nations which ought to love each other so well, and which . . . hang upon each other so constantly',[98] when he actually got there, American feeling against England was very bitter. 'All Americans to whom I spoke felt that it was so.'[99] Trollope believed that this was a mistaken as well as an unfair reaction: 'it seems to me that a great nation should not require an expression of sympathy during its struggle. Sympathy is for the weak rather than for the strong.'[100] Nevertheless, he ended his book uneasily, recognising that it would need more than books to guarantee future transatlantic 'good feeling'. 'When this war be over between the northern and the southern states, will there come upon us Englishmen a necessity of fighting with the Americans? If there do come such necessity . . . it will indeed be hard upon us, as a nation, seeing the struggle that we have made to be just towards the States generally, whether they be North or South.' And he then drew a European parallel. 'In that contest between Sardinia and Austria, it was all but impossible to be just to the Italians without being unjust to the Emperor of Austria.'[101] This was not his only European parallel. He added a character-istically Trollopian supplement. 'If we must fight, let us fight the French, "for King George upon the throne". The doing so will be disagreeable but it will not be antipathetic to the nature of an Englishman.'[102]

Trollope was not allowed by his critics in 1861 to get away with any of his generalisations – or his supplement – although, of course, the critics contradicted each other. The fact that the American constitution did not refer specifically to secession did not mean that there was no case for secession: 'to assert that whatever the constitution does not sanction is illegal, is to call it an abominable despotism'.[103] Before discussing the ineradicable differences between North and South, he should have visited the South.[104] 'Nothing throughout this book impresses us so constantly as the consciousness of how little Mr Trollope knows about the South.'[105] In any case, Northern sympathies were dangerous. *Fraser's* believed 'after long observation of this deplorable struggle' that 'there is very little wisdom and very little worth on either side'.[106] On slavery and its implications, Trollope had been unfair to the negroes. He had neglected 'some elements of the Negro character which seem to give a better promise for the future'.[107] 'It is not for the black man that our fears arise. Can any man familiar with the South fail to see that whatever slavery may be for the black man, it is ruin materially and morally for the white.'[108] The forecast that the terms of secession would be dictated by the North was as unproven as the forecast that the North would prove to be very strong. 'There is no man, either American or English, whose ratiocinations on these subjects are worth the paper they are written on. . . . As well might one endeavour to bale the vast Croton reservoir at New York with a lady's thimble as to gauge the dimensions and prospects of the vastest convulsion the world has ever seen.'[109] As for possible war – and the relative merits of war with the United States or with France – 'we do not believe that English people generally give Americans as a nation the preference over other foreigners, nor have they any reason to do so'. 'The blood relationship is a mere sentimental dream, conjured up for the purpose of fine writing.'[110]

The critics, some of whom praised the writings of other commentators on the United States[111] and the War, posed questions which Trollope did not ask and made generalisations of their own. In particular, they asked what North American experience revealed about 'the real merits of democracy' and 'wherein it undoubtedly failed'.[112] Trollope had praised the Americans of the North on two grounds – 'they were educated and they were rich'. Yet the education nourished small men at the expense of great men – 'the average of political intelligence . . . may be much higher in the American States than in European countries, but it is an average which is gained by depression as well as by elevation'[113] –

and the quest for riches was at best only loosely related to happiness. One critic of Trollope quoted John Stuart Mill, who 'confessed' that he was not 'charmed by the ideal of life held out by those who think that the normal state of human beings is that of struggling to get on'. Mill had concluded that while the Northern and Middle States of America had the Six Points of Chartism and no poverty, 'all that these advantages seem to have done for them' was that 'the life of the whole of one sex is devoted to dollar hunting, and of the other to breeding dollar-hunters'.[114] The review of *North America* in *Fraser's* was followed immediately by John Ruskin's 'Essays on Political Economy', the sequel to his *Cornhill* papers, challenging the whole mid-Victorian approach to wealth.

Not all the critics concentrated on such problems of values, while the *Cornhill* itself did not disapprove of Trollope defending with 'great good humour and strong good sense the real virtue of money-making'.[115] In other places *North America* was condemned for its verbosity, for its lack of organisation, for its little inaccuracies.[116] It seemed a mistake, too, that Trollope had included 'the inevitable Declaration of Independence' in an appendix, even though he might never have read it.[117] 'Character and manners', however, they usually felt that he handled well.[118] They quoted little directly in Trollope's words, although one of them selected for his readers a remarkable Trollopian passage on the American corn trade (which eventually was to transform Trollope's England more than the Civil War):

Statistical accounts do not bring any enduring idea . . . I was at Chicago and Buffalo in October 1861. I went down to the granaries, and climbed up to the elevators. I saw the wheat running in rivers from one vessel into another, and from the railroad up into the huge bins on the top stores of the warehouse. I saw corn measured by the forty-bushel measures with as much ease as we measure an ounce of cheese, and with greater rapidity. I ascertained that the work went on weekday and Sunday, day and night incessantly; rivers of wheat and rivers of maize ever running. I saw the men bathed in corn as they distributed it in its flow. I saw bins by the score laden with wheat, in each of which bins there was space for a comfortable residence. I breathed the flour, and drank the flour, and I felt myself to be enveloped in an ocean of breadstuff.[119]

Trollope placed himself in the middle of the picture. Yet even here he was no prophet. He saw the corn feeding the millions of the American East and the coming millions of the American West, but he did not foresee it (as Cobden did) pouring across the Atlantic Ocean and ruining English farmers. He rested content with a contemporary reaction. 'Events in these days march so quickly that they leave men behind, and our dear old Protectionists at home will have grown so sleek upon American flour before they have realised the fact that they are no longer fed from their own furrows.'[120]

The critic in *Blackwood's* attacked Trollope's method of arguing as much as the content of his argument. He personified too much and when excited or in difficulty resorted to metaphor. 'Abstract questions or metaphysical discussions which would have worn a very dry aspect . . . become bright, picquant, and interesting when personified and seen through the medium of familiar imagery.'[121] Sometimes the personification (of a drunken husband, for example, or a 'small chimney sweeper' or a 'Billingsgate heroine') led him – and his readers – completely astray: sometimes the metaphors clashed with each other. He was particularly misleading when he discussed national relationships in terms of individual relationships. What consolation was there, for instance, in the statement that 'the States of America will master their money difficulties because they are born of England not of Austria. What! Shall our eldest child become bankrupt by its first trade-difficulty – be utterly ruined by its first little commercial embarrassment? The child bears much too strong a resemblance to its parent for me to think so.'[122]

This reviewer described Trollope as 'among the most amusing and popular of our novelists' who had established 'agreeable relations with his audience'. 'It is not often that a good novelist makes a good politician', however, he went on. Bulwer did, but Trollope was no exception. 'We think that his just and fairly-earned reputation will continue to rest upon his clever and always entertaining novels.'[123] 'We shall grudge the time he may spend in writing any more books of travel, or politics,' he concluded, 'if they deprive us of one of the brilliant successors of *Barchester Towers*.'[124]

## IV

In considering Trollope's travel reflections it is always necessary to remember, as he himself put it, that he was well aware that his own muse was not Clio: 'I appeal to her frequently, but ever in vain.'[125] Historians appeal to Trollope – and he certainly appeals to them – but they would be wrong (and some of them are) to take everything he says at face value as 'evidence'. As the travel books show, the evidence always requires to be interpreted.[126] Literary critics will be more tempted to relate Trollope's travel books to his fiction than to the writings of recent historians or of his historically minded contemporaries. They may argue negatively, as an early critic did, that to include the American Declaration of Independence as an appendix to *North America* is no more odd than to insert into *The Three Clerks* long passages on the organisation and promotion system of the British Civil Service.[127] More positively, however, they will ask questions about the relationship of Trollope's 'travel material' to his novels.

Four aspects of the relationship are interesting. First, however tempted Trollope was to generalise in his travel books, he also showed exceptional interest in and a capacity to deal with particulars. It is the particulars, above all the particulars of encounters and conversations, which will command most interest for critics of the novels. Second, he showed from time to time – though seldom as strikingly as Dickens – that he had a remarkable gift for phrase, not least when he conveyed a sense not of perspective but of immediacy, or when the note of irony, so strong in the *Autobiography*, gives a twist to the obvious.[128] Third, he was forced in his travel books to consider his 'public', and his asides to them can and should be compared with the asides (and the less explicit devices) in his novels. Fourth, he very occasionally touches on the art (and problems) of the novelist in his travel books, for example in his chapter on 'Literature' in *North America*,[129] and, like his comments on Post Offices, these constitute a distinctive 'source'.

One of the best instances of Trollope's concern for particulars is his delightful description in *The West Indies* of his meeting in Port Antonio, Jamaica, with a coloured girl whose lover had left her.[130] 'Whence she came or who she was I did not know and never learnt.' The meeting might have been awkward for two reasons. She was coloured, and the lover who had abandoned her was not a Christian but a Jew. She was a Baptist. Trollope had Sterne in mind as he told the story to his readers. Yet the flavour is entirely his own. He also brings himself directly into the conversation not as observer but as active participant. 'Now I hate Baptists', he remarks *en passant*, 'as she did her lover – like poison; and even under such pressure as this I could not bring myself to aid in their support.'[131] The conversation – and it was unsolicited – ends with the girl saying, 'I don't t'ink I'll be happy no more. 'Tis so dull: goodbye'; and Trollope adds, 'Were I a girl I doubt whether I also would not sooner dance with a Jew than pray with a Baptist.'[132] He also clearly establishes his own stance, doubtless to reassure his readers. 'I am not a very young man; and my friends have told me that I show strongly that steady married appearance of a paterfamilias which is so apt to lend assurance to maiden timidity.'[133]

This is by no means the only record of a specific conversation in *The West Indies*, and it is fair to add that whatever Trollope might have thought about the general prospects for negroes in the future he had no inhibitions about talking to particular negroes freely and generally. He had lively accounts to give also of dancing and bathing. He recognised that 'in the West Indies it is absolutely necessary that these people should be treated with dignity. . . . They like familiarity but are singularly averse to ridicule; and though they wish to be on good terms with you, they do not choose that these shall be reached without the proper degree of antecedent ceremony.'[134] Trollope was the best possible judge of 'the proper degree' in Kingston as in London. He also showed conspicuous curiosity about everything, not least food. Avocado pears make their way into his list of food preferences at a time when there could have been little idea of eating an avocado pear in London.[135]

There are lively personal encounters also in *North America* (though not in *Australia and New Zealand*). A chapter which deals *inter alia* with 'The Frontier Man'[136] is free from unnecessary abstraction as it proceeds to reveal a man with 'romance, high poetic feeling, and above all manly dignity'. 'All the odious incivility of the republican servant has been banished.' Trollope, always interested in talking to women, reveals the frontier wife too, in this case a wife deserted by her husband. 'I have known what it is to be hungry and cold, and to work hard till my bones have ached. I only wish that I might have the same chance again. If I could have ten acres cleared two miles from any living being, I would be happy with my children.'[137]

It was when he passed from particulars to generalities again that Trollope reached barriers to thinking. 'That women should have their rights no man will deny. To my thinking neither increase of work nor increase of political influence are among them.'[138] There are parallel passages in *Australia and New Zealand*. 'Women all the world over are entitled to everything that chivalry can give them. They should sit while men stand. They should be served while men wait. They should be praised – even without desert. They should be courted – even when having neither wit nor beauty. They should be worshipped – even without love.'[139] How much irony is there here in what seems at first sight to be such a conventional, if eloquent, presentation of Victorian attitudes? However little or much, it is difficult to consider Trollope 'a feminist'.

Trollope was not able to convert his impressions of a different society (with the exception of Ireland) into a novel of the kind that Dickens wrote in *Martin Chuzzlewit*, where, as has been suggested, Dickens 'turned his limitations as a traveller into novelists's gold'.[140] Yet, like Dickens, he had an often impressive turn of phrase, particularly when there was an explicit or implicit cross-reference. 'The unfinished dome of the Capitol will loom before you in the distance, and you will think that you approach the ruins of some Western Palmyra.'[141] 'A man may lose himself in the streets, not as one loses oneself in London between Shoreditch and Russell Square, but as one does so in the deserts of the Holy Land, between Emmaus and Arimathea.'[142] A list of the names of gold mines in Victoria – 'New Chums', 'Old Chums', etc., again recalling mining passages in *The Three Clerks*, ends with 'the Gladstone'. 'Indeed, there are five or six Gladstone Companies,' he concludes, 'and to be fair . . . a Disraeli Company. I do not, however, find it quoted among those that are paying dividends.'[143]

None of these passages compares in quality, however, with the memorable poetic passages in Dickens's *American Notes*, such as his descriptions of Washington – 'It is sometimes called the City of Magnificent Distances, but it might with greater propriety be called the City of Magnificent Intentions'[144] – or of Boston – 'When I got into the streets upon this Sunday morning, the air was so clear, the houses were so bright and gay; the signboards were painted in such gaudy colours . . . that I never turned a corner without looking out for the clown and the pantaloon, who, I had no doubt, were hiding in a doorway or behind some pillar close at hand.'[145] By contrast, Trollope's Boston was a pale imitation of London. 'There is an Athenaeum, and a State Hall, and a fashionable street – Beacon Street – very like Piccadilly, as it runs along the Green Park – and there is a Green Park opposite to this Piccadilly, called Boston Common.'[146] In 'melancholy' Washington Trollope walked unimpressed through its 'ragged collection of unbuilt broad streets'; Dickens was more involved in the scene when he wrote, 'after walking about it for an hour or two, I felt that I would have given the world for a crooked street'.[147]

Dickens and Trollope each visited the manufacturing town of Lowell, and in their accounts of this fascinating community both their strengths are plain. That they both went there is a sign of the interest taken by early or mid-nineteenth travellers in visiting industrial places. 'Lowell and its Factory System' was Dickens's sub-title, and he was impressed above all else by the factory girls, all of whom had the 'deportment of young women, not of degraded brutes of burden.' The rooms in which they worked were as clean and 'well ordered' as they were, and they lived in pleasant boarding houses, where there were 'joint stock pianos' and books from circulating libraries. The town itself had 'quaintness and oddity of character', once again associated in Dickens's imagination, as Boston had been, with the sparkle of newness: 'the very river that moves the machinery in the mills (for they are all worked by water power) seems to acquire a new character from the fresh buildings of bright red brick and painted wood among which it takes its course; and to be as light-headed, thoughtless, and brisk a young river, in its murmurings and tumblings, as one would desire to see'.

Dickens 'carefully abstained from drawing a comparison between the factories and those of our own land', although he adjured his readers to ponder on the differences between Lowell and 'those great haunts of misery' in their own country. He suggested too that the 'large class' of his readers who would feel that the workpeople of Lowell were thinking 'above their station' should think again for themselves. 'Are we quite sure that we in England have not formed our idea of the "station" of working people from accustoming ourselves to the contemplation of that class as they are, and not as they might be?'

The title of Trollope's chapter on Lowell, 'Cambridge and Lowell', itself suggests an unusual contrast. Cambridge with

Harvard was to New England what Oxford and Cambridge were to all England; Lowell was 'in little what Manchester is to us in as great a degree'. Like Dickens, Trollope began with the factory girls, 'neat, well dressed, careful, especially about their hair, composed in their manner, and sometimes a little supercilious in the propriety of their demeanour'. And then he thought again of Harvard. They had been admitted 'as it were, to a philanthropical manufacturing college'. 'This is all very nice and pretty at Lowell, but I am afraid it could not be done at Manchester.' Dickens would not have made that judgement. Nor would he have gone on to deal in some detail (adding quotations from documentary sources) with the economics of water power as compared with steam and the history of Lowell. For Trollope Lowell was 'a commercial Utopia': it could not be duplicated. Chicago, not Lowell, offered an example of what would happen elsewhere in the United States, for it had grown fast and was beyond control. There were things that philanthropy could not do. Moreover, the philanthropists of Lowell had learnt from the mistakes of England, where industry had developed first. 'In our thickly populated island any commercial Utopia is out of the question.' Once again Trollope had reached the frontiers of conventional thinking.

It is clear from his travel books that he never wanted to distance himself too far from his public even when he was far away from them in space. He draws his public in from the start. 'On reaching Sydney,' he begins *Australia and New Zealand*, 'the traveller should remember that he is visiting the spot on which our Australian empire was commenced, amidst difficulties of which we in England in these days think very little.'[148] He ends *North America* with a contrast between begging in Ireland and working in the United States, a land of 'self-asserting, obtrusive independence', and here he only just distances himself from those members of his public whose attitudes to Ireland were significantly different from his own. 'I myself am fond of Irish beggers. It is an acquired taste – which comes upon one as does that for smoked whisky, or Limerick tobacco. But I certainly wish that there were not so many of them at Queenstown.'[149]

It is in *North America* that he has most to say of 'literature', devoting a whole chapter to it.[150] 'As consumers of literature the Americans are certainly the most conspicuous people on the earth.'[151] Dickens sold more than Tennyson and Buckle – 'men and women after their day's work are not always up to the *Civilization'* – and (here we have the characteristic Trollopian gloss) 'as a rule they are generally up to *Proverbial Philosophy*, and thus perhaps, may have had something to do with the great popularity of that very popular work'.[152]

Before turning to copyright, a subject which preoccupied Dickens,[153] Trollope once more emphasised his sense of obligation to a broad public, drawing India into the picture as well as Australia and New Zealand and the United States. 'The English author should feel that he writes for the widest circle of readers ever yet obtained by the literature of any country.'[154] Wherever Trollope travelled to see the world, he knew that he had readers. And he knew how they often looked to what he had to say more than to the books of their own writers. 'General literature is perhaps the product which comes last from the energies of an established country. . . . The production of books must follow the production of other things and the growth of literature will be slow.'[155]

There was no sign, however, that Trollope expected his travel books to be read *in situ*, although he referred at the end of *North America* to 'his readers on either side of the water';[156] and the *Cornhill Magazine*, which by a coincidence printed its review of *North America* next to a paragraph on Buckle's death – and an exalted section on 'the profession of literature' – noted that it would 'give pain' in America. 'Everyone who has winced under the severities of blame will sympathise with the Americans if they are angry at this exposure of their faults. But the castigated author, when he has any true metal in him, extracts its virtue from the bitter medicine. . . . Will not the energetic Americans do the same?'[157] Trollope would not have worried too much provided that there were 'energetic' people to read him. It is a final irony that, for all his eagerness to travel busily around the world, and to comment freely on men, women, manners and events, many of the people who have gained the greatest satisfaction from his work are those who have always preferred to stay comfortably behind – not necessarily at home, in Barsetshire, a place where, unlike most of the places Trollope visited, dreams can come true.

NOTES

1  *An Autobiography* (1950 edn) p. 129.
2  Ibid., pp. 164, 166.
3  Ibid., p. 349.
4  Ibid., p. 364.
5  The author's first duty, Trollope wrote, is that 'he shall tell the truth, and shall so tell that truth that what he has written may be readable' – *North America* (1862) I.3. For Trollope's sense of the 'real' and his capacity to create the 'illusion of reality', see J. M. Cohen, *Form and Realism in Six Novels of Anthony Trollope* (1976).
6  'The Family that Goes Abroad', first published in the *Pall Mall Gazette*, 3 Aug. 1865.
7  *The West Indies and the Spanish Main* (1859) p. 11; *North America*, II.108; *Australia and New Zealand* (1876 edn) p. 101.
8  *South Africa* (1879 edn) pp. 388–9.
9  'No doubt the story of the Maori may be told with poetry', he writes (*Australia and New Zealand*, II.39), but 'such an attempt is not my way.' 'As far as I have told it, I have endeavoured to tell it with truth.'
10  *Autobiography*, p. 161. See Frances Trollope, *Domestic Manners of the Americans* (1832).
11  *North America*, I.1.
12  See J. S. Whitley and A. Goldman (eds), *Charles Dickens: American Notes for General Circulation, 1842* (1972) p. 11. See also A. Nevins, *American Social History as Recorded by British Travellers* (1934).
13  *Fraser's Magazine*, LXII (1862) 256.
14  *An Autobiography*, pp. 27–8, describes his early 'banishment' to Belgium.
15  Ch. 4 describes his appointment in Ireland: 'since that time who has had a happier life than mine?' (p. 61). For his British tour, see p. 88.
16  Preface to *An Autobiography*, p. xii.
17  Ibid., p. 129.
18  *North America*, II.391.
19  Ibid., p. 23ff.
20  *Fraser's Magazine*, LXVI.256.
21  *Punch*, XXXIV (1858) p. 8. The first of the *Travelling Sketches*, 'The Family that Goes Abroad', appeared in the newly founded *Pall Mall Gazette* on 3 August 1865. *Punch* did not review the complete volume. For Trollope on Palmerston, see his biography (1882): curiously, he did not mention him in his *Autobiography*. See also Asa Briggs, 'Trollope, Bagehot and the English Constitution', *Victorian People* (1954).
22  *Autobiography*, ch. 17.
23  Ibid., p. 314.
24  Ibid., p. 315.
25  It does, however, include a 'conventional Yankee woman'. For Trollope's views on American women, see *North America*, I.295–302.
26  *Autobiography*, p. 341. See also p. 326 for Frederic's resolve to follow 'a Colonial career', a not unfamiliar Trollopian theme.
27  Ibid.
28  Ibid., p. 345.

29 'I cannot be at ease with all the new people and the new things', he wrote, complaining also that he found himself 'too old to be eighteen months away from home.' See *The Letters of Anthony Trollope*, ed. Bradford Allen Booth (1951) pp. 290–1.

30 See, for example, *The New Zealander*, published in 1972.

31 *Athenaeum*, 16 June 1877. None the less, there is one interesting passage in the novel about travel (ch. 77): 'When an intelligent Japanese travels in Great Britain or an intelligent Briton is in Japan, he is struck with no wonder at national differences. He is on the other hand rather startled to find how like his strange brother is to him in many things.' Curiously, he went on, English – American relations were more difficult.

32 See T. H. S. Escott, *Anthony Trollope* (1913).

33 R. C. Terry, *The Artist in Hiding* (1977) p. 193.

34 'Tourists Who Don't Like Their Travels', which first appeared in the *Pall Mall Gazette*, 6 Sep. 1865.

35 *Australia and New Zealand*, p. 100.

36 'The Alpine Club Man', first published in the *Pall Mall Gazette*, 2 Sep. 1865. For controversy about the death of four members of Edward Whymper's Alpine party in July 1865 – and its significance – see *inter alia* D. Robertson, 'Mid-Victorians Amongst the Alps' in U. C. Knoepflmacher and G. B. Tennyson, *Nature and the Victorian Imagination* (1977) pp. 113–17.

37 *The West Indies*, pp. 335–6 (ch. 21). *South Africa* is full of references to transport also – and to its effects.

38 Ibid., p. 349.

39 *North America*, II.390.

40 Ibid., II.396. Cf. I.59: 'I cannot say that I like the hotels in those parts or indeed the mode of life at American hotels in general.' On railways, see *South Africa*, p. 259: 'The question of a railway is of all the most vital to the new colony' (of the Transvaal).

41 *North America*, II.393–4.

42 See, for example, a well-known passage in his Letters: 'There is much that is higher and better and greater than one's country. One is patriotic only because one is too small and weak to be cosmopolitan' (*Letters*, pp. 178–9).

43 *North America*, II.392–3.

44 Ibid., I.303–4.

45 Ibid., I.304.

46 *The West Indies*, p. 57.

47 Ibid., p. 59.

48 This is one of the strangest features of his book. He preferred British Guiana to the rest: 'when I settle out of England . . . British Guiana shall be the land of my adoption' (ibid., p. 168); and had good words for Barbados, 'so respectable a little island' (p. 163 and ch. 13). 'Little England as it delights to call itself . . . owes no man anything, pays its own way and never makes a poor mouth' (p. 216).

49 Ibid., pp. 62–3. In slave-owning Cuba Trollope noted more 'evidences of capital' than in Jamaica (p. 136). In Bermuda he generalised again that 'no enfranchised negro entertains an idea of daily work' (p. 374).

50 Ibid., p. 63. He also condemned the current attitudes of the Anti-Slavery

Society (pp. 187, 220ff.).

51  Ibid., p. 92.

52  For Exeter Hall and its influence, see B. Semmel, *The Governor Eyre Controversy* (1962) esp. pp. 18–22. In *South Africa*, Trollope noted how the Boers were completely uninfluenced by such philanthropy.

53  *The West Indies*, p. 219.

54  E. Williams, *British Historians and the West Indies* (1966) pp. 90–101.

55  *The West Indies*, pp. 104–5.

56  Trollope liked British Guiana because it had 'no noisy sessions of Parliament as in Jamaica, no money squabbles as in Barbados. . . . The form of government is a mild despotism tempered by sugar' (ibid., p. 170). Bermuda would have been better also 'without a constitution of its own' (p. 377).

57  Ibid., pp. 122–3. He also criticised the system in the Windward Islands (p. 158).

58  See ibid., ch. 5, 'Coloured Men', where he called the coloured people and not the whites 'the ascendant race' (p. 73). 'That the mulatto race partakes largely of the intelligence and ambition of their white forefathers, it is I think useless, and moreover wicked, to deny' (p. 78). Trollope had no vision of black power. 'The West Indian negro knows nothing of Africa except that it is a term of reproach' (p. 56).

59  Ibid., p. 76.

60  Ibid., p. 75.

61  Ibid., pp. 84–5.

62  Ibid., p. 83. The 'appointed work' (whatever that was) would have been done.

63  He was contemptuous of 'farces' in Haiti and 'such like lands' (ibid., p. 118) and had this to say of the twentieth century: 'It may be that after all we shall still have to send out some white Governor with a white aide-de-camp and a white private secretary . . . to support the dignity of the throne of Queen Victoria's great-grandchild's grandchild. Such may or may not be. To my thinking it would be more for our honour that it should not be so' (p. 84).

64  Ibid., pp. 84–5. Trollope's anti-Imperial position is very clearly set out in C. A. Bodelson, *Studies in Mid-Victorian Imperialism* (1960) p. 50ff. For Trollope and the Boers in South Africa, see C. J. Eys, *In the Era of Shepstone* (1933).

65  *Australia and New Zealand*, I.22.

66  See *The English in Ireland* (1872); *Two Lectures on South Africa* (1880); *Oceana* (1886); and *The English in the West Indies* (1888). He also wrote *Lord Beaconsfield* (1890).

67  *South Africa*, ch. 20. Cf. p. 182, where he argues generally and reaches for once a prophetic conclusion. 'Having absorbed the Transvaal in 1877 and Cyprus in 1878, should we now in 1879 weld Zululand to Afghanistan? The task grows to such an extent that a new acquisition will be required to satisfy the ambition of each three months. . . . We are powerful, we are energetic, we are tenacious: but may it not be possible that we shall attempt to clutch more than we can hold? When once the subject peoples shall have begun to fall from our grasp, the process of dropping them will

be very quick.'
68   Williams, *British Historians and the West Indies*, pp. 90, 80.
69   'We do not put very much faith in Mr Carlyle – nor in Mr Ruskin and his
     other followers. . . . It is regarded simply as Carlylism to say that the
     English-speaking world is growing worse from day to day' (*An Auto-
     biography*, p. 354). It is necessary to add that this was a late opinion, when
     Carlyle's position itself had changed.
70   Ibid., p. 103.
71   *The West Indies*, p. 253. Cf. ibid., p. 89. 'Where white men and black men are
     together, the white will order and the black will obey, with an obedience
     more or less implicit according to the terms on which they stand.'
72   Ibid., p. 273.
73   Ibid., p. 389.
74   Ibid., pp. 94–5.
75   Ibid., p. 102.
76   Semmel, *The Governor Eyre Controversy*, surprisingly does not mention
     Trollope once.
77   Quoted in W. L. Burn, *The British West Indies* (1951) p. 144.
78   Ibid., *The West Indies*, p. 389.
79   *North America*, II.430–1.
80   Ibid., II.88–9.
81   Ibid., I.3, where he compared himself with de Tocqueville and other
     'philosopho-political' or 'politico-statistical' writers. He described himself
     as 'a man who professes to use a light pen and to manufacture his article for
     the use of general readers'. Somewhat similar points were to be made in
     *South Africa*. The coloured people of the Cape 'though idle are not as
     apathetic as savages, not quite as indifferent as Orientals' (p. 4).
82   *North America*, II.65.
83   *South Africa*, p. 316.
84   Ibid., p. 317.
85   Ibid., p. 23. Later in the book Trollope somewhat qualified this statement
     when he drew contrasts between British and Boer attitudes and the
     attitudes of blacks to each (e.g., p. 226). He also distinguished between
     Zulus and Kafirs as 'Natives' (ch. 10). 'I liked the Zulu of the Natal capital
     very thoroughly' (p. 169).
86   See *South Africa*, p. 292. 'That Englishman should live under a policy
     devised or depending on Negroes I believe to be altogether impossible.'
87   Ibid., p. 22.
88   Ibid., p. 94.
89   *North America*, I.1.
90   For *The Times* on the War, see H. Brogan (ed.), *The Times Reports the
     American Civil War* (1975).
91   *North America*, I.10. Cf. p. 272: 'The South chose violence, and prepared for
     it secretly and with great adroitness. If that be not rebellion, there never
     has been rebellion since history began.'
92   Ibid., I.12, See also II, ch. 3, 'The Causes of the War'.
93   Ibid., II.65.
94   Ibid., II.85–6.
95   Ibid., II.89.

96  Ibid., II.452.
97  Ibid., II.454.
98  Ibid., I, p. 3.
99  Ibid., I.268. 'The name of an Englishman has become a by-word for reproach' (p. 282). See also p. 364ff. and II.457ff. None the less, he never detected 'any falling off in the hospitality and courtesy generally shown by a civilised people to passing visitors' (II.171).
100  Ibid., I.281.
101  Ibid., II.455.
102  Ibid., II.462. He thought of Canada as a possible *casus belli* (p. 460) and here his anti-Imperialism came out strongly. He always envisaged Canadian independence.
103  *Blackwood's Edinburgh Magazine*, XCII (1862) 374.
104  *Home and Foreign Review*, I (1862) 116.
105  *Fraser's Magazine*, LXII.257
106  Ibid., p. 260.
107  *Home and Foreign Review*, I.117.
108  *Fraser's Magazine*, LXII.264.
109  Ibid., p. 259.
110  *Blackwood's Edinburgh Magazine*, XCII.378. The critic added that Trollope himself used a better argument against a war with the United States – that 'sixty millions sterling of stock – railway stock and such like' – were held there by Britain.
111  Among the books and articles praised were J. Stirling, *Letters from the Slave States* (1857) and H. Martineau's 'Brewing of the American Storm' in the June issue of *Macmillan's*. There was no reference to E. V. Dicey's articles in the same periodical. In a letter to the *Spectator*, 16 Aug. 1862, Dicey used the phrase 'a people's war'.
112  *Blackwood's Edinburgh Magazine*, XCII.373. The argument about the 'lessons' of American democracy was of key importance in the debates on parliamentary reform later in the 1860s. See *Essays in Reform* (1867).
113  *Home and Foreign Review*, I.127.
114  Ibid., p. 128.
115  *Cornhill Magazine*, VI (1862) 106. 'I do not believe', Trollope had written, 'that Dives is as black as he is painted or his peril is so imminent.'
116  See, in particular, *Fraser's Magazine*, LXII.256.
117  *Home and Foreign Review*, I (1862) 110.
118  Ibid., p. 113. 'It seems like cutting blocks with a razor', therefore, 'when he devotes time and space to telling us that all the States in the Union return an equal number of senators.'
119  *North America*, I.231–2, quoted in *Home and Foreign Review*, I.114. The title of Trollope's chapter 11, from which the passage came, was 'Ceres Americana'.
120  *North America*, I.234.
121  *Blackwood's Edinburgh Magazine*, XCII.374.
122  Ibid.
123  Ibid., pp. 372–3.
124  Ibid., p. 390.
125  *North America*, II.435.

126   R. Foster, 'Appreciating the Usual', in the *Times Literary Supplement*, 27 Mar. 1981, touches on some of these themes.

127   *Home and Foreign Review*, I.110.

128   None the less, *Blackwood's*, XCII.389, found the stylè of *North America* 'slipshod', like the argument.

129   *North America*, II, ch. 15.

130   *The West Indies*, p. 32ff.

131   Ibid., p. 36.

132   Ibid., p. 38.

133   Ibid., p. 33.

134   Ibid., p. 22.

135   Avocados are mentioned twice – on pp. 21 and 28 along with breadfruit and mangoes. See *The American Senator* (1877) ch. 27. 'Men care more for what they eat than anything else.'

136   *North America* I, ch. 9.

137   Ibid., I.198–200.

138   Ibid., II.408.

139   *Australia and New Zealand*, II.99.

140   J. S. Whitley and A. Goldman, Introduction to *American Notes*, p. 23.

141   *North America*, II.3.

142   Ibid.

143   *Australia and New Zealand*, II.56–7.

144   Dickens, *North American Notes* (1842) ch. 8. A cheap edition of this appeared in 1859.

145   Ibid., ch. 3.

146   *North America*, I.26.

147   Ibid., II.2–3; *North American Notes*, ch. 8. In his *Memorandum Book, 1855–1865*, Dickens had written revealingly of 'representing London or Paris or any other great place – in the new light of being actually unknown to all the people in the story, and only taking the colour of their fears and fancies and opinions.' See also the illuminating chapter on *Bleak House* in J. Hillis Miller, *Charles Dickens: The World of His Novels* (1959). Edward Dicey (*Macmillan's Magazine*, VI.285) saw Boston in a completely different light from Dickens.

148   *Australia and New Zealand*, p. 3.

149   *North America*, II.464.

150   Ibid., II, ch. 15.

151   Ibid., II.411.

152   Ibid., II.414. For Martin Tupper, author of *Proverbial Philosophy*, see the excellent study by D. Hudson, *Martin Tupper, His Rise and Fall* (1949).

153   See *The Letters of Charles Dickens*, III (1974) 232, for a particularly strong statement. For Trollope's invòlvement with American copyright questions see his *Autobiography*, ch. 17.

154   *North America*, II.415.

155   *Australia and New Zealand*, II.107. Trollope was concerned with newspapers as well as books (see ibid.) and he shared Dickens's view of the low quality of the American Press. A rather different line was taken by Edward Dicey in his article in *Macmillan's Magazine*, VI.150–1.

156   *North America*, II.441.

157   *Cornhill Magazine*, VI.106.

# Trollope and Ireland

## JANET EGLESON DUNLEAVY

When Anthony Trollope accepted a Post Office appointment in
Ireland, his ignorance of the country that was to be his home and
the people who were to be his friends and neighbours for eighteen
years was almost complete. Like many another Englishman, he
had 'learned to think that Ireland was a land flowing with fun and
whisky, in which irregularity was the rule of life, and where
broken heads were looked upon as honourable badges'. It was an
impression shared by those to whom he confided his plans – a few
friends and an elderly cousin who served as the Trollope family
lawyer. To the twenty-six-year-old Trollope, however, the
position of surveyor's clerk in Connaught, the western Irish
province that sets its rocky cliffs against the cold Atlantic, offered
an escape from a life that had become unbearable: for him, it was a
chance to go not *to* Ireland but *from* England. For seven years he
had clerked in the Post Office in London, at a salary that had left
him constantly in debt at the mercy of a particularly obnoxious
money-lender; for seven years he had been wretched, feeling
himself trapped in a meaningless job, in an office he hated, under
supervisors who frequently upbraided him (with some justice, he
admits) for his idleness, his habitual tardiness, and his insubor-
dination.[1] Still, when he first saw Dublin Bay and realised that he
would soon set foot on Irish soil, his feelings were not unmixed.
Many English men and women lived abroad, and for a short time
the Trollope family had settled in Belgium. But to a young
Englishman the Continent was a familiar place where he might
expect to meet not only countrymen but former friends and acquaintances. Although English-governed for over seven hundred
years and English-speaking for the most part, Ireland was a
foreign country that attracted few English tourists. 'On the 15th of
September, 1841, I landed in Dublin,' Trollope wistfully recalled
in his *Autobiography*, 'without an acquaintance in the country, and

with only two or three letters of introduction from a brother clerk in the Post Office.' In all Ireland, he declared, 'there was not a single individual whom I had ever spoken to or seen'. Like many other recollections in the *Autobiography*, these cannot be accepted literally: in fact, Trollope had been at Harrow with Sir William Gregory, whose estate (Coole Park, in Co. Galway) was but a day's journey from Banagher, Co. Offaly, where Trollope held his first Irish post. But they express the desolation of the young Englishman who had turned his back on London to make a life for himself in a country known to him only through the disparaging anecdotes of his peers.[2]

Before long Trollope's mood changed. 'The Irish people did not murder me, nor did they even break my head.' Indeed, he found them to be 'good-humoured, clever, . . . economical, and hospitable'. Moreover, almost immediately his fortunes began to improve, for the cost of living in Connaught was much lower than it had been in London, and in addition his new position carried a small increase in salary plus a travel allowance. For the first time in his life young Trollope, who had been humiliated at Harrow by his day-student status, his unfashionable clothing, and his lack of money, who had sunk deep into debt to keep up with his fellow clerks from more affluent families in the London Post Office, had the means to live like a gentleman. More important, perhaps, he was received as a gentleman by his neighbours, who were not at all what Gerald Griffin, the Banim brothers, Lady Sydney Morgan, William Carleton, Charles Lever and Samuel Lover had led English readers to expect. Connaught was not a wilderness populated by wild-eyed rogues and savages. In the towns the new surveyor's clerk was entertained by lawyers, doctors, prosperous merchants, garrison officers, and their families; the Big House landlords of the countryside invited him to dinners, balls and hunts. He renewed his acquaintance with Sir William Gregory, who welcomed him to Coole Park. Even his superiors treated him with courtesy and respect. He bought a horse and found time to ride to hounds. For the first time that he could remember, life became 'altogether . . . very jolly' for him.[3]

Years earlier, Trollope had resolved that one day he would make his mark as a writer, but life divided between a boarder's bed in Marylebone and a clerk's desk in St Martin's-le-Grand had not been conducive to such work. In Ireland, however, according to Michael Sadleir, Trollope 'needed only the atmosphere of political declamation and good-natured wrangling in which his Irish friends perpetually lived to rouse his own potential enthusiasm for politics'. From verbal discussion it was but a short step to written pronouncements: his 'literary ambition and his love of politics grew rapidly and side by side'.[4] Travelling alone on horseback, on Post Office business, Trollope sharpened the powers of observation his nineteenth-century gentleman's education had developed.[5] On long journeys he again fell into his schoolboy habit of creating in his mind imaginary situations that could occur in the places through which he passed. But in those boyhood adventures he had been the central character. He now assumed a more appropriate role, that of interested observer, in the fictions he shaped in his imagination.

Trollope found, in Ireland, both a subject and a narrative position well suited to his occupation, inclinations and abilities. He could become, he believed, the Englishman who knew Ireland; he could dramatise, on a stage constructed from his own careful observations, the cares and conflicts of a people whose subtle and complex ties to England continually caused national debate; he could explain the sources and limitations of social and political power in Ireland, where England was the designated model, but where, beneath the surface structure of Government, law, and land tenure – as he quickly learned – currents of cultural difference and historical accident flowed and eddied, rubbing stone against stone.[6] John Halperin has argued that Trollope's fascination with politics is manifest 'from his earliest writings', articles on social and political conditions in Ireland, to 'almost the last thing he wrote', his memoir of Lord Palmerston.[7] His interest in politics was matched by and compounded with his lifelong fascination with Ireland, manifest from his first novel, which predates the articles mentioned above, to the novel left unfinished at his death.[8] Between these two stretch fifty-seven other separate works, some set in Ireland, some focused on Irish characters, and some which introduce Irish men and women as figures essential to an understanding of the social, economic and political life of nineteenth-century England. The Irish Question, a major issue in the British Parliament during Trollope's lifetime, dominates four of the novels: *The Macdermots of Ballycloran*, *The Kellys and the O'Kellys*, *Castle Richmond* and *The Landleaguers*. It affects, through situation or character, developments in four others: *Phineas Finn*, *Phineas Redux*, *The Prime Minister*, *An Eye for an Eye*. Like the guns of

Elizabeth Bowen's *Last September*, it echoes distantly, in the attitudes of minor figures and in passing allusions, through many more.[9]

The Irish Question was, of course, not a single recurrent issue of nineteenth-century England but a series of related issues that 'haunted the Victorians,' in the words of E. W. Wittig, 'just as, in a different form, it haunts modern England'.[10] The eighteenth century had closed in an atmosphere of fear and suspicion: throughout its last decade the United Irishmen had been gathering strength among young members of the landlord class, and an Irish–French conspiracy, led by Wolfe Tone, had brought French forces to Irish soil in the aborted Rising of '98. England had responded with the Act of Union (1800), by which Ireland lost its status as a separate kingdom and became part of the United Kingdom. Three years later another insurrection provided the nationalists with another eloquent martyr, Robert Emmet, whose speech from the dock continued to inspire anti-Unionists throughout the nineteenth century.

At first England attempted to disperse anti-Union sentiment with economic improvements: the Grand Canal was completed in 1804; grants supporting the building and repair of roads were approved in 1822; laws governing banking and commerce were changed to the advantage of Irish investors in 1821 and 1826; a Board of Works was established in 1831; a Poor Law Enquiry, promising redress of grievances, was created in 1836. Moreover, the economic and social position of Irish Catholics was relieved in 1829 by a parliamentary vote of Catholic Emancipation, which removed the last of the Penal Laws, and a National School system was set up in 1831. Nevertheless, when Trollope arrived in Ireland few Englishmen would have expected to find life 'altogether . . . very jolly' there. For reasons which most Englishmen, unfamiliar with the true structure of Irish society, could not understand, the Government's improvements did not change the lives of most of the people of Ireland. Agitation for repeal of Union continued, gathering strength in 'monster meetings,' and resulting, under the leadership of Daniel O'Connell, champion of the struggle for Catholic Emancipation, in the formation of the powerful Repeal Assocation. Through agrarian crime – arson, vandalism, and maiming of cattle – demands were made for agrarian reform. Boycotts were organised against landlords and tenants who would not support the Anti-Tithe Pledge.[11] Within three years after Trollope's arrival, the Government made a futile attempt to suppress anti-Union sentiment by arresting and trying Daniel O'Connell and his associates, a move that merely increased membership in protest organisations, radicalised moderates, and strengthened the influence of those calling for outright rebellion. The Young Irelanders, like their counterparts on the Continent, planned and drilled in anticipation of revolution in 1848. Also like their counterparts on the Continent, as well as their predecessors of 1798, they drew strength from young dissidents of the landlord class. In 1846, however, the Great Famine – far worse in its effects and farther reaching in its consequences than anything the Young Irelanders might have accomplished – began to devastate the countryside, requiring extraordinary relief measures that did little for the suffering populace, and diminishing all hope among the nationalists for a general rising. During the next decade landlord attempts to achieve economic recovery from the effects of the Famine were hampered by the Tenant Right League, which again attacked the land-tenure system, dismissing reforms perceived as improving only the lot of the landlords. At the same time the call for legislative independence for Ireland was renewed, this time under the new banner of Home Rule rather than Anti-Unionism. During the 1860s the Fenian Brotherhood threatened revolution. Its officers were arrested and transported, but in its place, through the next two decades, both the Land League and the Home Rule party continued to press for land reform and self-government, with Charles Stewart Parnell, another young dissident from the landlord class, emerging to lead them. By the end of the century the question was not whether there would be still greater changes in the laws affecting landlord–tenant relationships in Ireland, but what such laws would contain; not whether there would be legislative independence in Ireland, but when and how.

Trollope was of course acutely aware of the violence and protests in Ireland about which his countrymen read in their quiet English homes, but he dismissed their conclusions concerning the Irish people, Catholic and Protestant, whom he knew as friends and neighbours. He also knew that the impression created by newspaper reports – of an Ireland aflame, an Ireland in turmoil and chaos – was false. To be sure, the incidents described in the newspapers did occur, but, like the economic improvements with which Parliament had hoped to win support for the Union, each touched but a limited number of people. In general, the Ireland of his daily experience was relatively peaceful. To his mother in Italy, who worried about his safety in Ireland, Trollope wrote that he himself was acquainted with the dangers of Irish life only from what he read in English newspapers.[12] He saw that newspaper editors, knowing their readers but not knowing Ireland, focused on threats to landlords and merchants; that accounts of violence and mob action were reported fully, while the distress of the poor was understated and the causes of social unrest were not examined; that class and religious differences were exploited. To the editor of the *Examiner* in 1848 he offered a series of letters describing and analysing true conditions in West Cork, Kerry and Clare, as he had seen them at first-hand.[13] He had no sympathy for Irish nationalists; he was an Englishman who firmly believed in the advantages of belonging to the Crown. Yet even the Government, in Trollope's opinion, was misled by inaccurate reports of Ireland. In his novels, Trollope attempted to present a more balanced picture, showing the wretched conditions that drove men and women to acts of desperation. A recurring scene in these novels depicts the interior of a small cabin in which a mother and infant, sometimes also the father of the family, occupy the few broken sticks of furniture, their rags insufficient to cover their nakedness, while other children, naked and gaunt, huddle together on the mud floor.[14] In *The Prime Minister*, written in the 1870s, Trollope's best-known Irish character, Phineas Finn, warns a fellow Liberal MP that sentiment for Home Rule is far stronger in key Irish counties than their English colleagues have suspected, and that the Lord Lieutenant is mistaken in thinking the country 'admirably managed' because 'Dublin ladies dance at the Castle, and the list of agrarian murders is kept low'.[15]

A striking feature of Trollope's Irish novels is the skill with which he wove together fictional elements and political observations on the one hand and the anomalies of Irish life and the character of the countryside on the other. For this he was not always admired by his contemporaries: unsigned notices published in the *Spectator* and the *Saturday Review* (May 1847; May 1860; Dec. 1883) deplore the 'needless minutiae' of *The Macdermots of Ballycloran*, suggest that the Famine was the only part of *Castle Richmond* 'about which Mr Trollope really cared', and describe *The Landleaguers* as 'a long pamphlet, under the guise of fiction, upon Irish troubles'.[16] Writing about the Palliser novels and the Chronicles of Barsetshire, recent critics not only have found Trollope's verisimilitude more to their taste but have perceived in his selection of detail a depth of meaning missed by his contemporaries.[17] Trollope's ability to recreate the emotional tenor of inhabitants of a particular place as well as the visual reality of the place itself is especially marked in the Irish novels, which have received less critical attention than his other works, and which were set in areas for the most part still relatively unchanged. To this day, for example, starting from Drumsna, unaided by local residents, a stranger to Leitrim can use the opening pages of *The Macdermots of Ballycloran* to go directly to the derelict house that inspired the novel and from there north through Keshcarrigan to Aughacashel, east and south to Ballinamore, then south along a good road to Mohill, returning west to Drumsna, and continuing on through Drumsna to Carrick-on-Shannon – all places vividly described by Trollope and peopled with his characters.[18] This circle will show, moreover, that Keshcarrigan is still a crossroads village; that in Aughacashel an abandoned cabin by the side of a stream fits the description of the site on which Pat Brady's brother was arrested; and that the bridewell beside the bridge in Ballinamore, although recently converted into a shop, still shows its history in the angle and windows of its rear walls. In Mohill the lane where the Widow Mulready used to keep a shebeen remains dark and narrow – a good place, surely, for plotting revenge and taking secret oaths. The courtyard in Carrick-on-Shannon where Thady Macdermot was hanged still may be seen from the riverbank. Leitrim's soil is no more fertile today than it was in Trollope's time: it sustains scrub growth reluctantly; rocks abound; short, gnarled trees are bent by prevailing winds.[19]

Much of the world of *The Kellys and the O'Kellys* also remains to be examined. In the village of Dunmore, in Co. Galway, Dunmore House is now in ruin, but from its large front door kind-hearted Biddy still could hurry down the drive, through the gate, and to the shop that was once Kelly's Hotel (the Kelly's Hotel used by Trollope in his novel) to ask for help for her unfortunate mistress.[20] On the road to Ballindine, the land rises, just as Trollope described it, where Martin would have had his farm. There the scrubby growth and poor soil of the protuberant ground are like other areas of the western countryside known as 'Toneroe' to local inhabitants, although for this particular place the name is neither recorded in deed or validated by local memory.[21] In Cork, the ruins of MacDonagh's Court near Kanturk are situated on the Blackwater where stood, according to Trollope, Desmond Court of *Castle Richmond*. Although stories told about the two houses, the one existing in fact, the other in fiction, have certain similarities, Trollope's description of Desmond Court more closely matches Castlemagarret in Co. Mayo, with which Trollope also was familiar.[22] The geography of the novel, however, corresponds to the geography of the Kanturk-Mallow countryside rather than to the geography of Mayo. Visitors to the Cliffs of Moher easily may find the spot where the O'Hara cottage stood and where Mrs O'Hara of *An Eye for an Eye* pushed the faithless Fred Neville to his death. To the east, on the River Shannon, is Killaloe, where Phineas Finn was born. To the north, in Co. Galway, live descendants of tenant farmers whose fictional counterparts, the tenant farmers of the Earl of Tulla, sent Phineas to represent them in Parliament. From Galway north into Mayo many of the roads travelled in Trollope's fiction by Captain Yorke Clayton, Frank Jones, Gerald O'Mahoney, Rachel O'Mahoney and other characters of *The Landleaguers* have been widened to accommodate residents of the area in which Trollope set Philip Jones's estate, who no longer journey to Galway City by boat: farming, however, continues to be a way of life there for much of the population, the soil remains rocky and shallow, and those who make their living from it continue to rely on drainage projects to keep their fields from flooding.

Throughout his career, Trollope's opinions on Irish political issues were closely tied to what he knew from personal observation and experience of the Irish countryside and of social and economic conditions that prevailed there. His perception of the subtle relationships and unexpected stratifications of a deeply textured society at a time when it eased most English minds to think of Ireland as a dichotomy of Anglo-Saxon, Protestant landlord and Celtic, Catholic cottager informed his choice of characters and governed the ways in which he allowed them to behave toward one another. (Contrary to statements made by some critics, however, Trollope's accuracy of observation did not extend to differences in Hiberno-English regional dialects, nor do his characters always use the Irish language as they should.[23]) Through their behaviour and the events that befall them he contrasted the sources of power and influence that existed in the two cultures not as separate streams but as currents within the same river.[24]

The privileged members of nineteenth-century Irish society were, as depicted by Trollope, the affluent peers: men such as Lord Tulla of *Phineas Finn*, whose seat is Castlemorris in Co. Clare, but who owns almost all the land of Loughshane, Co. Galway, which is managed by an agent and represented in Parliament by the man of Lord Tulla's choice; Lord Claddagh of the Palliser novels, who controls a borough in Co. Mayo; and Lord Birmingham of *The Macdermots of Ballycloran*, absentee owner of Mohill. Behind their fictional power lies the historical fact that the Reform Acts of 1832 and 1866–7 did not entirely disenfranchise pocket boroughs and rotten boroughs in Ireland. These men, therefore, are able to exert in Trollope's novels what their historical counterparts regarded as a right and a privilege: direct influence over parliamentary representation. Until the Reform Bills of 1866–7 remove his influence, for example, Lord Brentford of the Palliser novels dispatches the Liberal representative of his choice from Loughton, his pocket borough in England. For twenty years, until a family quarrel and pique over a patronage request refused by the Party leads to his withdrawal of support, Lord Tulla of *Phineas Finn* provides a seat in Parliament for his hard-drinking high-living brother, George Morris. At the same time he assures the Conservatives of representation from Galway. Meanwhile Lord Claddagh's neighbouring Irish borough guarantees a place in the House of Commons to his youngest son, Laurence Fitzgibbon.

Not all Victorian peers either in fact or Trollopian fiction had strong political interests, however; not all Trollopian peers, therefore, exercise their political power directly. Beyond the injunction understood by his agent that nothing should prevent Mohill from continuing to provide handsomely for him, Lord Birmingham of *The Macdermots* cares little what happens to his Irish estates or to the people living on them. Like Lord Dillon, a real-life peer whose actual property in the nineteenth-century corresponded loosely with the area owned by the Trollopian lord, Birmingham's major concern is that he should not die in Ireland, and the precautions he takes to assure himself that no such fate should overtake him are, similarly, to set foot on Irish soil as rarely as possible.[25]

As a bachelor, Lord Ballindine of *The Kellys and the O'Kellys* also has little interest in politics and poses no great threat to the parliamentary process. To be sure, his interest in horses has caused him to exceed his income for some years – a situation which, if continued, might lead by necessity to increased financial pressures on his tenants, with resulting unrest and political consequences. But 'a good match' (Victorian English for a wife with money) plus his own prudence prevails: once married, he settles down to manage the family estate that had been much neglected by his absentee grandfather and becomes a commendable example of what Trollope no doubt considered to be a responsible peer. By contrast, the ambition of Lord Ballindine's grandfather, deceased before the start of the novel, had been for a place in the court of the Queen of England, not in the Houses of Parliament: having been named Lord of the Bedchamber, he had left his lands in Roscommon, Mayo and Sligo in the hands of an agent, Simeon Lynch. Lynch (the name suggests some connection with one of the powerful merchant families of Galway, although Simeon seems to have accumulated property entirely by his wits) gradually had allowed the leases on the estate to expire, had told the old Lord by letter that no new tenants could be found, and had then leased the lands to himself and through him to subtenants, diverting most of the income from the estate into his own pockets. By the time the old Lord's son, a captain in the Queen's army, father to Lord Ballindine of the novel, discovered that Lynch was playing a game no doubt as familiar to Trollope from actual accounts as from Maria Edgeworth's *Castle Rackrent*, with which he also was familiar, financial loss to the O'Kellys (Lord Ballindine's family) was severe. It is this diminished estate that is inherited by Lord Ballindine at the start of the novel, along with his grandfather's title. His legacy includes the dubious pleasure of having Simeon Lynch's son for a school-fellow at Eton, on money that should have been his own, and an Ireland in which such men as Simeon Lynch and his son are able to rise to positions of power and influence through the failure of irresponsible peers to assume the obligations as well as the privileges of inherited rank.[26]

Whatever Lord Ballindine has lost as a result of the negligence of his grandfather, however – whatever the long-range effects were of men such as the old Lord on real-life Ireland – the tenants of O'Kelly's Court and Dunmore House (the home of Simeon Lynch) do not suffer immoderately at the hands of the unscrupulous agent. Other tenants subject to other agents in other

Trollopian novels are not so fortunate. In *The Macdermots of Ballycloran*, the Ballycloran tenantry prefer Thady Macdermot, the unkingly remnant of an ancient family of kings who still clings to a parcel of land and regards his cottagers as feudal vassals, to a Carrick attorney, Hyacinth Keegan, the turncoat Protestant Tory son of a poor, Roman Catholic process server who has 'taught himself to believe that what was legal was right, and . . . knew how to stretch legalities to the utmost'.[27] Thady is almost as poor as his tenants, but an ancient code adhered to by both establishes his right to be master and their right to expect fair treatment from him. For Keegan there are no such honourable traditions: they expect – and receive – the worst from him. Lord Birmingham's tenants in Mohill are even less fortunate; they can expect little charity from Mr Cassidy, Lord Birmingham's agent, although in London the hypocritical lord is Charity itself: 'presiding genius of the company for relieving the Poles; . . . vice-presiding genius for relieving destitute authors, destitute actors, destitute clergymen's widows, [and] destitute half-pay officers' widows; . . . [and] patron of the Mendicity Society [and] the Lying-in, Small Pox, Lock, and Fever Hospitals'. Mr Cassidy is 'a fat, good-natured man, . . . a good man, as good to the poor as he can be'. But he is the agent, not the landlord, and his assigned task, which he performs virtuously (pocketing, of course, the standard commission – not a farthing more – for himself), is to collect the landlord's rents. On his income from his commission he occupies a big house in the centre of town, distinguishable by its 'elegance, . . . neat, slated roof, brass knocker . . . large sash windows, and iron railings', while from his gable ends hang mud hovels, each with a roof 'about three feet above the ground' and a front so narrow that the doorway takes 'nearly the whole facing to the street'. Through the doorway of one hovel may be seen the emaciated tenant family and the furnishings of the single room they call their home: a 'low stool' and 'a few rotten boards propped upon equally infirm supports'.[28]

In Trollope's Ireland men like Simeon Lynch and Mr Cassidy stood between absentee landlord and tenant, exacting their share of profits from the negligence of one and the helplessness of the other. Politics, the kind practised in Parliament, was of no concern to them: they marched the tenants to the polls and returned the vote required by the landlord. They did not figure in the reports and charts presented to Parliament by commissions on relief of the poor, land valuation, and tenants' rights. But, as Trollope knew, they played an important part in the social and economic life of nineteenth-century Ireland.

Trollope also knew that not all estates owned by absentee landlords were managed by agents. Some landlords leased their land in large parcels at full value to men of no property who, as Trollope observed, sublet it in small patches, charging rents which 'took the whole labour of their tenants and the whole produce of the small patch, over and above the quantity of potatoes absolutely necessary to keep that tenant's body and soul together'. This system produced a lease-holding middle class, Protestant as well as Catholic, in which young men, lacking traditional values, were 'brought up to do nothing. Property was regarded as having no duties attached to it. Men became rapacious, and determined to extract the uttermost farthing out of the land within their power, let the consequences to the people on that land be what they might.' The result: 'a state of things engendered on Ireland which discouraged any produce from the land except the potato crop, which maintained one class of men in what they considered to be the gentility of idleness, and another class, the people of the country, in the abjectness of poverty'.[29]

One measure passed by Parliament for the relief of tenants impoverished by this system was the Poor Law. However, as Trollope complained in *Castle Richmond*, as a result of political manipulation, the rates charged landlords and tenants varied from electoral district to electoral district, tending to be highest in the areas where there was the most poverty – and the least political influence.[30] Since the poorest tenants already were paying the highest rents they could afford, their share of the Poor Rate was deducted from their rent, not added to it. Thus, as the share of the Poor Rate to be paid increased, rental income decreased. When poverty became more widespread (during the less publicised failures of the potato crop as well as during the Great Famine) tenants were unable to pay any rent at all. At such times the Poor Rate levied against landowners soared even higher, despite the fact that their incomes had been diminished. As a result, many landowners soon found themselves – like Trollope's Lady Desmond – deeply in debt, their estates heavily encumbered. Lady Desmond's financial distress is diminished, of course, by her daughter's fortunate marriage, but the only choice left to those who could not be rescued so easily by a novelist's pen was often –

as Trollope observed – to give up their land, either by leasing to the self-styled gentlemen of no property described above, or by selling out entirely to speculators who cleared the tenant farmers from their smallholdings, forcing them to emigrate.[31]

Despite his admiration for Lord Palmerston (who coined the slogan 'Tenants' right is landlords' wrong') Trollope seems to have had more sympathy for the goals of the Tenant Right League, founded in 1850 by Sharman Crawford, Gavan Duffy, and others, than for the Poor Law, as a means of ending the abuses that gave rise to the kind of poverty he depicted in *The Macdermots of Ballycloran* and *Castle Richmond*. In *Phineas Finn*, written in the late 1860s, a Tenant Right bill is introduced to the House by Julius Monk, a Cabinet minister of independence and integrity much admired by the young Phineas. The Liberals oppose the measure, in a move familiar to students of modern parliamentary history, not because they have valid objections to it, but for reasons based solely on party management and party discipline: they do not wish it to become an issue in the present session; they prefer that a similar measure be introduced in the future by the party's Chief Secretary for Ireland. For the sake of his own career, Phineas is advised against joining Monk. Young, idealistic and relatively inexperienced, unwilling to support factionalism against what he considers to be the best interests of the people whom Parliament is supposed to represent, Phineas ignores this advice, even though his maverick behaviour leads his Liberal colleagues to distrust him. He is forced to resign his position as Under-Secretary for the Colonies (his only source of income beyond a small allowance from his father); for the time being (until he reappears in *Phineas Redux*) he must put an end to what had appeared to be a promising parliamentary career.[32]

Phineas Finn's sacrifice of public office in the novel in which he begins his political career has sometimes been interpreted as an indication of Finn's nationalist sentiments, leading some critics to identify him as a fictional counterpart of John Sadleir, the MP from Galway and Tenant Right advocate of the 1850s who, with William Keogh, formed the political team derisively known in Parliament as the 'Pope's Brass Band'. Far from being an ardent Papist or seeking Church support, however, Finn is one of several Trollopian characters who embody Trollope's own commitment, expressed in letters and in his *Autobiography* as well as in his novels, to ecumenism.[33] Furthermore, Finn is a product of a mixed marriage: his father was Roman Catholic; his mother, Protestant. Following the common practice of such unions in nineteenth-century Ireland, the boy was brought up in the religion of his father, his sisters, in the religion of their mother.[34] As for being a nationalist, Phineas is too much of a practical politician for that, even if his idealism did lead him to join a Cabinet minister in support of Tenant Right. No Cabinet ministers in either fact or Trollopian fiction backed the incipient Irish party of the 1850s and 1860s, nor were the MPs of this group yet sufficiently numerous during these years (in *The Prime Minister*, Finn declares there to be 'about twenty') to have the significant impact realised later under Parnell. The verisimilitude of Phineas Finn's support of Monk's measure in *Phineas Finn* (and his later approval of disestablishment in *Phineas Redux*) springs therefore not from any identification with a single historical person but from the fact that the positions he assumes are credible, given his class, education and family background and the opportunities these would have provided for direct observation of all facets of the nineteenth-century Irish social, economic, and political scene.[35] These opportunities also would have provided Finn with awareness of the contradictions as well as the complexities of Irish social and political life, the ineffectual size of the Irish Party, and the odds against radical change, so long as neither Tories nor Liberals were dependent upon Irish votes to achieve or remain in power.

Finn's experiences, the observations that lead to the formation of his Trollopian attitudes, and the political stance he assumes as a result contrast, of course, with those of O'Mahony in *The Land-leaguers*, whose ill-informed Irish-American background leads him to advocate extreme positions which Trollope frankly and openly disapproved.[36] If today Finn appears to be a West Briton, Trollope an English apologist, and O'Mahony a patriot, it must be remembered that such a post-1916 view of Trollope's novels is coloured by the fact that twentieth-century Ireland is an established republic, Irish Nationalism is now respectable, and less than one hundred years after Trollope's death the sun has set on the British Empire. These were not the political realities of England in the nineteenth century – or of Trollope's Ireland.

NOTES

1 Anthony Trollope, *An Autobiography* (Berkeley and Los Angeles, Calif.: University of California Press, 1947) pp. 37–52. Michael Sadleir, *Trollope: A Commentary* (New York: Farrar, Straus, 1947) pp. 120–2, cautions against a too literal acceptance of Trollope's account of himself, pointing both to the public morality of the Victorians and to contemporary conventions of autobiography as reasons to regard it as exaggerated. To this may be added the observation that Trollope's *Autobiography* was written after he had fictionalised a number of events and people in his life (cf. – as just one example – Mr Clarkson of *Phineas Finn*, the obnoxious moneylender of the *Autobiography*): to what extent were his recollections taken from memory, to what extent were they altered by the novelist's imagination? Clearly, as Trollope was not dismissed from his job during his seven years in the Post Office in London, he could not have been quite so derelict in his duties as the *Autobiography* suggests; at the same time, it is worth noting that neither was he singled out during this period for reward or promotion.

2 Cf. Sadleir's caveat, noted above, and Sadleir's account of the Trollope–Gregory relationship: *Trollope: A Commentary*, pp. 67, 144.

3 *Autobiography*, p. 54.

4 Sadleir, *Trollope: A Commentary*, pp. 140–1. Cf. John Halperin, *Trollope and Politics: A Study of his Pallisers and Others* (New York: Barnes and Noble, 1977) pp. 1–23.

5 The unpublished correspondence of members of the O'Conor family contemporary with Anthony Trollope outlines the kind of accomplishments that were expected of educated young men and women, especially in writing: see summaries indexed under Education and Travel in Gareth W. Dunleavy and Janet E. Dunleavy, *The O'Conor Papers* (Madison: University of Wisconsin Press, 1977). They were instructed by their elders to record their daily observations in their diaries, following rhetorical models; when they travelled, they were required to write letters full of descriptive detail. In *Anthony Trollope: His Public Services, Private Friends and Literary Originals* (New York: John Lane, 1913) p. 29, T. H. S. Escott describes Frances Trollope's advice to her son in similar terms. According to Escott, she particularly encouraged Anthony's descriptive writings, urging attention to details.

6 Among those who contributed significantly to Trollope's understanding of Ireland were Sir William Gregory, mentioned above, and Carlo Bianconi, whose horse-drawn coaches provided land transportation in Ireland before the railways were built. The former was a Big House landlord on excellent terms with his tenants (his wife of later years was Lady Isabelle Augusta Gregory, a founding member of Ireland's Irish Literary Theatre and director of the Abbey, whose own plays drew upon tenant life at Coole Park for character, content and language). Bianconi had extraordinary insights, as a result of operating his coach service, into the complex social and economic relationships that characterised Ireland in the middle of the nineteenth century.

7 Halperin, *Trollope and Politics*, p. 2.

8 Cf. Robert Tracy, 'Instant Replay: Trollope's *The Landleaguers*, 1883', *Eire-Ireland*, XV, no. 2 (Summer 1980) 30–46.

9  Cf. Lady Eustace's remarks to Lord Fawn in *The Eustace Diamonds*, World's Classics edn (London: Oxford University Press, 1973) p. 80.

10  E. W. Wittig, 'Trollope's Irish Fiction', *Eire–Ireland*, IX, no. 3 (Autumn 1974) 97.

11  The practice of boycotting was common in Ireland long before the events of 1880, involving Captain Boycott of Lough Mask House, gave the practice its now familiar name.

12  Anthony Trollope to Frances Trollope, Spring [1848?], no. 14, in *The Letters of Anthony Trollope*, ed. Bradford A. Booth (London: Oxford University Press, 1951) p. 6.

13  Published 25 Aug. 1849; 30 Mar., 6 Apr., 11 May, 1 and 18 June 1850.

14  Cf. *The Macdermots of Ballycloran* (London: Chapman and Hall, 1867) pp. 73–4; *Castle Richmond* (Leipzig: Bernhard Tauchnitz, 1860) II.177–85.

15  *The Prime Minister*, World's Classics edn (London: Oxford University Press, 1973) I.111. Similar observations concerning the uninformed attitude and complacency of the Lord Lieutenant and his staff may be found in George Moore's *A Drama in Muslin* and *Parnell and His Island*. Cf. Janet Egleson Dunleavy, *George Moore: The Artist's Vision, the Storyteller's Art* (Lewisburg, Pa.: Bucknell University Press, 1973) pp. 83, 87–8; A. Norman Jeffares, '*A Drama in Muslin*', in *George Moore's Mind and Art*, ed. Graham Owens (New York: Barnes and Noble, 1970) pp. 1–20.

16  Reprinted by Donald Smalley (ed.), in *Trollope: The Critical Heritage* (New York: Barnes and Noble, 1969) pp. 547, 113, 518.

17  Cf. John Halperin, *Egoism and Self-Discovery in the Victorian Novel* (New York: Burt Franklin, 1974) pp. 61–78; C. P. Snow, *Trollope* (London: Macmillan, 1975) pp. 13, 109–12.

18  Trollope's spellings of Irish place-names, while close and for the most part phonetically accurate, do not conform to present usage; however, until recently (and in many parts of the country even today) place-name spelling was not standardised, and pronunciation often determined the several ways in which a name might be spelled.

19  So faithfully has Trollope recreated this area, indeed, that his fiction has become 'fact' in local lore. In 1979, when this writer asked a local resident who owned the derelict house before it had become a ruin, the answer was 'the Macdermots', with the additional information that it used to be called Ballycloran House. Neither Trollope's name for the house nor his name for its owners is associated with the house in Land Valuation records, however; both appear to have been invented by Trollope, although the surname Macdermot (spelled variously) is common and may be found in stories, annals, and records of this part of Ireland dating back to the first known documents of the early Middle Ages.

20  I am indebted to James Greaney of Dunmore for the opportunity to examine nineteenth-century photographs of this area in his possession.

21  Toneroe, as a place-name, comes from Irish *tón*(back side, used in place names to refer to a knobby part of a hill, as opposed to a smooth slope) plus *ruadh* (reddish brown, the colour of vegetation where the soil is poor).

22  While faithfulness to geographical detail is one of the hallmarks of Trollope's fiction, he was not above moving houses when such a move served his artistic purpose. *The Kellys and the O'Kellys* offers another

example: no Big House matching the description of Kelly's Court stands, is remembered as standing, or is recorded as having stood in the location described by Trollope, so far as this writer can ascertain, and red stone is not found in this area but further south, in Cork or Carlow. As Castlemagarret apparently was moved by Trollope from Mayo to Cork to serve as a model for Desmond Court of *Castle Richmond*, so the original of Kelly's Court may well have been moved by him from Cork to Carlow.

23  Cf. C. P. Snow, *Trollope*, p. 13; John William Clark, *The Language and Style of Anthony Trollope* (London: André Deutsch, 1975) pp. 100–18.

24  Trollope's awareness of conditions in Ireland and the causes of violence and unrest is evident even in his last novel, *The Landleaguers*, written twenty years after he had left Ireland and begun with a negative attitude toward the Irish that he could not sustain. Cf. Robert Tracy, in *Eire–Ireland*, XV, no. 2, 42–4.

25  *Phineas Finn* (London: Oxford University Press, 1973) I.13, 311–12; *The Macdermots of Ballycloran*, p. 75. For statements concerning Lord Viscount Dillon, the author is grateful for having had the opportunity to consult unpublished correspondence in the O'Conor Papers, Clonalis House, Castlerea, Co. Roscommon.

26  *The Kellys and the O'Kellys* (London: Chapman and Hall, 1867) p. 191.

27  *The Macdermots of Ballycloran*, pp. 6, 86.

28  Ibid., pp. 73–4.

29  *Castle Richmond*, pp. 59–60.

30  Trollope's complaints are echoed in letters of Denis O'Conor, MP for Co. Rosscommon from 1831 until his death in 1847. Cf. summaries of Denis O'Conor's correspondence in Dunleavy and Dunleavy, *The O'Conor Papers*.

31  *Castle Richmond*, pp. 60, 63–4.

32  *Phineas Finn*, II.263, 272–6, 327. Trollope's apparent sympathy with the Tenant Right League does not carry over, however, in sympathy for the Land League, which he deplored. Cf. Robert Tracy, in *Eire–Ireland*, XV, no. 2, 41–2.

33  *Autobiography*, p. 62; *The Kellys and the O'Kellys*, p. 372; *Castle Richmond*, pp. 47, 59, 90–3, 184, 188; *The Landleaguers*, pp. 4, 5, 16.

34  *Phineas Finn*, I.2. The practice continued until prohibited by the *Ne Temere* decree of 1907 (effective 1908). Similarly, the mother of George Henry Moore, MP, father of the novelist, was Catholic, although she was of the same family as Denis Browne, the 'hanging judge' of Connaught, a Protestant, and the Marquess of Sligo, who also was Protestant.

35  What is more likely is that Finn was developed by Trollope not as a fictional counterpart of any one historical figure but as a composite of several. As Robert Tracy (in *Eire–Ireland*, XV, no. 2, 30) has pointed out, Trollope's fictional counterparts of historical figures usually are minor characters.

36  Cf. 'The State of Ireland', *The Landleaguers*, pp. 251–60.

# Trollope's Country Estates

## JULIET McMASTER

'It is a comfortable feeling to know that you stand on your own ground', says Archdeacon Grantly to his son, as he surveys his prosperous estate of Plumstead Episcopi. 'Land is about the only thing that can't fly away. And then, you see, land gives so much more than the rent. It gives position and influence and political power, to say nothing about the game' (*Last Chronicle*, II.178).[1] The Archdeacon is at this time concerned to teach a great lesson to his son, who is inclined to defect from country gentlemanhood, and deliberately lays out the glories of his estate – 'fox-covers at Plumstead, and a seat among the magistrates of Barsetshire, and an establishment full of horses, beeves, swine, carriages, and hayricks' (II.179) – to tempt his son, like Satan displaying the kingdoms of the earth. Though Trollope knows quite well how to satirise the conservatism of such characters as Grantly, he too is imbued with a deep respect for the values that are rooted in the land.

'In an evil hour', Trollope tells us portentously in the first chapter of the *Autobiography*, his father took land on a long lease, and proceeded to build on it. 'He was felt to be entitled to a country house', he explains, and continues the dreary saga of the progressive blasting of all his father's ambitions. 'As a final crushing blow, an old uncle, whose heir he was to have been, married and had a family' (*Autobiography*, pp. 2–3). How many of Trollope's plots, as well as the aspirations of his life, have their well-springs in the frustrated longings of this early time! To envisage how comfortable a feeling it is to know you stand on your own land, and all the manifold threats and dangers involved in getting there, staying there, or trying to stay there, became one of his constant activities as a novelist. As he tells us in the first chapter of *The Macdermots of Ballycloran*, it was in musing over the spectacle of a deserted and ruined Irish estate that he found the impulse to write his first novel. Ballycloran, 'a picture of misery, of useless expenditure, unfinished pretence, and premature decay',[2] sounds rather like a description of his father.

Richard Gill, in his book on the country house in English fiction, says that 'Trollope might seem the country-house novelist par excellence, if only because his fiction exhibits the greatest number of houses. Symbolically, however, he did the least with them.' He claims that the houses and estates in Trollope's novels, though numerous, 'are not dramatically rendered in relation to their inhabitants, nor symbolically expressive of their condition and fate'.[3] I can only say, not so. It is true that Trollope is prodigal of description of the many country estates that are his settings, and often gives us more than we need. But Portray Castle, Carbury Manor and Clavering Park express their owners, devious Lizzy Eustace, steadfast Roger Carbury and stern Sir Hugh Clavering, as exactly almost as Pemberley expresses Mr Darcy, or Gardencourt Mr Touchett.[4] Owner and estate match, and together signify a way of life. Mr Longstaffe of Caversham, *nouveau riche*, a bit of a dandy, and 'intensely proud of his position in life, thinking himself to be immensely superior to all those who earned their bread' (*The Way We Live Now*, I.116), is very like Sir Walter Elliot of Kellynch Hall in *Persuasion*, who also cares intensely for appearance and status, and who equally sacrifices his duties as proprietor to the pursuit of prestige. The one surrounds himself with supernumerary flunkeys, the other with mirrors, and both from love of display accumulate debts they can't pay, and so burden the estate that is the source of their pride. Like Jane Austen,[5] Trollope tells us about his characters while he tells us about their estates.

He also shares Jane Austen's moral concern with the responsibilities attached to the proprietor of a considerable estate. 'Wealth must always bring its responsibilities, but a landed proprietor is especially in a responsible position', wrote Sir George Gilbert Scott, author of *Secular and Domestic Architecture* (1857). He goes on:

> To him the poor man should look up for protection; those in doubt or difficulty for advice; the ill-disposed for reproof or punishment; the deserving, of all classes, for consideration and hospitality; and *all* for a dignified, honourable, and Christian example. . . . He has been placed by Providence in a position of authority and dignity, and no false modesty should deter him

from expressing this, quietly and gravely, in the character of his house.[6]

The meretricious expression is hardly Austen's or Trollope's, but they would share the sentiment, as well as the aesthetic principle of the consonance of physical surroundings with moral character. An estate-owner is to be judged according to the way in which he fulfils his role as landlord and squire, and performs his duties as well as collecting his perquisites.

Sir Hugh Clavering, for instance, is equally a bad husband, husbandman and man.[7] *The Claverings* opens with a memorable scene set in the gardens of Clavering Park. The dried-up August garden expresses both the withering of the love of Harry and Julia, as she delivers her news that she is jilting him, and the landlord's neglect; 'care and labour were but scantily bestowed on the Clavering Gardens, and everything was yellow, adust, harsh, and dry' (p. 1). The needy on the estate are neglected like the gardens and are scantly supplied with comforts. 'Indeed, there was never much of such kindnesses between the lord of the soil and his dependants. A certain stipulated dole was given at Christmas for coals and blankets; but even for that there was generally some wrangle between the rector and the steward' (p. 31). Sir Hugh neglects the breeding of partridges, and then makes the poor head of game a reason for staying away, and turning his home into a 'prison' for his wife. 'I cannot stand this place', he declares (p. 43), and so dooms himself; for in this novel, which as the title indicates is as much about a family heritage as about the hero's loves, the worthy heir must eventually inherit the estate. Sir Hugh and his brother go down in a yacht at sea, the craft ballasted with his failings as landlord. Trollope is a sterner moralist than usual in so summarily meting out poetic justice to him and poor Archie:

> Both of the brothers had lived on the unexpressed theory of consuming, for the benefit of their own backs and their own bellies, the greatest possible amount of those good things which fortune might put in their way. I doubt whether either of them had ever contributed anything willingly to the comfort or happiness of any human being.   (pp. 469–70)

The reader is reassured that all will now be well at Clavering Park when he hears that the new baronet and his son are discussing 'the

alterations which they would make in reference to the preservation of pheasants' (p. 510).

As Sir Hugh the loveless man and landlord is balanced against
Harry, so the estate-hungry Mr Longstaffe of Caversham is
contrasted with Roger Carbury of Carbury; the absentee Marquis
of Brotherton in *Is He Popenjoy?* with his home-loving brother,
Lord George; and Captain Aylmer of *The Belton Estate*, who
chooses to rent out his inherited country home, with Will Belton,
who vigorously farms his own land. Devotion to the estate, and a
proper observance of the duties pertaining to it, remain virtues
that Trollope admires, even though he often chooses to satirise the
do-gooders (particularly among the women of a family) who take
their duties to the poor to absurd lengths. Some of his heirs, when
they come into their inheritance, are even inclined to pity themselves for the sacrifices they must make. Ralph Newton, when he
finally inherits Newton Priory and its ample income, asks
pathetically, 'What does it amount to when it's all told? You keep
horses for other fellows to ride, you buy wine for other fellows to
drink, you build a house for other fellows to live in. . . . You have
to work like a slave, and everybody gets a pull at you' (*Ralph the
Heir*, II.209). Needless to say, Ralph is not one of Trollope's model
squires, even though he is 'Newton of Newton'.

Trollope goes beyond Jane Austen in showing his characters
not just in relation *to* their estates, but in relation *with* them. We
see often the development of love for an estate, the process of
inheritance, the sequential performance of duties about the place,
and the interconnection of an estate with its owner's state of mind.
When Kennedy, the laird of Loughlinter, is deserted by his wife in
*Phineas Redux*, he makes his estate desolate too. Harry Gilmore in
*The Vicar of Bullhampton*, jilted by his fiancée, halts the alterations
that are being made to his house for his bride in the midst of the
operations, so that the house will be abrupted like his engagement.
'I will not have another stroke of work done here', he commands
the workmen in his bitterness (p. 441). He is like Edward in the
ballad, imposing his own state of mind on the physical objects that
surround him.

> 'And what will ye do wi' your tow'rs and your ha',
> Edward, Edward? . . .'
> 'I'll let them stand till they doun fa'.'

The character in Trollope's novels most fully connected with the land is Will Belton. He is Trollope's Heathcliff, violently and irrecoverably in love with his cousin, and feeling his love as some elemental force that is deeply connected with the earth.

> He loved her. He could not get over it. The passion . . . clung to him in his goings out and comings in with a painful, wearing tenacity. . . . As he watched the furrow, as his men and horses would drive it straight and deep through the ground, he was thinking of her. . . . Then he would turn away his face, and stand alone in his field, blinded by the salt drops in his eyes. . . . And when he was quite alone, he would stamp his foot on the ground, and throw abroad his arms, and curse himself. (*The Belton Estate*, p. 253)

Clara's vacillation between her two men, too, is intimately bound up with their estates, and their relation to Belton Castle, her own home.

The owner of a country estate, as he collects around him his family and his guests, his tenants and his servants, and administers his domain, is for Trollope what a captain at sea is for Conrad, a kind of god, with special powers as well as special responsibilities. Land gives more than the rent, Trollope reiterates – 'It gives position and influence and political power.' It gives, particularly, personal power of almost supernatural force in hands that know how to use it. Lady Glencora in her domains at Matching and Gatherum can both propose and dispose. It is a function of her role as hostess that she can smoothly arrange to marry off her penniless cousin Adelaide to the equally penniless man she loves, and find funds for them. She can do almost anything she likes with people by dint of having them down to Matching. After his trial, when Phineas Finn regards himself as a broken man, Lady Glencora manages with almost divine finesse to take him in hand when he arrives: 'She was one of those women whose minds were always engaged on such matters, and who are able to see how things will go. . . . She had considered it all, arranged it all, and given her orders with accuracy' (*Phineas Redux*, II. 362). Accordingly, Phineas is reunited with Madame Max under Lady Glen's auspices, and in course of time duly married.

Trollope was fascinated by these personal powers of the hostess of a country estate, especially in the match-making line. Mrs

Montacute Jones is another such manager as Glencora. In *Is He Popenjoy?* a minor plot has to do with the angling for and netting of young Lord Giblet, whom his hostess has destined to be the husband of Miss Patmore Green. She promotes flirtation in her London house, continues her campaign to hook the unwilling young man at a house-party at Rudham Park, and proposes to finish the business at her own Scottish estate of Killancodlem. 'We go from here to Killancodlem next week [she tells him]. You must come and join us.'

> 'I've got to go and grouse at Stranbracket's,' said Lord Giblet, happy in an excuse.
> 'It couldn't be better. They're both within eight miles of Dunkeld.' If so, then ropes shouldn't take him to Stranbracket's that year. 'Of course you'll come. . . . And she will be there. If you really want to know a girl, see her in a country house.'
> But he didn't really want to know the girl. . . . 'I should like it ever so,' he said.   (II.175)

Once at Killancodlem, we hear afterwards, 'the lover didn't make the least fight . . . , but submitted himself like a sheep to the shearers' (II.235). On this occasion at Rudham Park not only is Lord Giblet netted for Miss Green, but Guss Mildmay finally hooks the wayward Jack de Baron. 'He ought not to have gone to Rudham, when he knew that she was to be there', Jack reflects bitterly, after he has been fairly caught (II.208).

A large part of *Ayala's Angel* has to do with the means by which Ayala is persuaded to marry Colonel Jonathan Stubbs, whom she has determined not to marry. It is done by having her at Stalham Park under the powerful auspices of Lady Albury, who is quite unscrupulous in the business. Ayala is happy enough to leave her joyless quarters in London to go to the country estate – 'heaven had been once more opened to her', we hear (p. 211). Once there, she is taken over. She is to ride to hounds, and suitable horses and riding habit are provided by Lady Albury, who brooks no refusal. 'We've settled it all', she replies summarily to Ayala's objections (p. 214). Notwithstanding the favourable circumstances Lady Albury has created, Ayala staunchly refuses Stubbs again. But a second visit to Stalham is to settle the matter. 'It was clear to Lady Albury that Ayala must surrender now that she was coming to

Stalham a second time, knowing that the Colonel would be there'
(p. 439); and she cunningly arranges for the two to come down on
the same train. A further step in the campaign is a gift of a pearl-
coloured silk dress and shawl, in which Ayala looks stunning.
Once she has accepted and donned this she is like a beast decked
for the slaughter, and she is doomed. Ayala is one of the many
Trollope heroines who specialise in saying no, but even she cannot
resist the powerful magic of Lady Albury and Stalham Park, and
at last she must yield with a good grace. 'We talked you all over',
Lady Albury tells her when Ayala is safely engaged to Stubbs,
'and made up our minds, between us, that if we petted you down
here that would be the best way to win you. Were we not right?'
(p. 537). Yes, she was right. And luxurious pampering on a well-
appointed estate becomes again a means of exerting power.
'Stalham', suggesting the stalled ox, is like 'Killancodlem', where
the guests are equally coddled for the owner's own purposes,
preparatory to consumption.

It is interesting that Trollope pronounces little or no moral
judgement against these manipulations. Jane Austen's Emma is
made to suffer the pangs of remorse for her comparable man-
oeuvres – because 'with unpardonable arrogance [she had]
proposed to arrange everybody's destiny' (*Emma*, III, ch. 11); and
Trollope's own Mrs Carbuncle in *The Eustace Diamonds*, who is an
inveterate guest but has no estate, is shown as wicked and
heartless in her brazen campaign to marry her niece to the boorish
Sir Griffin. But the ladies of considerable estates have no qualms
of conscience, and nor does their author judge them harshly for
their matchmaking. It is almost as though their status as
proprietors of large country estates makes them independent of
the laws that pertain to ordinary mortals – as though they were
wizards or fairies. Lady Albury even performs the fairy god-
mother's trick of endowing her Cinderella with a beautiful gown.[8]
Lord Giblet, though quite shamelessly hunted down, is not made
a reproach to his manipulator. 'I'm told he's the happiest man in
the world, and the very best husband', Mrs Montacute Jones
writes with satisfaction after the event (*Is He Popenjoy?*, II.248). He
would have married someone sooner or later, suggests the
narrator, and why not Miss Green as well as another? The motives
of the matchmakers are in general benevolent, and that seems
sufficient justification. 'Keep a good house, and give nice parties',
Mrs Montacute Jones advises her protegée. 'Try and make other

people happy. That's the goodness I believe in' (II.235). By and large, we understand, Trollope believes in it too.

Of course his estate-owners have a power for doing evil as well as good – though it is usually the neglectful ones, the absentee landlords, who use their power for evil (those who elect to remain on their estates seem already to demonstrate themselves to be good fellows by that very act). The Earl De Courcy, for instance, has spent his prime straying in London and foreign watering-places, and it is only gout and lumbago that force him home to be a savage host and bitter father of a loveless race (*The Small House at Allington*, I.221ff).

The Marquis of Brotherton in *Is He Popenjoy?* is Trollope's most sustained study of a landlord who uses his estate to control and punish his family. Both his title and his family name 'Germain' are ironic, for far from being motivated by brotherly affection he conducts a long campaign of persecution against his dutiful and plodding brother, Lord George, and reminds even his devoted mother of Cain (I.300). At the outset he is content to live abroad in Italy and leave the family estate, though not the income, in the care of his brother, mother and sisters. They tend it faithfully, though they can't afford to keep up the status of the family, and the ladies laboriously sew petticoats for the poor. When his younger brother marries, however, the Marquis bestirs himself, and presently produces an Italian lady and a year-old child whom he claims to be his wife and son (the legitimacy or otherwise of this child is never proved). And now the landowner flexes his muscles. His mother, brother and sisters, he declares, must pick up their traps, leave Manor Cross, and go elsewhere – a long way if possible. The mother, in a flurry of pathetic deference to her elder son, pleads that she may be allowed the Dower House, Cross Hall, which is after all her own. Brotherton is annoyed that she won't do his bidding at the first word, and makes himself unpleasant. He moves into Manor Cross himself for a short period, but finding he prefers the power of eviction to the dubious pleasure of occupation, he presently vacates his house and allows his mother and sisters – but not his brother – to return. The Dower House is accordingly let on lease, while the Marchioness returns with relief to the Manor, and to total dependence on her capricious landlord.

This is what he wants, for her tenancy gives him power. 'When people are dependent on me I choose that they shall be dependent', he says grimly (II.158). He gives orders from afar on whom the family may or may not receive in the house, and keeps them in perpetual terror of eviction. In spite of all his tyranny – or more likely because of it – his mother idolises him, and is 'prepared to lay herself at the feet of her eldest son' (I.203). But his sister Lady Sarah is ready to stand up to him, and brother and sister spar over the legitimate power of the land's legal incumbent, and its limits:

> He turned sharply round and looked at her for an instant. . . . And as he did so she remembered the peculiar tyranny of his eyes, the tyranny to which, when a boy, he had ever endeavoured to make her subject, and all others around him. Others had become subject because he was the Lord Popenjoy of the day, and would be the future Marquis; but she, though recognising his right to be first in everything, had ever rebelled against his usurpation of unauthorised power. He, too, remembered all this, and almost snarled at her with his eyes. (I.205)

Brotherton is one of Trollope's finer villains – not the less so because his portrait is touched with some compassion when he hears the news of the death of his son, 'a rickety brat who was bound to die' (II.202). His stature as a creation has a great deal to do with his stature as Marquis and landowner. His power to play god on his estate – a Hardyesque god, who takes pleasure in making his creatures wince – gives him a dimension beyond the humanly fallible beings that are the most characteristic creations in Trollope's chosen realistic mode. His tyrannical caprice and 'monstrous tyranny' on his estate lead some people to wonder whether he is insane (I.229). As a madman in possession of immense power in his own domain, he is Trollope's Captain Ahab on a country estate, obsessed with imposing his own will on his subordinates. 'It is unreasonable – monstrous!' exclaims his sister when he proposes to throw out his aged mother. 'It is terrible that any man should have so much power to do evil' (II.156). The fate of the *Pequod*, however, does not overtake Manor Cross, for the Marquis and his rickety brat are eliminated in order that Lord George, the 'pattern landlord' (II.308), and his son the real Popenjoy should inherit the Brotherton estate.

The inheritance plot is of course one of Trollope's specialities. The final windfall inheritance is a staple of the novel in general, but Trollope was intensely interested in the *process* of inheritance, and of land rather than money, and makes that his central subject in novels such as *Orley Farm*, *Ralph the Heir*, *Sir Harry Hotspur of Humblethwaite*, *The Belton Estate* and *Mr Scarborough's Family*. The entail, by which the estate is protected from the depradations of the individual for the continuing good of the family, was a moral and legal institution that fascinated him. His conservative model, Roger Carbury in *The Way We Live Now*, has the free disposal of Carbury Manor, but nevertheless 'felt himself constrained, almost as by some divine law, to see that his land went by natural descent' (I.132) – that is, to the nearest male relative, even if he happens, as in this case, to be a bounder. Trollope pondered endlessly over the 'divine law' of inheritance by primogeniture. He sympathised with Will Belton and even with the rogue Scarborough in their efforts to break entails and assert their individual wills in the disposal of land. But, all the same, with his plots he ultimately endorses the system, showing how land, unlike portable property, has a propensity to gravitate of itself to the right inheritor. It is appropriate that Melmotte, who can so successfully juggle shares in the realm of high finance, at last comes to grief when he plays fast and loose in the purchase of a country estate, Pickering. 'You must be aware, Mr. Melmotte,' the respectable attorney Bideawhile tells him severely, 'that the sale of a property is not like an ordinary mercantile transaction' (II. 237). The speculator in fictional companies comes to grief when he handles *real* estate at last.

In *The Belton Estate* Will Belton makes a chivalrous attempt to break the entail on Belton so that it will go to his cousin Clara, the daughter of the last owner, rather than to himself. We are to admire Will for his gallant self-sacrifice (and Trollope emphasises the extent of the sacrifice by showing us how much Will does long to be 'Belton of Belton'), but all the same the weight of the plot forces Will to abandon his attempt and to provide for his cousin by marrying her instead of breaking the rule of male inheritance. In *Ralph the Heir* we are led to understand that the illegitimate Ralph would be a better landlord than the ne'er-do-well legitimate one. We sympathise with the efforts of Sir Gregory Newton to secure the estate for his worthy son, but when the arrangement is almost concluded we recognise his paraded triumph as hubris. 'His father was almost excessive in the exuberance of his joy', reflects Ralph (II.26). Sure enough, nemesis overtakes him on the hunting field, and he dies before the deeds are executed whereby his son can inherit Newton Priory. The illegitimate son has never been eager for the inheritance in any case. 'I should be the owner of Newton Priory, and people would call me Mr. Newton. But I shouldn't be Newton of Newton', he confesses (I.190). And in fact even the tenantry, who respect him and have benefited from his care as they have never benefited from the legitimate son, share his conservatism and prefer the feckless and indebted heir: 'It was in proper conformity with English habits and English feelings that the real heir should reign' (II. 85). The real heir will, after all, be Newton of Newton. There is a fitness in the strictly legal inheritance of an estate according to principles of primogeniture that subsumes moral deserts. The worthy Ralph gets the girl, but the legitimate one must get the estate.

The women who do inherit country estates, usually by the death of their husbands, and for their life only, generally find them to be intolerable burdens. Land becomes their nemesis, as it does for Melmotte. Lady Ongar, Lady Eustace and Lady Laura Kennedy all marry their husbands for money, have disastrous marriages, and live through the deaths of their husbands to inherit their ample acres. In each case Trollope takes us with the widow to her estate, the extensive symbol of the price for which she has sold herself, and shows how her glories turn to ashes in her mouth. Lady Ongar at Ongar Park is at first bravely determined to fulfil all the duties of the estate-owner:

> She was determined that she would work hard; that she would understand the farm; that she would know the labourers; that she would assist the poor; . . . and, above all, that she would make all the privileges of ownership her own. Was not the price in her hand, and would she not use it? She felt that it was very good that something of the price had come to her thus in the shape of land, and beeves, and wide, heavy outside garniture. (*The Claverings*, p. 122)

But the fact that her price takes the shape of land is her undoing, for the estate becomes a constant reproach to her for having sold herself. It is not thus that an estate should change hands. After two weeks she is utterly defeated by Ongar Park, and leaves it, never to return. 'The apples had indeed quickly turned to ashes between her teeth. . . . She had the price in her hands, but she felt herself tempted to do as Judas did, – to go out and hang herself' (pp. 126–7). Lizzie Eustace is not burdened with a similarly tender conscience, but she too feels uncomfortably exposed on her Scottish country estate, Portray Castle, and becomes subject to it as she is never subject to her more portable property, the Eustace diamonds. Lady Laura, who accepts the laird Kennedy and his estate though she really loves the impecunious Phineas Finn, is similarly haunted by Loughlinter once Kennedy has got himself out of the way by dying. Both Lady Ongar and Lady Laura find themselves longing to heap their widows' riches and estates on the young men they had first loved, Harry Clavering and Phineas, as though to pass on their handsome property to a man would in some way justify them. Lady Laura 'allowed her fancy to revel in the idea of having [Phineas] with her as she wandered over the braes' (*Phineas Redux*, II.327); Lady Ongar reflects: 'She herself had learned to hate the house and fields and widespread comforts of Ongar Park. . . . But it would be a glory to her to see [Harry] go forth, with Giles at his heels, boldly giving his orders, changing this and improving that' (*The Claverings*, p. 162). It is surprising, in fact, that these morally scrupulous ladies should feel justified in handing their husbands' estates to former suitors: such a transaction would give an air of premeditation to their acts – making them resemble James's Kate Croy, who wants her fiancé to court a rich invalid so as to bring back a fortune when she dies. But the recurring motif is another of Trollope's ways of showing how country estates have a power of their own to shrug off the illegitimate inheritor.

Trollope has an acute sense of the taboos and rituals that go with the sacred institution of landowning. In his second novel, *The Kellys and the O'Kellys*, he shows some knowledge of the primitive beliefs that surround the threshold and the rooftree. The Irish peasant landlady, the widow Kelly, recognises that by allowing a stranger to cross your doorstill you give him power over you. 'I tell you what,' she tells her son of the attorney who has served a notice of prosecution on the family, 'you shouldn't iver have let Daly inside the house: he'll make us pay: . . . av' he hadn't got into the house, he couldn't've done a halfporth' (p. 250). More sophisticated characters, too, show curious superstitions about particular places as connected with experiences that have happened to them, and feel the need to propitiate the local manes by going back to a given spot to right some wrong: so Will Belton insists that Clara should at last accept him by the very rock on the Belton estate where she had first rejected him, and Ayala takes Jonathan

Stubbs back to the site of her refusal to tell him how much she loves him – 'here on this very spot' (*Ayala's Angel*, p. 544). That is a phrase that is repeated many times in Trollope's novels, a testimony to his intense sense of experience as related to locale.

He frequently makes comic use of the time-honoured relation between host and guest. Besieged in his own demesne by troublesome guests of his wife's asking, Palliser finally rebels by doing the unthinkable – turning out his own guest, Major Pountney, who has overstepped the bounds of acceptable behaviour for a guest. It is a resounding incident, as it spurs the usually tractable Duke to upset all his wife's elaborate arrangements for extensive hospitality. In *Ayala's Angel* there is a whole comic subplot on the relations of Sir Thomas Tringle with his son-in-law Mr Traffick, who both literally and figuratively hangs up his hat successively in Sir Thomas's town and country residences. Sir Thomas's hints to his unwanted guest are broad enough, but Mr Traffick has found comfortable and inexpensive quarters, and is resolved to put up with everything short of outright dismissal – the one gesture that is denied to the host. Sir Thomas becomes so desperate that he is actually glad when Traffick breaks the knees of his favourite mare, Phoebe, because it gives him a grievance he can gleefully make the most of. Trollope knows to a nicety the rules between host and guest:

> Mr. Traffick had done him this injury, and he now had Mr. Traffick on the hip. There are some injuries for which a host cannot abuse his guest. If your best Venetian decanter be broken at table you are bound to look as though you liked it. But if a horse be damaged a similar amount of courtesy is hardly required.    (*Ayala's Angel*, pp. 278–9)

Sir Thomas can finally give Traffick his explicit marching orders only from his place of business, where his obligations as host are in abeyance.

When Augustus Scarborough, the new heir, invites his crony Mr Jones to Tretton Park without first consulting his father, he commits a filial sin that is tantamount to Prince Hal's when he dons his father's crown before the breath is out of his body. So Mr Scarborough interprets it, and he summarily dismisses Jones, to whom he owes no obligations as host since he is Augustus's guest, not his. 'He is a most agreeable young man, I'm sure', says the father smoothly; 'but I do not care to entertain an agreeable young man without having a word to say on the subject' (*Mr Scarborough's Family*, p. 190). Thereafter there is war between father and son.

No one knew better than Trollope the extensive rituals connected with the preservation of game on an estate, or dwelt on them so lovingly. 'There is something doubtless absurd', he concedes, 'in the intensity of the worship paid to the fox by hunting communities. The animal becomes sacred, and his preservation is a religion' (*Phineas Redux*, II.375). Nevertheless, he delighted in showing characters like Lord Chiltern who treat the fox with proper devotion. Due care in the preservation of partridges and foxes is an indispensable duty for a landowner. It is one of Palliser's more forgivable shortcomings that he is deficient in this respect – not from lack of principle, but from want of knowledge and love of the sport. The issue of Trumpeton wood, where it is rumoured that foxes have been trapped, becomes a whole subplot in *Phineas Redux*: the Duke and his people are hard put to it to ensure that the foxes there are reproducing properly. 'That horrid wood, where the foxes won't get themselves born and bred as foxes ought to do,' Lady Glencora calls it. 'How can I help it? I'd send down a whole Lying-in Hospital for the foxes if I thought that that would do any good' (*Phineas Redux*, II.314).

Another sacred component of the estate is its timber, particularly its oaks, which are often viewed by the characters as a synecdoche for the estate itself. Recurrently we are shown the new incumbent wandering among the oaks on his estate, and telling himself that they are now all his own. Trees, old ones, are particularly holy because they can't be bought with new money. The trees in the otherwise unlovely Clavering Park ensure that the new family will be able to make all well with the estate. 'There are fine trees, you see,' Lady Ongar tells Florence, whose husband will inherit them, 'which are the only things which one cannot by any possibility command. Given good trees, taste and money may do anything very quickly' (*The Claverings*, p. 503). The books in the library are likewise viewed as intrinsic and almost alive. It is the books that can announce to Mountjoy Scarborough and Lady Ongar that they have no business pretending to the estates the books belong to. Mountjoy, one of Trollope's many rakish heirs, picks out a book at random from the shelves at Tretton Park, and finds 'of this he could make neither head nor tail. . . . He looked round the room and tried to price the books, and told himself that three or four days at the club might see an end of it all' (*Mr Scarborough's Family*, p. 511). When Mountjoy inherits Tretton Park, we are to understand, it will go to the dogs.

The servants, so essential for the proper maintenance of a country estate, are not nearly so much in evidence as the foxes, the timber, the books or the wine. This is partly because Trollope considers the best service to be unobtrusive. The crowd of footmen at Caversham and the large complement of idle servants at Aylmer Park are signals that the proprietors care more for status and display than for the real comfort of the house's inmates. In such establishments the proprietors in fact become subject to their own staff, and Clara Amedroz deserves her author's applause when she declares, in the face of the 'not-before-the-servants' brand of propriety, 'I don't care a straw for the servants' (*The Belton Estate*, p. 348).

Trollope often presents, I have been suggesting, owners of estates who have almost superhuman powers. He deals with what he calls a 'divine law' of legitimate inheritance, with the rituals and taboos of hospitality, with hunting the 'sacred' fox, with the supersititious propitiation of local manes, with those mysterious forces by which estates enforce themselves almost independently of human agents. Much of this suggestion of the supernatural is figurative or even jocular. Trollope is not a Gothic novelist, nor a writer of romance, and magic and the supernatural are not his subjects. He is prosaic and down-to-earth, and proud of it. Nevertheless, his fables suggest that for him land has a transcendent value. The proprietors of country estates are members of a ministry more fully demonstrated as sacred than that of all the bishops, deans, prebendaries and curates in the see of Barchester.

## NOTES

1 My references are to the World's Classics editions of Trollope's novels, by volume (when there are more than one) and page number. I use short titles for brevity.

2 *The Macdermots of Ballycloran*, with an introduction by Algar Thorold (London and New York: John Lane, 1906) p. 3. This novel was not printed in a World's Classics edition.

3 *Happy Rural Seat: The English Country House and the Literary Imagination* (New Haven, Conn., and London: Yale University Press, 1972) p. 251.

4 I have written of the symbolic consonance of house and owner elsewhere, in *Trollope's Palliser Novels: Theme and Pattern* (London: Macmillan, 1978) p. 180ff.

5 For a full discussion of the significance of the estate in Jane Austen's novels,

see Alistair Duckworth, *The Improvement of the Estate: A Study of Jane Austen's Novels* (Baltimore and London: Johns Hopkins Press, 1971).

6  *Remarks on Secular and Domestic Architecture* (London: John Murray, 1857) pp. 141–2.

7  Michael Sadleir has commented on the relation of building to owner's character in this case: 'Clavering itself – cold, square and hard as the bitter man who owns it – is set for ever in the reader's memory as the inevitable home of Sir Hugh Clavering' – *Trollope: A Commentary* (London: Constable, 1927) p. 183.

8  Mrs Mackenzie, another fairy-godmother figure, also provides a gown by which Margaret Mackenzie attracts her 'prince' in *Miss Mackenzie*.

# Trollope's Idea of the Gentleman

## ARTHUR POLLARD

'No English novelist ever had this sense [for the minute social gradations] more subtly attuned than Trollope. Think of the interplay between the Greshams and the Courcys or the Pallisers and Frank Tregear. There wasn't a step between the lower-middle class and the highest aristocracy that he didn't know by instinct.' Thus C. P. Snow in an essay on 'Dickens and the Public Service'.[1] Jane Austen had no doubt about the social distinctions between these extremes, but everybody is 'middle-class' now. The extent of change that had already taken place between her time and theirs was disturbingly evident to sensitive Victorians, not least to Trollope and not least in what it was that constituted a gentleman.

Indeed, this was an issue to which Trollope often referred but about which he felt able to speak most candidly only in what he knew would be published posthumously:

> As what I now write will certainly never be read till I am dead, I may dare to say what no one now does dare to say in print, – though some of us whisper it occasionally into our friends' ears. There are places in life which can hardly be well filled except by 'Gentlemen'. The word is one the use of which almost subjects one to ignoring. If I say that a judge should be a gentleman, or a bishop, I am met with a scornful allusion to 'Nature's Gentlemen'. . . . A man in public life could not do himself a greater injury than by saying in public that the commissions in the army or navy, or berths in the Civil Service, should be given exclusively to gentlemen. He would be defied to define the term, – and would fail should he attempt to do so. But he would know what he meant, and so very probably would they who defied him. (*An Autobiography*, ch. 3)

What then would he mean? Trollope clearly had in mind certain professional and social dimensions, and though he would allow for social fluidity – 'The gates of one class should be open to the other' – he insisted on hierarchy, on the uselessness of pretending that any good can 'be done by declaring that there are no gates, no barrier, no difference'. In the reference to 'Nature's Gentlemen', however, he noticed the view that the idea of the gentleman embraced other than social considerations. He agreed that it did, but not to the exclusion of such considerations.

The respective importance of social standing and moral quality is interestingly illustrated in three articles on the subject of the gentleman. In an anonymous contribution to the *Cornhill Magazine* we read that 'the word implies the combination of a certain degree of social rank with a certain amount of the qualities which the possession of such rank ought to imply; but there is a constantly increasing disposition to insist more upon the moral and less upon the social element of the word'.[2] This article is disposed to insist upon the feelings and manners of a gentleman – that is, nothing so deliberate as explicit moral conduct, though it found them especially in 'the two great cognate virtues – truth and courage'.[3] J. R. Vernon in the *Contemporary Review* rejects utterly those 'things external merely – rank, wealth, power, show' and in a heavily moral interpretation proceeds from 'nobility of thought and intention' to consider gentlemanly behaviour as it respects, first, the self and then, more extensively, others, in the process bringing out the importance of self-respect, integrity, generosity, thoughtfulness, tact, and ease of manners.[4] W. R. B[rowne] in the *National Review* also rejects the criteria of birth, wealth and outward manners in favour of a simple definition of the gentleman as 'one to whom discourtesy is a sin and falsehood a crime'.[5] None the less, he spends much time on four 'main sub-divisions' of the *genus* gentleman, namely, the squire, the parson, the professional man, and the man of business, finding it most difficult for the last-named to sustain truth and thereby his status as gentleman.[6] These reviews are themselves some indication of the way things were moving. Trollope's novels are a more extended commentary on the same phenomenon.

For him clearly the idea of the gentleman involved a fairly well-defined degree of social exclusiveness. Nobility, aristocracy, squirearchy, gentry, these groups are the repository of gentlemanly values, even though in their ranks there may be found individ-

uals who are not gentlemen. Together they represent a society of
established families, bound by tradition, living often on land and
in houses that had descended from one generation to another
through the centuries, possessed of 'those far-reaching fibres and
roots by which . . . the solidity and stability of a human tree should
be assured' (*The Prime Minister*, ch. 9), 'secure in their own identity
and confident of their social position'.[7] Mr Wharton's metaphor of
the 'human tree' indicates the importance of family, birth and
marriage as the institutions upon which rank and status are
sustained.

Sir Peregrine Orme, undoubtedly one of Trollope's most sympathetic characters, exemplifies it thus:

> In judging a position which a man should hold in the world,
> Sir Peregrine was very resolute in ignoring all claims made by
> wealth alone. Even property in land could not in his eyes create
> a gentleman. A gentleman, according to his ideas, should at any
> rate have great-grandfathers capable of being traced in the
> world's history; and the greater the number of such, and the
> more easily traceable they might be on the world's surface, the
> more unquestionable would be the status of the claimant in
> question.   (*Orley Farm*, ch. 3)

It is this regard for family that sets up the inconsistency in the
Duke of Omnium, generous in theory about the unimportance of
family but determined, if possible, that his children by their
marriages should sustain 'the blue blood and the rank' (*The Duke's
Children*, ch. 48). A duke could not step down to the gentry to see
his daughter marry Frank Tregear; the gentry in their turn kept
their barriers. Emily Wharton rejected one of her own class for
such a shady adventurer as Lopez and suffered (*The Prime
Minister*), and Georgiana Longstaffe was thought to have thrown
herself away on the respectable Jew Brehgert. For Harry Clavering there is the dilemma of choosing between a social equal, Julia
Ongar, soiled by giving herself in an earlier marriage to a *roué*, and
a socially inferior but morally acceptable girl, Florence Burton,
sister to 'the man who dusted his boots with his handkerchief'
(ch. 26). In this instance, however, Trollope seems to have rejected the view expressed in *The Three Clerks* that 'a man from the
ordinary ranks of the upper classes, who has had the nurture of a
gentleman, prepares for himself a hell on earth in taking a wife

from any rank below his own' (ch. 31). But then Florence was different. Most piquant of all these situations was that of Frank Gresham, heir to a centuries-old line, Gresham of Greshamsbury, living on its own land, but now impoverished by the extravagance of his mother, a scion of the aristocracy, the consequence of his father's aspiration beyond his rank. The de Courcy relatives insist that 'Frank must marry money' rather than Mary Thorne, but at the end it is found that this illegitimate but lovable and upright girl is the heiress to the money that has done much, by way of mortgage, to prop up the Gresham house. In revealing her newly enriched status Dr Thorne, her uncle, declares: 'I wish . . . that her birth were equal to her fortune, as her worth is superior to both' (ch. 46).

She presumably would not have done for Sir Peregrine Orme. Not even land sufficed for him, though (and because) it was the object of others to acquire it. Mary indeed inherited her wealth from her self-made industrialist uncle, Sir Roger Scatcherd, who had built Boxall Hill; and the ultimate aim of Melmotte in *The Way We Live Now* was to achieve the status of a landed gentleman, to which he aimed by the fraudulent signature of documents that paved the way to his downfall. Even for wealth, wealth was not sufficient. Yet that social fluidity which the Duke of Omnium had noted in considering his own children's fortunes – 'The peer who sat next to him in the House of Lords, whose grandmother had been a washerwoman and whose father an innkeeper, was to him every whit as good a peer as himself' (*The Duke's Children*, ch. 48) – was usually achieved by money. Mary Thorne's money rescues the Greshams, and Miss Dunstable's ointment-millions elevate Dr Thorne himself by marriage to the occupation of Chaldicotes and a place in Barchester society. Dean Lovelace in *Is He Popenjoy?* claims that 'it is a grand thing to rise in the world' (ch. 61). Trollope, I think, would have claimed that it depended on the way it was done. The Dean himself was not wholly approved of by his creator; and the aspirations of a Moffat (acceptable for the money he derived from his tailoring trade), which entail the repudiation of his engagement to Augusta Gresham in his pursuit of a better catch, result only in a well-merited, and by Trollope thoroughly applauded, horse-whipping from her brother Frank. Money could not make a gentleman. Its mode of acquisition and its use said much as to whether its possessor was a gentleman or not.

In the opening chapter of *Dr Thorne* Trollope writes, 'Buying and selling is good and necessary; it is very necessary, and may, possibly, be very good; but it cannot be the noblest work of man; and let us hope that it may not in our time be esteemed the noblest work of an Englishman.' The taint of trade and especially the temptations of trade made it difficult for Trollope to find gentlemen there. In particular, the getting of money led men, he felt, to all kinds of dubious devices, epitomised in the fraudulent share-dealings of *The Way We Live Now* – 'dishonesty magnificent in its proportions and climbing into high places', as he described it in the *Autobiography* (ch. 20).

Likewise, politics could often attract the mere adventurer. None more than Trollope respected the title of Member of Parliament; the entrance to the House of Commons he described as 'the only gate before which I have ever stood filled with envy' (*Can You Forgive Her?*, ch. 45), but through it, he recognised, had proceeded many who were not gentlemen – 'Dishonesty, ignorance and vulgarity do not close the gate' (ibid.). Adventurers such as Lopez and Melmotte saw it as a means of climbing the social ladder, and rogues such as George Vavasor of keeping out of the bailiffs' hands. The distaste with which Sir Thomas Underwood finds himself having to associate with such a ruffian as Griffenbottom (*Ralph the Heir*) is sufficient testimony that gentlemen had to associate in the House of Commons with many not of their kind. Even such a man of honour as Phineas Finn concluded that it was no place for someone not of independent means (*Phineas Redux*, ch. 79).

If wealth and public office did not provide a sure means towards social recognition as a gentleman, where then did the professional men and the clergy stand? These two categories have a special interest in that Trollope himself was for long a civil servant, his father was a lawyer and his grandfathers were clergymen. I do not think that there is any doubt that such civil servants as Johnny Eames and those in *The Three Clerks*, whatever be the misdemeanours some of them committed, qualify in Trollope's eyes socially as gentlemen. It is in *The Three Clerks* that Trollope makes his famous attack on the introduction of competitive examinations in the Civil Service. He deplored the pursuit of success not only for its effects on those who failed but also, and more, on those who won. Thus ambition drove Alaric Tudor so much that he adopted a double standard:

In other matters it behoves a gentleman to be open, above-board, liberal and true . . . but in the acquirement and use of money . . . his practice should be exactly the reverse; he should be close, secret, exacting, given to concealment, not over-troubled by scruples. (ch. 17)

Thus ambition – and eventual exposure and disgrace.

As with the civil servants, so with the lawyers. Trollope had undoubted gentlemen such as Judge Staveley and Felix Graham and Mortimer Gazebee, but there are also the Chaffanbrasses and the Furnivals, in whose professional and personal behaviour he found much to criticise. What we witness here, as indeed with the clergy, is that rank did less to protect status than it did with the gentry and the aristocracy.

The clergy are an interesting group, not least because Trollope was himself so fascinated by them. There is the famous and oft-quoted meeting, on the engagement of their offspring, of the wealthy, socially self-confident Archdeacon Grantly and the neurotic, poverty-stricken curate Crawley, with the former's remark, 'We stand . . . on the only perfect level on which such men can meet each other. We are both gentlemen' (*The Last Chronicle of Barset*, ch. 83). Most of Trollope's clergy are gentlemen. Two or three are not. One such is Dean Lovelace:

With great care and cunning workmanship one may almost make a silk purse out of a sow's ear, but not quite. The care which Dean Lovelace had bestowed upon the operation in regard to himself had been very great, and the cunning workmanship was to be seen in every plait and every stitch. But still there was something left of the coarseness of the original material. (*Is He Popenjoy?*, ch. 2)

Some made even worse attempts. Of such were the oily chaplain Slope in *Barchester Towers* and Mr Prong in *Rachel Ray* with his vain attempts at a dignified appearance and with his virtues – 'sincere, hard-working, sufficiently intelligent . . . – but deficient in one vital qualification for a clergyman of the Church of England; he was not a gentleman'. Trollope acknowledges the difficulty of defining gentility, but 'it is caught at a word, it is seen at a glance, it is appreciated unconsciously at a touch by those who have none of it themselves' (ch. 6). Mr Prong was not a graduate, merely a literate from Islington, one of those whom Trollope identified as 'less attractive, less urbane, less genial, – in one significant word, less of a gentleman' (*Clergymen of the Church of England*, p. 60). In that sense he was outside the pale, and Mr Crawley was within, just as was Mr Saul in *The Claverings* – even though, as Harry puts it, 'he isn't quite one of our sort' (ch. 48); but then their sort was 'the clerical country gentlemen [who] understood it all as though there were some secret sign or shibboleth between them' (ch. 33).

In social terms Mr Prong was not a gentleman. What then of those who passed by these criteria but whose conduct was far from gentlemanly, the frequenters of the Beargarden, chief among them Sir Felix Carbury, or someone capable of such violent behaviour as Lord Chiltern, or George Hotspur, 'a gambler, a swindler, . . . a forger and a card-sharper [who] has lived upon the wages of the woman he has professed to love' (*Sir Harry Hotspur of Humblethwaite*, ch. 16)? We have reached the moral qualities of gentility. They include essentially 'honour, honesty and truth, out-spoken truth, self-denying truth, a fealty from man to man' (*Dr Thorne*, ch. 36). They will result in a man being 'faithful to his friends, unsuspicious before the world, gentle with women, loving with children, considerate to his inferiors, kindly with servants, tender-hearted with all, – and at the same time frank, of open speech, with springing eager energies, – simply because he desires it' (*Phineas Redux*, ch. 68). Here is self-confidence without assertiveness, openness without ostentation, self-control, naturalness, generosity and courtesy.

By these standards Carbury and Hotspur obviously do not qualify. But further, it may be asked, do not those whom Trollope describes as 'Nature's Gentlemen' pass the test? In this context Mary Thorne provides some interesting comment:

If she were born a gentlewoman! And then came to her mind these curious questions: what makes a gentleman? what makes a gentlewoman? What is the inner reality, the spiritualised quintessence of that privilege in the world than men call rank? . . . And she answered the question. Absolute, intrinsic, acknowledged individual merit must give to its possessor, let him be whom, and what, and whence he might. So far the spirit of democracy was strong within her. Beyond this it could be had but by inheritance, received as it were second-hand, or twenty-second-hand. And so far the spirit of aristocracy was strong within her.    (*Doctor Thorne*, ch. 6)

The passage from *Phineas Redux* quoted above ends, 'These things which are the attributes of manliness, must come of training on a nature not ignoble.' Trollope's choice of this final adjective with its moral *and* social connotations is interesting.

The *Cornhill* article had summarised gentlemanly virtues as truth and courage. Not dissimilarly Trollope speaks of the 'love of honest, courageous truth' (*The Prime Minister*, ch. 31). Deviousness and dishonesty characterise the behaviour of such people as Melmotte and Lopez and Alaric Tudor, Felix Carbury and the Beargarden set, Fred Neville in his treatment of Kate O'Hara, Sowerby in his dealings with Mark Robarts, and Burgo Fitzgerald in his planned elopement with Glencora, to name no others. One might have expected better of those who were supposed to be gentlemen. Even some who are better regarded are shown to behave ambiguously – Frank Greystock in his relations with Lizzie Eustace at the expense of Lucy Morris or Paul Montague in his never fully explained association with Mrs Hurtle. Against this last, as against the behaviour of so many in *The Way We Live Now*, stands the unsullied integrity of Roger Carbury, the country gentleman wedded to ancient virtues, 'living on his own land among his own people, as all the Carburys before him had done' (ch. 6).

Ideally, this was the way in which a gentleman should occupy his time. He would not be engaged in trade and, if he had to earn a living, the professions – the Church, the law, the Civil Service, the Army – would provide it. If he did not, he would act as a magistrate or he might seek a place in Parliament – as a *county* member. Attendance at the House of Commons and visiting London for the season were the only good reasons for being in the metropolis at all: other occasions would be merely the necessary constraints of business, consultation with lawyers and the like. Otherwise, in the eyes of an unsympathetic observer – such as Elias Gotobed – life for the country gentleman was a round of hunting and shooting over one's own and others' estates in winter, shooting in Scotland in August and for the rest of the year fishing, cricket, tennis and the races: 'It is the employment of his life to fit in his amusements so that he may not have a dull day' (*The American Senator*, ch. 29). Not all were so devoted to such a single-minded pursuit of this kind of life as Lord Rufford here considered, but, in essence, this description does convey an idea of many of the activities of the country gentleman.

Manner, deportment, pursuits all served to distinguish the gentleman. All were the outward manifestations of that decorum, of 'what is done and not done', that proceeded from his sense of position as leader of society, seeing and fulfilling his responsibilities to himself, showing loyalty to members of his own class and carrying out his obligations to those dependent upon him. As Sir Harold Nicolson remarked, 'Every society invents for itself a type, a model, an exemplar, of what the perfect member of that society ought to be'.[8] That was what Trollope endeavoured to portray in what he realised was the ultimately indefinable but none the less perfectly recognisable character of the gentleman.

NOTES

1   In *Dickens 1970*, ed. M. Slater (1970) pp. 142–3.
2   *Cornhill Magazine*, V. (1862) 330.
3   Ibid., p. 336.
4   *Contemporary Review*, XI (1869) 562–3.
5   *National Review*, Apr. 1886, p. 261.
6   Interesting statistics on 'The Business Interests of the Gentry in the Parliament of 1841–47' by Professor W. D. Aydelotte are to be found in an appendix to G. Kitson Clark's *The Making of Victorian England* (1962).
7   Anthony Lejeune, quoted in M. Bence-Jones and H. Montgomery-Massingberd, *The British Aristocracy* (1979) p. 20.
8   Quoted ibid.

# Trollope's Dialogue

## ROBERT M. POLHEMUS

The dialogue is generally the most agreeable part of a novel: but it is only so as long as it tends in some way to the telling of the main story.

Anthony Trollope, An Autobiography, ch. 12[1]

Dialogue, the verbal interchange of questions, comments, admonitions and points of view, *is* 'in some way' the 'main story' of Trollope's fiction. It is there that we mainly find the grace, the spontaneity and the reverberant meanings of his world, as well as the underlying variousness and delicacy of his art and personality. He sees the evolving human condition as one of dialogue, a continuing synthesis of voices – often incongruous voices – within the community and within the self. This dialogue, significantly, can be internal as well as external: he often represents the meditative consciousness and decision making processes as inward conversation, as such common Trollopian constructions as 'she asked herself' and 'he told himself' show.[2] Character reveals, defines and redefines itself in conversational interplay.

The most important times in life, as Trollope depicts it, come when people talk to each other or to themselves. In many of his best passages, the narrator seems to fade out, or to comment almost irrelevantly on the outer and inner voices: the characters go on speaking, interacting, displaying their many sides and influencing the nature of their world. Their discourse shapes and clarifies their ideas, expresses their ruling passions and full selves, and also lets us see the movements and the themes of the particular story we are reading.

Henry James praised Trollope for his 'good ear',[3] and anyone who has read Trollope seriously has recognised his ability to write good dialogue. But the art of dialogue, as C. P. Snow remarked, needs to be studied in textual detail.[4] My aims here are modest

but, I believe, worthwhile: I want simply to point out a few
specific but highly representative passages from the two Phineas
Finn novels and from two Barchester chronicles which make clear
the suggestive quality and range of effects that Trollope typically
achieves in his dialogue.[5] Because Trollope wrote so much,
critical discussion of his fiction tends to slide easily into generalisation, and we need to read his actual words closely if we care to
know the pleasures, felicities and values of his text. By quoting
him at length, I mean to indicate the kind of sympathetic
attention – the 'good ear' – that his dialogue demands if it is to be
properly understood and appreciated.

I

In *Phineas Redux*, two of Trollope's most famous characters,
Plantagenet and Glencora Palliser, quarrel over her spirited
defence of Phineas Finn and her continuing assertions of his
innocence against a murder charge:

> . . . the Duchess, wherever she went, spoke of the trial as a
> persecution. . . .
> 'Glencora,' he said to her, 'I wish that you could drop the
> subject of this trial till it be over.'
> 'But I can't.'
> 'Surely you can avoid speaking of it.'
> 'No more than you can avoid your decimals. Out of the full
> heart the mouth speaks, and my heart is full. What harm do I
> do?'
> 'You set people talking of you.'
> 'They have been doing that ever since we were married; – but
> I do not know that they have made out much against me. We
> must go after our nature, Plantagenet. Your nature is decimals,
> I run after units.'[6]

That brief interchange between the political champion of decimal
coinage and his wife characterises these figures and their prickly
marriage. It renders his drive for order, his analytic, matter-of-
fact mind, and his fear of loose, hostile talk; it shows her intuitive
faith in others, her energy, her susceptibility to synthetic integrity,
and her emotionalism. It displays her wit and his stolidity, her

satirical playfulness and his touchy sense of decorum. They both share their author's feeling for the importance of speech, but in different ways. She needs expression as an outlet for her turbulent spirit; he feels he has to protect himself and his family from the critical voice of public opinion. We have a speaking picture here of a unique couple, of two kinds of people, of a telling Victorian skirmish in the war between the sexes, of two ways of life.

That passage is itself a sequel to an earlier debate on the same subject when Glencora bemoans Phineas's fate to her husband and his mentor, the Duke of St Bungay:

'My dear,' said the elder Duke, 'I do not think that in my time any innocent man has ever lost his life upon the scaffold.'

'Is that any reason why our friend should be the first instance?' said the Duchess.

'He must be tried according to the laws of his country', said the younger Duke.

'Plantagenet, you always speak as if everything were perfect, whereas you know very well that everything is imperfect. If that man is – is hung, I –'

'Glencora,' said her husband, 'do not connect yourself with the fate of a stranger from any misdirected enthusiasm.'

'I do connect myself. If that man be hung – I shall go into mourning for him. You had better look to it.'[7]

This conversation lets us see Glencora's impetuousness and her husband's conventional nature, his propriety, and his voice of allegiance to commonwealth – something which Trollope rightly esteems as very precious. It also highlights one of the major themes of the Phineas books and the whole Palliser series: the necessity for some kind of primacy of faith in, and connection with, another. Long before E. M. Forster, the Duchess speaks the gist of his famous epigraph, 'Only connect', with all that that memorable phrase implies.

Later, Glencora rails at Palliser and the sober-sided counsel for Phineas about how she would bribe juries, subvert the legal process, and do anything she could to secure the acquittal of a man she feels certain is innocent. The men naturally mouth disapproval, but the Duchess exclaims, 'A woman, I know, can't do much; – but she has this privilege, that she can speak out what men only think.'[8] That gives us an insight into the brilliance and wit of the dialogue spoken by so many women in Trollope's fiction and his intense sympathy – if not at times downright identification – with women in the novels. It also implies, I think, the revelatory impulse in his dialogue. As women's speech is to the world of action in Glencora's remark, so, for Trollope, is literature to life. Authors, like women, can at least get things out in the open. For him it seems that fiction plays the same role in life that dialogue does in novels: it expresses true meanings for those who can read perceptively.


## II


In *Phineas Finn*, Phineas and Violet Effingham go riding. Violet is his friend Chiltern's beloved, but, though she cares for Chiltern, she has turned him down; Phineas wants to woo her now for himself. Chiltern's sister Lady Laura Kennedy, whom Finn had wanted to marry and who can no longer trust herself to see Phineas because she realises she loves him better than her own husband, wants Chiltern settled at home and married to Violet. As they ride Violet and Finn talk of how to get Chiltern back living at home.

'We must put our heads together, and do it. Don't you think it is to be done?'

Phineas replied that he thought it was to be done. 'I'll tell you the truth at once, Miss Effingham', he said. 'You can do it by a single word.'

'Yes; – yes', she said; 'but I do not mean that; – without that. . . .' He had been bold to speak to her about Lord Chiltern as he had done, and she had answered just as he would have wished to be answered. . . .

Presently they came to rough ground over which they were forced to walk, and he was close by her side. 'Mr Finn,' she said, 'I wonder whether I may ask a question?'

'Any question', he replied.

'Is there any quarrel between you and Lady Laura?'

'None.' . . .

'Then why are you not going to be at Loughlinter? She has written me expressly saying you would not be there.'

He paused a moment before he replied. 'It did not suit', he

said at last.

'It is a secret then?'

'Yes; – it is a secret. You are not angry with me?'

'Angry; no.'

'It is not a secret of my own, or I should not keep it from you.'

'Perhaps I can guess it', she said. 'But I will not try. I will not even think of it.'

'The cause, whatever it be, has been full of sorrow to me. I would have given my left hand to have been at Loughlinter this autumn.'

'Are you so fond of it?'

'I should have been staying there with you', he said. . . . 'When I found how it must be, and that I must miss you, I rushed down here that I might see you for a moment. And now I am here I do not dare speak to you of myself.' . . . Violet, without speaking a word, again put her horse in a trot. He was by her side in a moment, but he could not see her face. 'Have you not a word to say to me?' . . . he asked.

'No; – no – no;' she replied, 'not a word when you speak to me like that.'9

What happens here is that in the symmetry of this dialogue Violet expresses her own 'main story' in the novel: that is, she will accept Chiltern and refuse Phineas. As for Finn, his charm, openness, and willingness to make himself vulnerable – those things that endear him to women – show through here, but so does his tempered feeling. Violet's 'no' to Phineas, her 'yes' to the idea of Chiltern's presence, and Phineas's 'left hand' reveal the precise emotional state of these two. Finn thinks he is now deeply in love with Violet, as he had once thought himself in love with Laura, but with that strange and perfect choice of words, 'I would have given my left hand' (not, 'I'd give my right arm' or 'right hand'), he unwittingly pays a left-handed compliment to both ladies. His love is qualified. Violet here is trying to find out about her friend Laura's marriage and Phineas's relationship to Laura, so that she can gauge the depth and steadiness of his feelings and act accordingly. This conversation is of immense consequence, though neither the characters nor the narrator seems consciously to know or acknowledge it. The words spoken have a telling precision which may not at first be obvious. To be good readers of Trollope, we have to be good listeners, and make independent, running judgements about the dialogue without much help from the author.

## III

Dialogue, then, is what makes Trollope's novels so subtle, so full of nuances, so much more intelligent and complex than anyone would generally gather from the narrative commentary. In his best work, Trollope usually leaves it to us to infer the full import of what his people say, and that is what sometimes gives his fiction the illusion of being an unmediated, realistic vision of life: nothing appears to stand between us and the characters. Neither these figures nor the author will *seem* to have the grasp that readers can have on the meaning of what is said and why it matters. Critics note Trollope's respect for his characters – a 'novelist', he says, must sometimes 'submit' to his characters, by which he means that their personalities should sometimes be strong enough to overwhelm the author's opinions and conceptual desires – but he respects the independence and intelligence of his audience too. He understates the significance of his dialogue, and rhetorically this mode of understatement flatteringly assumes the readers' critical awareness. It works to draw us into his creation and take responsibility for seeing and judging the intimations and importance of what is being said.

Take, for instance, the first encounter between Phineas Finn and Madame Max Goesler; this ostensibly trivial dinner-party conversation is crucial in arousing and determining her feeling for him. Through dialogue and gesture of conversation, Trollope, in an apparently off-hand way, brings us to know and wonder about the personality and psychology of each and the meaning of their interaction. Phineas, Trollope says, has two things near his heart at this point – political patronage and Violet Effingham – and Madame Max manages to touch on both subjects. They begin by talking politics; in words that suggest not only the particular tragedy of Lady Laura, but also one of the great subjects of the whole Palliser series, she remarks,

'The one great drawback to the life of women is that they cannot act in politics.'
'Ah, which side would you take?'

'. . . Indeed, it is hard to say. Politically I should want to . . . vote for everything that could be voted for, – ballot, manhood suffrage, womanhood suffrage, unlimited right of striking, tenant right, education of everybody, annual parliaments, and the abolition of at least the bench of bishops. . . .'

'That is a strong programme', said Phineas.

'It is strong, but that's what I should like. . . . But then, Mr Finn, there's such a difference between life and theory; – is there not.'

'And it is so comfortable to have theories that one is not bound to carry out', said Phineas.[10]

Phineas's conventional irony could be male condescension and the self-serving platitude of a smugly ambitious youth. Madame Max immediately tests him to find out what kind of stuff he is made of, though Trollope leaves it for us to infer what exactly she is doing and why:

'Mr Palliser, do you live up to your political theories?' . . . Mr Palliser . . . gave a little spring in his chair as this sudden address was made to him. 'Your House of Common theories, I mean, Mr Palliser. Mr Finn is saying that it is very well to have far-advanced ideas, – it does not matter how far advanced, – because one is never called upon to act upon them practically.'

'That is a dangerous doctrine, I think', said Mr Palliser.

'But pleasant, – so at least Mr Finn says.'

'It is at least very common', said Phineas, not caring to protect himself by a contradiction.

'For myself,' said Mr Palliser gravely, 'I think I may say that I am always really anxious to carry into practice all those doctrines of policy which I advocate in theory. . . .' Mr Palliser, when he had made his little speech, turned away to the Duke's daughter. . . .

'I have called forth a word of wisdom', said Madame Max Goesler, almost in a whisper.

'Yes,' said Phineas, 'and taught a Cabinet Minister to believe that I am a most unsound politician. You may have ruined my prospects for life, Madame Max Goesler.'

'Let me hope not. . . . But to put joking aside, – they tell me you are sure to become a minister.'

Phineas felt that he blushed. . . . Could it be that people said

of him behind his back that he was a man likely to rise high in
political position? 'Your informants are very kind', he replied
awkwardly. . . .

　　After that Madame Max Goesler turned round to Mr
Grey. . . .[11]

In the odd sparring arena of social intercourse, Phineas proves
himself valiant by letting Madame Max put him in a bad light
before someone on whom he depends without bothering to defend
himself or in any way embarrass her. She finds him no toady, but a
good-natured man of honour who humours her without patronis-
ing her; and she rewards him by telling him just what will please
him. In fact, the impressions that this table-talk make do last.
Palliser never does quite believe Phineas to be sound; Marie
Goesler always has faith in Phineas; and he always feels that she
likes him and can lift his spirits.

　　Shortly after, she tests him again, knowing that he has fought a
duel with Chiltern over Violet and wants to marry her.

'What do you think of Miss Effingham?' said Madame Max
Goesler, again addressing him suddenly.
　　'What do I think about her?'
　　'You know her I suppose. . . . they tell me scores of men are
raving about her. Are you one of them?'
　　'Oh yes; – I don't mind being one of sundry scores.'
　　'But you do admire her?'
　　'Of course I do', said Phineas.
　　'. . . They say that women never do admire women but I most
sincerely do admire Miss Effingham. . . . I do believe that
nothing would make her marry a man unless she loved and
honoured him, and I think it is so very seldom that you can say
that of a girl.'
　　'I believe so also', said Phineas. . . . 'I cannot say that I know
Miss Effingham very intimately, but I should think it probable
that she may not marry at all.'
　　'Very probably,' said Madame Max Goesler, who then again
turned away. . . .

As Trollope composes this conversation, Phineas appears honourable, but not irresponsibly candid, reasonably honest, but protec-
tive of Violet's privacy and feelings; charming, but somewhat

callow. He seems to have a lot of maturing to do before he can be a match for Marie Goesler, and of course that is to be the plot of their relationship.

During the same party, Trollope subtly contrasts Phineas's behaviour with Lord Fawn's: these two men vie to impress Violet as the three of them talk about Madame Max, who by chance overhears the conversation:

'What a happy man you were at dinner!' continued Violet, addressing Phineas. . . . 'You had Madame Max Goesler all to yourself for nearly two hours, and I suppose there was not a creature in the room who did not envy you. . . . Lord Fawn I know intrigued.'

'Miss Effingham, really I must contradict you . . .', said Lord Fawn.

'You know Madame Max Goesler, of course?' said Violet to Lord Fawn.

'Oh yes, I know the lady; – that is, as well as other people do. . . . it seems to me that the world is becoming tired of her. A mystery is good for nothing if it always remains a mystery.'

'And it is good for nothing at all when it is found out', said Violet.

'And therefore it is that Madame Max Goesler is a bore', said Lord Fawn.

'Did you not find her a bore?' said Violet. Then Phineas, choosing to oppose Lord Fawn as well as he could on that matter, as on every other, declared that he had found Madame Max Goesler most delightful.

'And beautiful, – is she not?' said Violet.

'Beautiful!' exclaimed Lord Fawn.

'I think her very beautiful', said Phineas.'[12]

The conversation shows Phineas's talent for pleasing, his respect for women's feelings, and his ability to win their trust. Fatefully, Madame Max says to him at the end of the soirée, 'Mind you come and call on me – 193 Park Lane.' She responds to a sweetness in Phineas and a gift for intimacy. He really does engage in dialogue with women, and that is why he is popular.

## IV

I want to emphasise the richness and complexity of human intercourse that such Trollopian dialogue renders. As any perceptive
reader of the Phineas novels can plainly see, I have only begun to
suggest, by quoting out of full context and in truncated fashion,
the social and dramatic interest, the kinds of personal transac-
tions, and the intricate tones that these conversations carry. To
read Trollope's dialogue carefully is to experience his uncanny
sense of how people relate to one another in society – to know the
intricate mass of probings, shifting alliances, animosities, power-
plays, mating rites, ambivalent feelings, mental play, social
business, and sea-changes that he imagines human relationships
to be.

Even one little pronoun can illuminate his genius for revelation
in speech. Look at what the small word 'it', as two of his well-
known figures, Lily Dale and Archdeacon Grantly, utter it, can
tell us about love and ambition in his world.

In *The Last Chronicle of Barset*, Lily is talking to her friend Emily,
who is happily in love and engaged:

'I do envy you'. . . .
    'I can't give him up you know', said Emily.
    'I don't envy you him, but "it" ', said Lily.
    'Then go and get an "it" for yourself. Why don't you have an
"it" for yourself?'
    'I wish you would make up your mind to have an "it" for
yourself'. Emily Dunstable said to her again that night. . . .
    'I shall never have an "it" if I live to be a hundred', said Lily
Dale.[13]

That 'it' tells us about Lily's idea of love, her state of mind, and
ironically the reason for her morbid loyalty to Crosbie, the
pathetic ass who threw her over in order to marry miserably into
the aristocracy – she can't let go of her own 'it'. More significantly,
'it' implies enough to fill volumes about the subjective nature of
love; 'it' makes love the transformation of another into the projected emotion and desire of the self. 'It' suggests an anatomy of
Victorian love; 'it' identifies as a powerful cause of love envy for
the supposed happiness of another and thus makes love a self-
referential behaviour pattern which one is driven to imitate. The

pronoun makes clear the tension between the subjective ego and the objective other in what we now often refer to as love relationships.

In the celebrated opening of *Barchester Towers*, in which the quick death of old Bishop Grantly would, because of the imminent fall of a ministry, mean that his son Archdeacon Grantly would be named bishop, and a lingering death would mean the ultimate dashing of the son's professional hopes, Grantly has to undergo a spiritual crisis and ask himself whether he truly wishes his own father's death. When the Bishop finally does die, the unworldly, guileless Mr Harding commiserates with the son:

> 'You cannot but rejoice that it is over', said Mr Harding. . . .
> But how was he to act while his father-in-law stood there holding his hand? How, without appearing unfeeling, was he to forget his father in the bishop – to overlook what he had lost, and think only of what he might possibly gain?
> 'No; I suppose not', said he, at last, in answer to Mr Harding. 'We have all expected it so long.'[14]

'It' here encompasses both the death and the bishopric. In the apparently conventional cliché of polite conversation 'expected it', Trollope reveals, through Grantly's word choice, the conflict of his soul and the precise frustration of his heartfelt ambitions.

## V

Just as important as Trollope's subtle irony in Grantly's speech is the conflict in the Archdeacon's self-questioning inner voice. The tricky fate of having to relate to other people different from oneself and live up to their expectations is the nub of experience in Trollope. That means that the voices of others and, in general, of what we call society, public opinion or the world, get internalised in these figures. He often represents the mental life of characters as inward interrogation, debate and dialogue. Trollope, an acknowledged master hand at drawing interpersonal relationships, is also expert at rendering *intrapersonal relationship*. Like Grantly, his most interesting characters are made up of various, sometimes changing and conflicting social roles and attitudes.

Though it often takes the form of indirect discourse, this inner conversation, like the external dialogue, has an unmediated quality about it and also works rhetorically to involve the alert reader. Here is a passage on the interior life of Francis Arabin, the formal hero of *Barchester Towers*, which shows Trollope's use of illuminating but understated internal dialogue:

> He had, as was his wont, asked himself a great many questions, and given himself a great many answers. . . . Then he had asked himself whether in truth he did love this woman; and he answered himself, not without a long struggle, but at last honestly, that he certainly did love her. He then asked himself whether he did not also love her money; and he again answered that he did so. But here he did not answer honestly. It was and ever had been his weakness to look for impure motives for his own conduct.[15]

Notice that what the narrator says about Arabin's answer – that he does, indeed, love Eleanor's money – is *not* the truth that emerges. We have before us the unequivocal answer of Arabin's mind: he *does* love the idea of her money, and nothing that he says or does in the rest of the book, nothing that happens, supports the authorial comment that 'he did not answer honestly'. The narrator may pretend not to understand that the love for a woman and the love of her wealth can be tied to each other, but Arabin understands, Trollope understands and we understand. We also learn from this internal dialogue and from several other conversations that 'looking for the impure motive' in one's conduct is not a weakness but a great strength and spur to progress.

## VI

The stress on both inner and outer dialogue pulls us into a dialogue with the fiction. In *Barchester Towers*, Trollope presents this seemingly off-hand talk among clergymen who are visiting the old dying Dean:

> 'Poor Dr Trefoil; the best of men, but –'
> 'It's the most comfortable dean's residence in England,' said a second prebendary. 'Fifteen acres in the grounds. It is better than many of the bishops' palaces.'

'And full two thousand a year', said the meagre doctor.

'It is cut down to £1200', said the chancellor.

'No', said the second prebendary. 'It is to be fifteen. A special case was made.'

'No such thing', said the chancellor.

'You'll find I'm right', said the prebendary.

'I'm sure I read it in the report', said the minor canon. . . .

'What do you say, Grantly?' said the meagre little doctor.

'Say about what?' said the archdeacon, who had been looking as though he had been thinking about his friend the dean, but who had in reality been thinking about Mr Slope.

'What is the next dean to have, twelve or fifteen?'

'Twelve', said the archdeacon authoritatively, thereby putting an end at once to all doubt and dispute among his subordinates as far as that subject was concerned.[16]

It is a typical moment in a Trollope novel. Reading this without direct authorial guidance, I have the illusion of being a witness and interpreter with as much credibility as the narrator of what this conversation signifies. I infer that in the midst of death we are in life, that institutional identity provides continuity of life, that professional people are fascinated by the status and pay of members of their vocation, that this church is a very worldly organisation, that an organisation pecking-order functions even in extraordinary times, and that Grantly knows everything about the temporalities of his calling. This chatter makes fun of the religious institution, but it shows the animation of profession and the life force even at death's door.

In the fictive substance of such unobstrusive dialogue I find Trollope's essential humour and communal vision – not only in *Barchester Towers*, but in his work as a whole. His point is that even in casual talk everything matters, everything resounds with relationship – if you listen closely.

NOTES

1   *An Autobiography*, World's Classics edn (London, 1953) p. 205.

2   See David Skilton, *Anthony Trollope and His Contemporaries* (London, 1972) pp. 140–3, for an informative general discussion of internal monologue and debate in Trollope's characters. For a provocative discussion of self-dialogue in Trollope's fiction, see Walter M. Kendrick's *The Novel-Machine: The Theory and Fiction of Anthony Trollope* (Baltimore, 1980) pp. 83–106 (ch. 7).

3    Henry James, 'Anthony Trollope', repr. in *Trollope: The Critical Heritage*, ed. Donald Smalley (London, 1969) p. 529.
4    See C. P. Snow, *Trollope: His Life and Art* (New York, 1975) p. 156.
5    For a discussion of dialogue in *Barchester Towers*, see my *Comic Faith: The Great Tradition from Austen to Joyce* (Chicago, 1980) pp. 191–6. My ideas and comments in both the present piece and in *Comic Faith* on Trollope's use of dialogue have been informed by Lowery Pei's 'Anthony Trollope's Palliser Novels: The Conquest of Separateness' (Stanford dissertation, 1975) pp. 93–100.
6    *Phineas Redux*, World's Classics edn, pp. 194–5 (ch. 58).
7    Ibid., pp. 149–50 (ch. 54).
8    Ibid., p. 153.
9    *Phineas Finn*, World's Classics edn (London, 1951) pp. 396–8 (ch. 34).
10   Ibid., pp. 32–3 (ch. 40).
11   Ibid., pp. 33–5.
12   Ibid., pp. 40–2.
13   *The Last Chronicle of Barset*, World's Classics edn (London, 1958) pp. 107, 114 (ch. 52).
14   *Barchester Towers*, World's Classics edn (London, 1925) p. 5 (ch. 1).
15   Ibid., p. 323 (ch. 34).
16   Ibid., pp. 296–7 (ch. 31).

# Trollope Revises Trollope[1]

## ANDREW WRIGHT

Trollope's productive energy and enormous accomplishment, his admittedly obsessive drive to write every day in or out of season, offer – sometimes all too plausibly – the temptation to find the result insufficiently finished. To be sure, it is easy enough to discover in his novels a certain untidiness in plot-making, the assignment of different names to a single character, imperfect consistency in geography: Frank Robbins and John W. Clark are among the many readers of Trollope who have remarked on such matters.[2] Nor did Trollope ever undertake so comprehensive a revision of his work as did Henry James for the New York Edition (and that James relished the opportunity is made splendidly plain in the prefaces and in his letters). Of course, Trollope was never granted such an opportunity, but there is little evidence that he would have grasped the nettle with such forcefulness as did James. So much must be granted, but these facts sometimes conceal the attentive seriousness which Trollope devoted to his work, especially when these facts are coupled with the somewhat disingenuous disclaimers of the *Autobiography* on the doctrine of inspiration, together with his notorious comparison of the craft of fiction to those of the tallow-chandler and the cobbler.

Yet there is also in the *Autobiography* another and more credible account of the impulse behind the production of the forty-seven novels – not to mention the bulky record of his travels to the West Indies, to North America, to Australia and New Zealand, to South Africa; the studies of Cicero, Thackeray, Palmerston; the short stories and the journalism. In the *Autobiography* Trollope writes most persuasively of the force behind his enormous output: 'I was always going about', he says, 'with some castle in the air firmly built within my mind. Nor were these efforts in architecture spasmodic, or subject to constant change from day to day. For weeks, for months, if I remember rightly, from year to year, I would carry on the same tale, binding myself down to certain laws, to certain proportions, and proprieties, and unities.'[3] Explicitly this castle-building came about as a desperate alternative to the ruinous circumstances of his early life as the son of an improvident father, a neglectful mother, and a bullying elder brother. It was, again explicitly, an alternative to suicide. Given the circumstances, and given his intelligence and talent, it is no wonder that Trollope was able to produce more work of importance than any other first-class novelist before or since. Yet this urgent impulse has, not altogether surprisingly, been insufficiently taken into account. The centenary of his death provides opportunity to redress the balance. The present essay, however, is not a piece of speculation: it is a study of Trollope at work on his manuscripts.

Such study is in its infancy. In 'The Text of Trollope's *Phineas Redux*'[4] R. W. Chapman indicated almost by the way (the essay is a consideration of various textual anomalies in the World's Classics edition of *Phineas Redux*) that he had examined the manuscript of the *Autobiography* in the British Museum but acknowledged that he had made no very particular study of it; he even supposed, as he admitted in this essay, that there was no surviving manuscript of any of Trollope's novels. Robert H. Taylor, in 'The Manuscript of Trollope's *The American Senator* Collated with the First Edition',[5] produced a fine study of a kind that was not to be attempted again in such detail for many years. Later, Frederick Page provided in the Oxford Trollope edition of the *Autobiography* of 1950 'a printed text in accordance with Trollope's manuscript'. P. D. Edwards collated the manuscript of *He Knew He Was Right* in the Pierpont Morgan Library with the first edition for the University of Queensland edition of 1974. Mary Hamer's exemplary study of the *Framley Parsonage* manuscript at Harrow School[6] corrects some misapprehensions about Trollope's working habits, and will be discussed more fully in the course of the present essay; unfortunately about half the manuscript is missing, but the remaining portion provides adequate ground for demonstration of the steps taken by Trollope in the revision of that novel from first draft onward. And there is no lack of manuscript evidence. In a most valuable appendix to 'Trollope at Full Length',[7] Gordon Ray listed manuscripts of thirty-three novels and indicated locations for them, together with an assessment in each case of the level of correction: all bear signs of at least minor correction, eight of substantial or large-scale correction. (Since the publication of 'Trollope at Full Length', the manuscript of *The Way We Live Now* has been acquired by the Pierpont Morgan Library, and it can be added to the list.)

On the matter of his own writing, Trollope is explicit but less than fully particular in the *Autobiography*. But in 'A Walk in a Wood', published three years after the *Autobiography* was completed,[8] Trollope confessed that the bulk of his work of composition was done in advance of his sitting down to his desk, where – as the *Autobiography* and the Work Sheets at the Bodleian Library attest – he performed the act of writing with a quantitative exactness unknown in or unacknowledged by any other writer: 250 words per quarter of an hour in accordance with a diary that would enable him to know well in advance the day on which he would be finished writing even the bulkiest of three-deckers or four-deckers. He was exact – but human. In the Bodley Work Sheets, for instance, is the day-by-day schedule for *The Way We Live Now*, at the end of which is this note: 'Completed in 34 weeks (instead of 32) – but five weeks [he is wrong here – it was four] were occupied on Harry Heathcote, and therefore this novel "The Way We Live Now" has been done in 29 weeks. Dec. 22, 1873.' In one week he wrote but six pages, and beside that low number he wrote, 'Bad foot.'

The depiction in the *Autobiography* of himself as an ordinary workman has elicited a certain amount of derision, enough at least to obscure the overpowering novelistic purpose; and enough also to make the readers of the *Autobiography* scamp Trollope's own testimony as to his practice of revision: each day, as he says,

I always began my task by reading the work of the day before, an operation which would take me half an hour, and which consisted chiefly in weighing with my ear the sound of the words and phrases. I would strongly recommend this practice to all tyros in writing. That their work should be read after it has been written is a matter of course, – that it would be read twice at least before it goes to the printers, I take to be a matter of course. But by reading what he has last written, just before he recommences his task, the writer will catch the tone and spirit of what he is then saying, and will avoid the fault of seeming to be unlike himself.[9]

Since, as he says, he produced ten pages a day, his thirty-minute scrutiny of the 2500 words of the day before was indubitably particular; there was in addition at least one further reading before the manuscript went to the printer. Study of the manuscripts bears out the supposition that Trollope's examination of his work was far from superficial; and the published letters of Trollope to his publishers show, as Mary Hamer has pointed out in her essay on *Framley Parsonage*, that

> Trollope was more concerned with detail than is usually supposed from the evidence of imperfect proof-reading in his texts. He was scrupulous about proofs, asking that he should be sent the manuscript with the proof and that the corrected proofs or revises should be sent in duplicate. . . . He drew attention to the way a careless slip by the printer in producing revises had 'utterly destroyed the whole character of my own [?most] interesting personage'; he objected to having his punctuation altered.[10]

As David Skilton has shown more clearly than anyone else,[11] Trollope's creative work was in two stages that are blurred in the *Autobiography* but still discernible even there, the better so when considered in the light of his other remarks on the subject of composition. The preliminary step is what Trollope calls the work of 'conception':

> that work of observation and reception from which has come his power, without which his power cannot be continued, which work should be going on not only when he is at his desk, but in all his walks abroad, in all his movements through the world, in all his intercourse with his fellow-creatures. He has become a novelist, as another has become a poet, because in those walks abroad he has, unconsciously for the most part, been drawing in matter from all that he has seen and heard.[12]

So much goes on before the novelist sits down to the writing table: 'some hours of agonising doubt, almost of despair, – so at least it has been with me; – or perhaps some days'. This first step, however, is but a step: 'And then, with nothing settled in my brain as to the final development of events, with no capability of settling anything, but with a most distinct conception of some character or characters, I have rushed at the work as a rider rushes at a fence which he does not see.'[13] This account is helpful in coming to understand the declaration that 'the work which has been done quickest has been done the best'.[14] It helps explain also the looseness of the plots themselves. And in 'A Walk in a Wood', Trollope admits the following: 'To construct a plot so as to know, before the story is begun, how it is to end, has always been a labour of Hercules beyond my reach. I have to confess that my incidents are fabricated to fit my story as it goes on, and not my story to fit my incidents.' In the same place he even boasts that he did not decide that Lady Mason should have forged the codicil to her husband's will until he came to the chapter in which she acknowledges having done so; he admits also that he did not think of Lady Eustace's theft of her own diamonds until 'I was writing the page on which the theft is described'; he alludes to his having killed off Mrs Proudie immediately on hearing himself criticised for allowing her too much prominence in the Barsetshire novels.[15] But, as he says here, he had in his mind, again before sitting down to the writing table, what he calls 'plotlings':

> the minute ramifications of tale telling; – how this young lady should be made to behave herself with that young gentleman; – how this mother or that father would be affected by the ill conduct or the good of a son or a daughter; – how these words or those other would be most appropriate and true to nature if used on some special occasion.[16]

Much of the essay is given over to consideration, sometimes a little ponderous, of the kinds of wood in the various parts of the world in which this constructive work – this work of conception – can best take place, but toward the end Trollope returns with greater specificity to the subject of plotlings and their content. In the most propitious kind of wood, he says,

> gradually the scene forms itself for me . . . and words are weighed which shall suit, but do more than suit, the greatness or smallness of the occasion. . . . All this has to be thought of and decided upon in reference to those little plotlings of which I have spoken. . . . The first coarse outlines of his story he has found to be a matter almost indifferent to him. It is with these little plotlings that he has to contend. . . . Every little scene must

be arranged so that, – if it be possible – the proper words may be
spoken and the fitting effect produced.[17]

No wonder, therefore, that Trollope's manuscripts are so clean.
Since by his own admission he often had the very phrases of entire
scenes in his mind before picking up his pen, his labour was in
many respects merely clerical, transcriptive. Hence page after
page, indeed chapter after chapter, of his novels are as neat as fair
copies.

Study of five Trollope manuscripts, early and late, corroborates
his own declarations on the subject of writing and revision.
Particularisation also deepens the sense of Trollope's engagement
with his art. These are the five: *Orley Farm* (1862, manuscript at
the Carl H. Pforzheimer Library); *The Small House at Allington* (1864,
Huntington Library); *The Belton Estate* (1866, Huntington
Library); *The Duke's Children* (1880, Yale); *Mr Scarborough's Family*
(1883, Mr Robert H. Taylor). All five manuscripts were sent to
the printers: all bear indication of assignment by name to the
several compositors of the printing houses.

The transcriptions in the present essay are exemplary rather
than exhaustive, but the headnotes indicate all the places in the
manuscripts in which considerable alteration is to be found.

The following scheme has been employed:

1. Words within angle brackets have been cancelled by Trollope,
generally by means of a single straight or wavy line.
2. Italics are used to indicate words added by way of immediate
correction or in later revision.
3. An undeciphered word is indicated by a dash.
4. A doubtful reading is indicated as follows: [?].
5. Double angle brackets indicate a cancellation within a cancelled passage.
6. Citation is by chapter number; volume and page numbers (in
parentheses) refer to the World's Classics editions; variations in
accidentals have not been specially remarked, not because they
are unimportant – I know better – but because they would cause
too much clutter in an essay devoted to Trollope's working habits.

## ORLEY FARM

Trollope began writing this novel on 4 July 1860, and finished it on 15 June 1861. It was published in twenty monthly numbers beginning in March 1861 and in two volumes by Chapman & Hall, the first in December 1861, the second in September 1862. It is of special interest not only because it is one of Trollope's most absorbing works but also because it belongs to the period of what may be called his mature command of his medium: 'With the writing of *Orley Farm*,' Michael Sadleir says, 'Trollope may claim to have mastered once and for all the technique of his craft.'[18] Of the eighty chapters, nineteen contain more than merely cursory corrections; the remaining chapters are remarkably free from alteration. The nineteen are as follows: 1, 6, 10–12, 14, 16, 17, 19, 21, 22, 45, 46, 49, 57, 68, 72, 77, 79.

*Chapter 1    The Commencement of the Great Orley Farm Case*

The revisions in the course of this expository chapter show Trollope's effort to work out the circumstances of the signing of the codicil, by the terms of which Orley Farm was left to Lucius Mason. By his own admission in 'A Walk in a Wood' (see above), Trollope had not decided when he began this novel that Lady Mason should have forged her husband's signature to this codicil.

It is not true that a rose by any other name ⟨would⟩ *will* smell as sweet. Were it true I should call this story 'The Great Orley Farm Case'. But who would ask for the ninth number of a serial work burthened with so very uncouth a name: Thence and therefore, – Orley Farm.

I say so much at commencing in order that I may have an opportunity of expressing that this ⟨novel⟩ *book* of mine will not be devoted in any special way to rural delights. The name might lead to the idea that new precepts were to be given, in the pleasant guise of a novel, as to cream cheeses, pigs with small bones, wheat sown in drills, or artificial manure. No such aspirations are mine. I make no ⟨such⟩ attempts *in that line and declare at once that* agriculturalists will gain nothing from my present performance. Orley Farm, *my readers*, will be ⟨the⟩ *our* scene during ⟨some⟩ *a* portion of our ⟨sojourn⟩ *present sojourn*

together, but the name has been <selected> *chosen* as having
been for some time <well known> *intimately connected* with<a
particular> *certain legal* questions which <were much talked of in
some of> *made a considerable stir in* our courts of law.   (I.1)

The body of the will was in the handwriting of the widow as <the
codicil was supposed to be in that of Sir Joseph himself> *was
also the codicil. It was stated by her at the trial that the words* were dictated
to her by Usbech in her husband's hearing, and that the docu-
ment was then signed by her husband in the presence of them
both, and also in the presence of *two other persons*, a young man
employed by her husband as a clerk <also was there a [?] second
attending [?] witness [?], as there was a female servant in the
house> *and by a servant maid. These two last together with Mr Usbech
were the three witnesses whose names appeared in the codicil.* There had
been no secrets <with her or> *between Lady Mason and* her
husband as to his will. She had always, she said, endeavoured to
induce him to leave Orley Farm to her child from the day of the
child's birth, & *had* at last succeeded. In agreeing to this Sir
Joseph had explained *to her*, somewhat angrily, that he
<intended> *wished* to provide for Usbech's daughter, & that now
he would do so out of monies [?] *previously* intended for her, *the
widow*, and not out of the estate which would go to his eldest son.
To this she had assented without a word, and had written the
codicil in accordance with the lawyer's dictation, he the lawyer
suffering at the time from gout in his hand. Among other things
Lady Mason proved that on the date of the signatures Mr
Usbech had been with her husband for sundry hours.
     Then the young clerk was <— — testify> *examined.* He had he
said witnessed in his time four, ten, twenty, & under pressure,
he confessed to as many as a hundred & twenty business
signatures on the part of his employer Sir Joseph. He thought he
had witnessed a hundred & twenty, but would not take his oath
he had not witnessed a hundred & twenty one. *He did remember
witnessing a signature of his master about the time specified by the date of
the codicil, and he remembered the maid servant also signing at the same
time. Mr Usbech was then present, but he did not remember Mr Usbech
having the pen in his hand. Mr Usbech he knew could not write at that time
because of the gout, but he might no doubt, have written as much as his own
name.* He swore to both the signatures, his own and his master's;
& in cross examination swore that he thought it probable *that*

they might be forgeries. On re-examination he was confident *that* his own name, as there appearing, had been written by himself, but on re-cross-examination he felt that there was something wrong . . . . (I.3–4)

### Chapter 21    Christmas in Harley Street

Trollope betrays a certain anxiety about Lady Staveley's lapse of good manners in failing to invite Mrs Furnival (for she knows Mr Furnival to be married) to spend Christmas at Noningsby, although she has asked Mr Furnival to do so.

> It seems ⟨hard⟩ *singular* to me myself, considering the idea which I have in my own mind of the character of ⟨Mrs⟩ *Lady* Staveley, that I should be driven to ⟨say⟩ *declare* that about this time she committed an unpardonable offence not only against good nature but also against the domestic ⟨proprieties⟩ *proprieties*. But I am driven so to say, altho' she ⟨was perhaps⟩ *herself was of all women* the most goodnatured & most domestic ⟨woman of my acquaintance. I find it impossible to forgive her in that s⟩ *S*he asked Mr Furnival to pass his Christmas day at Noningsby, *and I find it impossible to forgive her that offence against the poor wife whom in that case he must leave alone by her desolate hearth.*
>
> (I.204–5)

### Chapter 57    The Loves and Hopes of Albert Fitzallen

Here Trollope faces the challenge of presenting Felix Staveley in a light which will make possible his continued acceptability to the reader, even though the young man is going to divest himself of Mary Snow, the girl beneath him in class whom he has intended to form into a worthy wife for himself. Trollope succeeds by revealing an attachment between Mary Snow and an apothecary's assistant whose name appears in the title of the chapter. Trollope also decided to add, in revision, a lengthy passage the purpose of which is to darken the picture of Mary Snow's father. This latter is indicated in the following sample:

> *Look at him as he stands there before the foul, reeking, sloppy bar, with the*

*glass in his hand, which he has just emptied. See the grimace with which he puts it down, as tho' the dram had been almost too unpalatable. It is the last touch of hypocrisy with which he attempts to cover the offence; as tho' he were to say, 'I do it for my stomach's sake; but you know how I abhor it.' Then he skulks sullenly away, speaking a word to no one, – shuffling with his feet, shaking himself in his foul rags, pressing himself into a heap – as tho' striving to drive the warmth of the spirit into his extremities! And there he stands lounging at the corner of the street, till his short patience is exhausted, and he returns with his last penny for the other glass. When that has been swallowed the policeman is his guardian.*

*Reader, such as you & I have come to that, when abandoned by the respect which a man owes to himself. May God in his mercy watch over us and protect us both!*

## Chapter 72    Mr Furnival's Speech

The trial depicted at the end of the novel is far from anti-climatic, though the reader has known for a long time that Lady Mason is guilty. That Trollope attended to the shadings in this important section of *Orley Farm* is indicated by the addition in the following passage:

And then it had become the duty of the prosecutors to prove the circumstances of the former trial. This was of course essentially necessary, seeing that the offence for which Lady Mason was now on her defence was perjury alleged to have been committed at that trial. *And when this had been done at considerable length by Sir Richard Leatherham, – not without many interruptions from Mr Furnival and much assistance from Mr Steelyard, – it fell upon Felix Graham to show by cross-examination of Crook the attorney, what had been the nature and effect of Lady Mason's testimony.* As he rose to do this, Mr Chaffanbrass whispered into his ear, 'If you feel yourself unequal to it I'll take it up. I won't have her thrown over for any etiquette, – nor yet for any squeamishness.' To this Graham vouchsafed no answer. He would not even reply by a look, but he got up and did his work.    (II.323–4)

## THE SMALL HOUSE AT ALLINGTON

This novel was begun on 20 May 1862 and finished on 11 February 1863. It was serialised in the *Cornhill* from September 1862 to April 1864. It was issued in two volumes by Smith, Elder in March 1864. *The Small House at Allington* occupies a special place in the hearts of a number of readers of Trollope. In the *Autobiography* – in the same paragraph in which he says, 'I believe that the work which has been done quickest has been done the best' – Trollope says of this novel, 'I do not think that I have ever done better work';[19] and Lily Dale has always been one of Trollope's best-loved heroines. In the *Autobiography*, however, Trollope also records his dissent: 'In the love with which she has been greeted I have hardly joined with much enthusiasm, feeling that she is somewhat of a female prig.'[20] The manuscript is remarkably clean, the hand-writing firm: the dominant impression formed by a study of the manuscript is of a confident and unhesitating author. For instance, chapter 23, 'Mr Plantagenet Palliser', gives first introduction to a character who later in the series called by his name will assume first importance; in the section of the chapter devoted to Palliser himself there are only the most minor and trivial alterations. Of the sixty chapters only eight contain considerable alteration: 9, 16, 20, 29, 31, 41, 43, 53.

*Chapter 31    The Wounded Faun*

In the penultimate paragraph, Trollope has worked on the response of Lily to the effort of Mrs Boyce to say 'one word' to her about Crosbie's having jilted her. The cancelled version and the revision are as follows:

<'I know Mrs Boyce is a very good woman,' said Lily as she walked home. But I find it quite impossible to like her. There are people that one is obliged to take upon position and not upon any merits that one discovers oneself.'> *I need hardly say what were Lily's sufferings under such a gaze; but she bore it, acknowledging to herself in her misery that the fault did not lie with Mrs Boyce. How could Mrs Boyce have looked at her otherwise than tenderly?*

(II.13)

## THE BELTON ESTATE

Trollope began the novel on 30 January 1865 and .completed it on 4 September of the same year. It was serialised in the *Fortnightly Review* from 15 May 1865 to 1 January 1866. It was published in three volumes by Chapman & Hall in December 1865. Trollope thought little of it: 'It has no peculiar merits, and will add nothing to my reputation as a novelist.'[21] But it is economically written and contains a gallery of well-drawn characters. Of the thirty-two chapters, only two contain alteration worthy of special remark: 10 and 28.

*Chapter 10    Showing How Captain Aylmer Kept His Promise*

Having promised his aunt not long before her death to do so, the young man of the chapter title – rather a Crosbie in character – proposes marriage with all due reluctance to the heroine, Clara Amedroz, and she accepts him without hesitation. He is brought up short by her directness, and she feels the want of enthusiasm on his part.

> The walk back to the house was not of itself very exciting, though to Clara it was a <short> *short* period of unalloyed bliss. No doubt had then come upon her to cloud her happiness, and she was 'wrapped up in measureless content'. It was well that they should *both* be silent <then>at such a moment. Only yesterday had been buried their dear old friend, – the friend who had brought them together, and been so anxious for their future happiness! And Clara Amedroz was not a young girl, prone to jump out of her shoes with elation because she had got a lover. She could be steadily happy without <much> *many* immediate <talk> <words> *words* about her happiness. <When they reached the house she again gave him her hand as – he had followed her up to the drawing room where for a season [?] their front door was closed behind them.> *When they had reached the house and were once more together in the drawing room, she again gave him her hand, and was the first to speak.* 'And you; are you contented?' she asked. Who does not know the smile of triumph with which a girl asks such a question at such a moment as that?    (p. 127)

*Chapter 28     Miss Amedroz is Pursued*

Again the proposal of Captain Aylmer is on Clara Amedroz's mind, but now it is a burden rather than a joy, not least because her cousin Will Belton's repeated and importunate proposals contrast so strongly.

> . . . she was now aware that she had accepted <the man she did not love and rejected him whom she did love> *the wrong man and rejected the wrong man.* She was steadily minded, now, at this moment, that before she parted from Captain Aylmer, her engagement with him should be brought to a close.    (p.372)


## THE DUKE'S CHILDREN

Two days after finishing the *Autobiography* Trollope commenced the novel which at first he called *The Ex-Prime Minister* – on 2 May 1876. He completed it on 29 October of the same year, but publication was delayed until 1879, when serialisation began in *All the Year Round* in the issue for 4 October; the final instalment appeared on 24 July 1880. It was published in three volumes by Chapman & Hall in May 1880. But the Trollope who in 1856 had refused to compress *Barchester Towers* ('I do object to reducing the book to two volumes – not because I am particularly wedded to three, but from a conviction that no book written in three can be judiciously so reduced'[22]) was more amenable two decades later, because – realist that he was – he recognised that his works were no longer so popular as in earlier years. The Work Sheets at the Bodleian Library provide evidence of this willingness. The section devoted to this novel is headed,

> The Ex-Prime Minister
> 4 volumes 8 parts
> 20 numbers
> Begun 2 May Ended 29 October 1876

Above this note, also in Trollope's hand:

> Afterwards called The Duke's Children

And below the main note:

> Reduced to 3 volumes. 16 numbers April
> and May 1878

There follows a Memorandum of Agreement, dated 3 June 1878, between Charles Dickens, the proprietor of *All the Year Round*, and Trollope, for a novel to be called 'Lord Silverbridge' – 'or by any other name' in three volumes. A letter from Trollope's son Henry,[23] sends the manuscript of the novel to the Red Cross Gift House as a gift for a forthcoming Red Cross sale. In the letter Henry Trollope says:

> As may be seen from a few words in his handwriting on a loose sheet inside the parcel the novel was written with the idea that it should come out in monthly parts, but it was published as a whole in 3 volumes in 1880. And it was shortened; – hence the erasures and corrections which are more numerous than my father usually made.

Accordingly the manuscript is a record not only of Trollope's customary review and alteration of his work but also of large-scale excision; and the samples provided here are among many passages containing important cancellation. Of the eighty chapters, all but two (29 and 44) are considerably revised; and the following are even more extensively revised: 1–4, 6, 7, 9, 11, 13, 14, 21, 34, 41, 51, 55, 56, 59, 67, 74 and 78.

*Chapter 1    When the Duchess Was Dead*

In the early chapters Trollope made large but most intelligent cuts. As the present sample demonstrates, he eliminated much of the recapitulation which ties *The Duke's Children* to *The Prime Minister*, the novel preceding it in the series. None the less, he indicates links in chronology and signalises the reappearance of certain of its leading characters. In this passage it is notable that Trollope reduced the number of Palliser children from four to three, but it is likely that this represents an early decision.

No one probably ever felt himself to be more alone in the world than our old friend the Duke of Omnium when the Duchess died. When this sad event happened he had ceased to be Prime Minister <but two years. Those who are conversant with the political changes which have taken place of late in the government of this country will remember that when the coalition ministry of which he had been the head was broken up, the old liberal party <<—>> *came* back to <<—>> *power* under the leading [?] of Mr Gresham. That arrangement did not remain in force very long; – but at the present moment we need not attend [?] to ministerial changes except to say that the Duke of Omnium had not yet obtained office.> During the first <year> *nine months he* <and the —> *and the Duchess* remained in England. Then they had gone abroad, taking with them their <four> *three* children. The eldest, Lord Silverbridge, had been at Oxford but had had his career there cut short by *some* more than ordinary youthful folly which had induced his father to agree with the College authorities that his name had <been> *better* be taken off the College books – *all which had been the cause of very great sorrow to the Duke.* The <two> other boy<s> <were> *was* to go<, one to Oxford & one> to Cambridge; but <their> *his* father had thought it well to give <them> *him* a <run for> twelvemonths *run* on the continent under his own inspection. Lady Mary, the only daughter, <had been the youngest of the four, and — — had been with them> was the youngest of the family, *and she also had been with them on the continent.* They remained the full year abroad, travelling with a large accompaniment of tutors, lady's maids, couriers, and, sometimes, friends. I do not know that the Duchess or the Duke had enjoyed it much but the young people had seen something of foreign courts and much of foreign scenery, and had perhaps perfected their French <and added something to their German>. The Duke had <some friends invited [?]> *gone to work at his travels with a firm determination* to create for himself enjoyment out of a new kind of life. He had studied Dante and had striven to arouse himself to ecstatic joy amidst the loveliness of the Italian lakes. But, through it all, he had been aware that he had failed. The Duchess had made no such resolution; – had hardly, perhaps, made any attempt; <and her expectations [?] had militated against her efforts. But> *but* in truth they had both sighed to be back among the war trumpets. They had both suffered much among the trumpets, and yet they longed to return. He told himself from day to day that, though he had been banished from the House of <Lord>

*Commons,* <—> still as a peer he had a seat in Parliament, and
that though he was no longer a <British> Minister still he might
be useful as a <British> legislator. She, in her career as a leader
of fashion, had no doubt met with some trouble; – with some
trouble but with no disgrace; and as she had been carried about
among the lakes and <pictures [?] and> *mountains, among* the
pictures and statues, among the counts and countesses, she had
once more[24] felt that there was no happiness except in that
dominion which circumstances had enabled her to achieve once
and might <again> enable her to achieve *again* in the realms of
London Society. <and so they had both sighed to be again
among the trumpets without any free communication of these –
thoughts among themselves>.    (I. 1–2)

### Chapter 13    *The Duke's Injustice*

The long passage cancelled by Trollope in this chapter contains
an account of the relationship between Mrs Finn (when she was
Madam Max Goesler) and the uncle of the present duke, related
in chapters 25 and 26 of *Phineas Redux*; the old duke's legacy is
recalled by the present duke in chapter 15 of *The Duke's Children*.
Still, there is reason to regret the cancellation, for it exhibits in
even sharper relief than in the final version how deeply the acid of
resentment has corroded his sense of fair-mindedness, the more so
on account of his fully realised sense of indebtedness to her for her
generosity.

No advantage whatever was obtained by Lady Mary's
interview with her father. He persisted that <she> *Mrs Finn* had
been untrue to him <and to the charge which she had accepted
from his hands.> when she left Matching without telling him all
that she knew of his daughter's engagement with Mr Tregear.
No doubt by degrees that idea which he at first entertained was
expelled from his head, – the idea that she had been cognizant
of the whole thing before she came to Matching; but even this
was done so slowly that there was no moment at which he
became aware of any lessened feeling of indignation. <The fact
at any rate <<—>> remained that she<<was>> had been aware
of this iniquity while she was holding intercourse with him
about his daughter <<—>> and that she had concealed it.

No doubt there returned at this time to the <<man's>> *Duke's* mind something of the feeling towards this woman which had been strong with him when first his <<—>> wife had proposed her to him as a friend. He too had thought, – he as well as Lady Cantrip and others, – that she had been in some degree mysterious and, in the same degree, objectionable. At any rate she was not one of his class. She had then been a widow and even up to this day he had heard nothing of her first husband except that he had died leaving her a rich woman. She had no doubt behaved well in <<— very>> peculiar circumstances. She might herself have been at this very moment a Duchess of Omnium, the old Duke having asked her to marry him. She had refused, – no doubt very wisely <<as had regarded>> *in reference to* her own happiness; – but there had seemed to him something noble in her refusal. The late Duchess had so regarded it, and had consequently opened her heart to the woman. He had gradually been carried along with his wife, and had submitted himself to an intimacy which had been contrary to his taste. Other matters had acted much in her favour; first <<but>> *and* chiefly, no doubt, his – appreciation of a certain modesty on her part. Intimate as she had been in the house she had never been <<forward>> *familiar* in her manner with himself. She had <<always>> borne herself *in those days* as though there <<was>> *must always be* something of a gulf between the Duke of Omnium and Madam Max Goesler, as she was then called. He was the last man in the world to tell himself that this was a consideration; but he had felt it as such. Then it had chanced that she had married a man with whom he had close political relations. And then, too, there had been the matter of the legacy, a very large legacy, left her by the old Duke as to which, though he had strenuously opposed her, still he had <<—>> admired her conduct. Of what the old man had left her she would take nothing, – and even at this very day there was lying packed up in the vaults beneath the premises of the Duke's bankers near Charing Cross a collection of diamonds, said to be worth a very great sum of money, which was in truth the property of this woman but which she had hitherto positively refused to accept. These things had, after a fashion, reconciled even his stubborn nature to his wife's friend. He had become, if not absolutely intimate with her, at least so much more intimate than with any other woman, that he had asked her to remain with his

daughter at Matching. Even when doing so he <<—>> remembered that she had been the mysterious widow of an unheard of
old husband; but still he had asked her. And she had betrayed
his trust! So he declared to himself; and he asked himself at the
same time what else he had a right to expect from the
mysterious widow of an unheard of old husband.>

To his thinking she had betrayed her trust . . . .    (I.122)

*Chapter 21    Sir Timothy Beeswax*

Trollope's wonderfully cynical portrait of Sir Timothy Beeswax,
whose principles are consonant with his name, is one of the best
things in *The Duke's Children*. The cancellations here remove some
of the darker strokes.

<There can be no doubt that m> *M*uch, no doubt, of Sir
Timothy's power, <much rather of his opportunities,> had been
from his <most [?]> praiseworthy industry. Though he cared
nothing for the making of laws, though he knew nothing of
finance, <what should now have been his own familiar
business,> though he had abandoned his legal studies, still he
worked <very> hard. And because he had worked harder in a
special direction than others around him, therefore he was
enabled to lead them. The management of a party is a <very>
great work in itself; and when to that is added the management
of the House of Commons, a man has enough upon his hands
even though he neglects altogether the <most> ordinary
pursuits of a Statesman. Those around Sir Timothy were
<very> fond of their party; but they were for the most part men
who had not condescended to put their shoulders to the wheel
as he had done. Had there been any very great light among them,
had there been a Pitt or a Peel, Sir Timothy would have *probably*
become Attorney General and <in due course> have made his
way to the bench; – but there had been no Pitt and no Peel and
he had seen his opening. He had studied the ways of members.
Parliamentary practice had become familiar to him. He had
shown himself to be ready at all hours to fight the battle of the
party he had joined. And no man knew so well as Sir Timothy
how to elevate simple legislative attempt into a good faction
fight <and so he had been successful.

His parliamentary career had been versatile. Though it might be true as he had once boasted that he had never changed his political <<friends [?]>> *principles*, he had more than once changed his political friends. Not having <<any such>> had political principles, he could not but be consistent. He had been Solicitor General to a Conservative minister, and had then, with many other Conservatives, joined the Coalition which had been made under the auspices of the Duke of Omnium. When that was broken up he remained for a while with the Liberals. But the Liberal government which was then formed by Mr Monk had in it from the first so much of weakness that Sir Timothy did not see his way to remain. It would <<fatigue>> *weary* the reader were he to be called on here to read the remarkably clever explanation which he then gave of his conduct. It was, however, so clever that it enabled him without a blush to <<attack>> *commence his attack upon* his late colleagues from the *very* day on which he left them, *and this he had done*, in a <<—>> *manner* that had greatly assisted Sir Timothy through defeat. Now he was reaping his reward; – not so great a reward as he hoped might come in time, for he looked forward to the glory of making a duke or two and of his own bosom, <<which could only be done>> *and this could be done only* when he <<had>> *should have* succeeded in getting rid of the lord who still was the Prime Minister of England <<— still a great reward>> >. He had so mastered his <—> *tricks* of conjuring that no one could get to the bottom of them; and he had assumed a look of preternatural gravity which made many young members think that Sir Timothy was born to be <an — — all> a King of men.    (I.202)

### Chapter 28   *Mrs Montacute Jones's Garden Party*

There is much cancellation in the manuscript as Lord Silverbridge becomes attracted to Isabel Boncassen, but – with a characteristic modesty – cannot believe that Mabel Grex would be jealous. Isabel is perhaps more jaunty in the fuller version presented here, and Lord Silverbridge more fully conscious of his own feelings. Mabel Grex addresses Lord Silverbridge:

'Now we've been round the haycocks, and really Lord Silverbridge, I don't think we have gained much by it. <I quite feel

that I haven't made myself pleasant, and you have been as cross as ever you can be.> These forced marches never do any good. <I dare say I shall meet you somewhere tonight, and then I hope I shall be pleasanter and you better mannered. Ta, ta.>' And so they parted.

He was thinking with a bitter spirit of the result of his morning's work <or of the absence of any result> when he <came> again found himself close to Miss Boncassen in the crowd *of departing people* on the terrace. <People were going away and were hurrying through to their carriages. Mr Sprottle had been sent on in advance and Miss Boncassen <<had been>> *was* hanging on her father's arm.> 'Mind you keep your <promise> *word*', she said. And then she turned to her father. 'Lord Silverbridge has promised to call.'

<'Your mother> *'Mrs Boncassen* will be delighted to make his acquaintance.'

<'We are dining today with Sir Oliver Crumblewit, the President of the Phrenological society. I suppose you won't go there.'

'Well; no; I don't think I know Sir Oliver.'

'And tomorrow with General Van Snuff, the great Dutch traveller.'

'I don't think I know the General either.'

'I dare say not. We always go to learned places; never anywhere else. On the next evening there is a grand meeting of vivisectors. You won't be there I dare say.'

'My Lord, you mustn't believe all the nonsense that my girl talks', said the father.

'Oh yes, I do', said Lord Silverbridge cheerfully as he made his way through the crowd. 'At any rate I shall be sure to come and call.' Then Miss Boncassen smiled and nodded to him familiarly. At that moment he saw that Lady Mabel was just at his other elbow. She also smiled and nodded, but it seemed to him that there was more of <<——>> *sarcasm* than of good humour in her smile.>

He got into his cab and was driven off towards Richmond. As he went he began to think of the two young women with whom he had passed the morning. <Of course he was still fully prepared to ask Lady Mabel to be his wife <<and>>. He assured himself that he was not the man to be put off his intention by the absurd nonsense of a few minutes. But surely> Mabel had *certainly* behaved badly to him. Even if she suspected nothing of his object did she not owe it to their friendship to be more courteous to him than she had been? And if she suspected that object, should she not at any rate have given him the opportunity? <Or could it be possible that she intended him to take what she had before said as a rejection in earnest, and that therefore she would not give him that opportunity? If so, – if he could feel convinced that it were so, – then why should he undergo the annoyance of a mere positive impulse? And yet her manner had hardly been such as in that condition of affairs he would have expected!>

Or could it be that she was really jealous of the American girl? No . . .    (I.272)

## MR SCARBOROUGH'S FAMILY

One of Trollope's last works, this novel was begun on 14 March 1881 and finished on 31 October. It was serialised in *All the Year Round* from 27 May 1882, to 16 June 1883. It was published in three volumes by Chatto & Windus in April 1883. The manuscript is about half in Trollope's hand; the other hand is that of his niece Florence Bland, to whom – according to Michael Sadleir – Trollope dictated when he was suffering from writer's cramp.[25] *Mr Scarborough's Family* bears witness to the struggle which Trollope had in this respect: he wanted to write himself rather than dictate, and a number of chapters begin in Trollope's hand, only to break off in obvious desperation. Revisions throughout are written by Trollope; clearly he read over the work of the previous day and made corrections while he was still fresh. The manuscript as a whole is not much revised; only the first chapter contains extensive alterations.

*Chapter 1    Mr Scarborough*

This passage, toward the end of the chapter, is of interest as showing a refinement in narrative management introduced in the revision. In the published version of the novel the actuality of both the marriages of Mr Scarborough (as Mr Sandover became) is not revealed until the end of the book, when the depth of his rascality is sounded: Mr Scarborough married twice, so that he could in due course *choose* which of his sons should be his heir.

> It is not necessary here that I should recapitulate all the circumstances of the original fraud < — — it had taken place in the first instance almost from accident, the false fact of Mr Sandover's marriage having been in the first instance received in England, and there the true fact of the subsequent marriage having been <<at that moment>> cancelled.> – *for a gross fraud had undoubtedly been perpetrated*. After the perpetration of that fraud papers had <undoubtedly> been prepared by Mr Sandover himself with a great deal of ingenuity and the matter had been so arranged that but for his own <profession> *declaration* his eldest son would undoubtedly have inherited the property.   (p. 11)

### Chapter 2    *Florence Mountjoy*

The delicate matter of Florence Mountjoy's relationship with her cousin Mountjoy Scarborough is treated here, she having been expected by her family and by old Mr Scarborough to marry the young man.

> It has been said that within two or three days after the communication he had left London. He had done so in order that he might at once go down to Cheltenham, and there see his cousin. There Miss < — > *Mountjoy* lived with her mother<; and there also occasionally was to be found her brother. Now John Mountjoy was a young man of fortune as far as three or four thousand a year went, was a Member of Parliament, was <<three or>> *four or five* years older than his sister, was supposed to be peculiarly prudent and wise, and was of all men the one whom Captain <<Mountjoy>> Sandover liked the least.
>
> But his sister liked him and approved of him, was proud of him,>. *The time had been when Florence Mountjoy had been proud of her cousin,* and, to tell the truth of her feelings, *though she had never loved him, she had* <at this moment in reference to her cousin was not <<she was no longer>> proud of him nor <<though she was still in some way proud of him>> did she love him> *almost done so.*   (p. 16).

*Chapter 10    Sir Magnus Mountjoy*

Florence Mountjoy's mother, having been informed that Augustus is the true heir, must respond to the monstrous suggestion that Augustus rather than his elder brother now marry Florence – and Mrs Mountjoy must be shown to contemplate this possibility without being thought monstrous herself.

> . . . to her eyes Mountjoy Sandover was so commanding that all things must at last be compelled to go ⟨right⟩ as he would have them. And to tell the truth there had lately come to Mrs Mountjoy a word of comfort, ⟨ — ⟩ which might be necessary if the world should be absolutely upset in accordance with the wicked skill of her brother – which even in that case might make ⟨things go right⟩ *crooked things smooth.* Augustus, whom she had regarded always as quite a Mountjoy because of his talent and appearance, and habit of command, had whispered to her a word. ⟨The world no doubt was about to be upset, – though such a reversion [?] —— ⟨⟨*was she felt*⟩⟩ confessed almost as all but impossible – ⟨⟨and Tretton⟩⟩ was to become his⟩. Why should not Florence be transferred with the rest of the property?    (p. 86)

*Chapter 56    Scarborough's Revenge*

This chapter deals with old Mr Scarborough's confrontation with the unfeeling younger son Augustus, and the articulation of the revenge which the old man has taken, by cutting Augustus out of his will altogether. For Augustus is guilty of having wished his father dead, thinking to take over the estate sooner rather than later. Old Mr Scarborough speaks thus to his sister.

> 'Words such as those spoken by a son to a father demand a little thought. Were I to tell you that I did not think of them would you not know that I was a hypocrite?'
> '⟨You⟩ *You* need not speak of them, John.'
> 'Not unless he came here to harass my last moments. I strove to do very much for him – you know with what return. Mountjoy has been at any rate honest and straightforward, and considering all things not lacking in respect. *I shall at any rate have*

*some pleasure in letting Augustus know the state of my mind.'*

'What shall I say to <Augustus> *him?*' his sister asked.

'Tell him <to> *that he had better* go back to London. <At any rate> I have tried them both, as few sons can be tried by their father, and I know them now. Tell him with my compliments that <I would rather not see him. I have no communication> *it will be better for him not to see me. There can be nothing pleasant said between us. I have no communication* to make to him which could in the least interest him.'

But before night came the Squire had <altered his mind in compliance with his sister's request and had agreed to see his son at twelve o'clock on the following day> *been talked over, and agreed to see his son. 'The interview will be easy enough for me,' he had said, 'but I cannot imagine what he will get from it. But let him come if he will.'*

Augustus spent much of the intervening time in discussing the matter with his Aunt . . . .    (p. 538)

## SUMMARY AND CONCLUSION

From the evidence of the manuscripts, together with that provided in the *Autobiography*, the letters, and the fugitive pieces (especially that signally revealing essay called 'A Walk in a Wood'), it is possible to reconstruct the processes by which Trollope wrote his novels. First, he was a strongly motivated writer, the compensatory day-dreams of his boyhood being made the stuff of fictions which gave point and focus to his life incomparable with any other activity. Second, a good deal of work preceded the actual putting of pen to paper, though Trollope thought out his novels in small blocks rather than as a whole; within these blocks, which he called 'plotlings', he appears to have worked out the direction and scope and even in some instances the actual wording of the episode that he would commit to paper on the following day. Third, he read and reread what he had written, making – on the whole – few alterations. The examples in the present essay are not typical; Trollope was more often than not content with what he set down in the first instance. Fourth, he was capable of large-scale revision if necessary, as in the example of *The Duke's Children*.

## NOTES

1  I wish to express my thanks to the following for permission to quote from manuscripts in their possession: the Bodleian Library (Trollope's Work Sheets [MS Don. c. 10]), Mr Robert H. Taylor (*Mr Scarborough's Family*), the Huntington Library (*The Belton Estate* [HM 1332] and *The Small House at Allington* [HM 1330]), the Carl H. Pforzheimer Library (*Orley Farm* [CHPL Misc. MS 640]), and the Beinecke Library of Yale University (*The Duke's Children*). Professor N. John Hall has very kindly shared his bibliographical mastery of Trollope with me and thus contributed to the possible usefulness of the present essay.

2  Frank Robbins, 'Chronology and History in Trollope's Barset and Parliamentary Novels', *Nineteenth-Century Fiction*, V (1951) 303–16; John W. Clark, *The Language and Style of Anthony Trollope* (London: André Deutsch, 1975).

3  *An Autobiography*, ed. Frederick Page (London: Oxford University Press, 1950) p. 42.

4  *Review of English Studies*, XVII (1941) 184.

5  *Papers of the Bibliographical Society of America*, XLI (1947) 123–9.

6  *Review of English Studies*, XXVI (1975) 154–70.

7  *Huntington Library Quarterly*, XXXI (1968) 313–40.

8  *Good Words*, XX (1879) 595–600.

9  *Autobiography*, p. 272.

10  *Review of English Studies*, XXVI.157.

11  David Skilton, *Anthony Trollope and His Contemporaries* (London: Longman, 1972).

12  *Autobiography*, pp. 230–1.

13  Ibid., p. 175.

14  Ibid., p. 174.

15  *Good Words*, XX.595.

16  Ibid.

17  Ibid., p. 600.

18  Michael Sadleir, *Trollope: A Commentary*, 3rd edn (London: Constable, 1945) p. 389.

19  *Autobiography*, pp. 174-5.

20  Ibid., p. 178.

21  Ibid., p. 196.

22  To William Longman, 20 Dec. 1856, in *The Letters of Anthony Trollope*, ed. Bradford Allen Booth (London: Oxford University Press, 1951) p. 25.

23  To R. Hudson, Red Cross Gift House, King Street, St James's, 11 Feb. 1918 (the Beinecke Library of Yale University).

24  In the World's Classics edition, 'once more' is 'often'.

25  See Sadleir, *Trollope: A Commentary*, p. 316.

# Trollope's *Autobiography*

## A. L. ROWSE

To a writer Trollope's *Autobiography* is the most revealing ever
written. Writers' autobiographies fall into a special class of their
own, and there are not many of them. Among these Trollope's is,
paradoxically, the most illuminating about writing; I say 'paradoxically' because at the outset he specifically disclaims any
intention of recording his inner life *à la Rousseau*. But he does so all
the same; for his inner life was devoted to story-telling, the world
of imagination he created for himself (or was born with, for he was
a born story-teller), which had consoled him through all the years
of misery of his boyhood and youth.

Everybody who knows about Trollope knows about that misery
– far worse and more prolonged, as Leslie Stephen noted, than
Dickens' short period in the blacking factory, which he so much
resented. Trollope wrote his autobiography in 1876, some six
years before his death. The peak of his success was over, and –
clear-eyed as always – he foresaw his eclipse. He was then famous
throughout the English-speaking world; he had had a successful
public career in the Post Office; he had had all those years of
passionate delight in the hunting field; he was well off, a popular
member of society, especially of the men's clubs he enjoyed; he
was happily married, and his own children created few problems.

But nothing consoled him for the humiliations he had endured –
i.e. inwardly, for outwardly he was the successful man, with the
bluff, blustering, euphoric personality. Writing for himself, as a
real writer does – and the public would not see it until after his
death – he says, in describing one humiliation he had received at
school (apparently over the usual sex-trouble, though he could
not bring himself to say it, and had been too innocent to know
what it was about, though the other boys did), 'All that was fifty
years ago, but it burns me now as though it were yesterday. What
lily-livered curs those boys must have been not to have told the

truth! – at any rate as far as I was concerned. I remember their names well, and almost wish to write them here.'

They were ordinary human animals; but we already begin to see in Trollope something of the stigmata of genius: the abnormal sensitiveness, the one skin too few, the tenacious memory, almost total recall.

This was but one example of the humiliations he received all through boyhood and adolescence, at school and at home. We cannot go into them in detail; the *Autobiography* tells us the story. The descent of the family from upper-class affluence to debt, insecurity, bailiffs in the house, skedaddling abroad – through his father's incompetence and his mother's extravagance (until, at fifty, she took to writing and rescued what was left of the family, four of the children dying of consumption). There was his father's extreme temper, impossible to live with, along with his hopeless impracticality – an Oxford don who should never have married, throwing away his substance on trying to farm ('Orley Farm'). The boy had to walk to school three miles twice a day, through mud and dirt, as a day-boy at Harrow, looked down on by the boarders – and the famous novelist noted the innate cruelty of boys. He himself was treated as 'a Pariah'. At Winchester his keep was not paid for, and the other boys knew it; he was the only boy who could not give their servant the regular tip at end of term, 'and the cause of the defalcation was explained to him. I never saw one of those servants without feeling that I had picked his pocket.'

Many boys would not have bothered, but this big masculine fellow was, underneath, extremely sensitive. He was unkempt, ill-clad, dirty and, no doubt, unattractive – while longing to be as other boys, and liked. The man who had made such a huge success of his life wrote that the 'disgrace' of his early life had remained with him always: 'the sufferings, disgrace, and inward remorse' of his first twenty-six years.

There was something even deeper. All his life he had had a 'craving' for love and, pathetically, the successful man described this as a weakness. In fact, he had been an unloved child, both by mother and father; at Winchester – in those days an exceptionally brutal school – his elder brother, to whom he was fag, used to beat him with a big stick. It is a wonder that Trollope grew up with a nature unwarped: he was a normal man, very masculine and undistractedly heterosexual, full of family affection and kindness, with tenderness underneath the gruff, bullying exterior.

One sees what a spur this was to latent ambition, once the discouraged, disgraced member of the family belatedly woke up: hence, in part, the unflagging industry, the enormous output. A deep motive – unrealised by himself, for Victorians were curiously unselfaware – was the desire *se faire valoir*, to assert himself in that clamorous assertive family all given to writing. Even when he began to publish, his mother discouraged him; she, who wrote nearly a hundred books when over fifty – of which only *Domestic Manners of the Americans* survives – told him, Anthony Trollope, that there was no future for him in novel-writing. Think of it! But then her favourite was always the oldest boy, Tom – who wrote another sixty books, popular history and novels, mostly on Italian subjects. A fairly simple motive with Anthony, youngest of them to survive, must have been that he would show them!

The deeper truth was that he was a born writer. Leslie Stephen says that the best way to begin on Trollope is with the *Autobiography*. When I first read it many years ago – before the resurrection of Trollope got into its full stride – I spotted at once that here was the clue. During all those years of humiliation Trollope consoled himself with the inner life of the imagination, telling himself endless tales, often with himself as the hero, weaving a connected saga; the fantasy world in which he lived and his real life grew and burgeoned. Psychologists today have the useful concept of 'compensation'. But it is odd that all the critics who questioned his genius and depreciated it should not have noticed this clue; nor that, even in the early years before he took to novels, he kept a journal for ten years, which he destroyed when he began to be successful.

Actually, as a writer, Trollope had a long, hard apprenticeship; he lived with his characters, 'learned to dwell on a work created by my own imagination, and to live in a world altogether outside the world of my own material life'. This is why the world he created has such extraordinary force and conviction, and why we remember so many of his characters: he had always lived with them. 'Of all in that gallery I may say that I know the tone of the voice, the colour of the hair, every flame of the eye, and the very clothes they wear. Of each man I could assert whether he would have said these or the other words.' He wrote best in 'some quiet spot among the mountains', where there were no distractions: 'I have wandered alone among the rocks and woods, crying at their grief, laughing at their absurdities, and thoroughly enjoying their joy.'

We recognise the inner sensibility, just as much as with Dickens, who used to laugh and cry while writing.

Later, Trollope says something still more interesting. 'So much of my inner life was passed in their company, that I was continually asking myself how this woman would act when this or that event had passed over her head, or how that man would carry himself when his youth had become manhood, or his manhood declined to old age.' That is to say that, in his inner mind, his characters grew and changed with the years, as in life; and this is rare indeed. So he is entitled to give advice to any intending writer that he has to live with his creations if they are to be any good: 'They must be with him as he lies down to sleep, and as he wakes from his dreams. He must learn to hate them and to love them. He must argue with them, forgive them, and even submit to them.'

Everything that this most professional of writers, who learned the hard way, has to say about writing is of the utmost fascination to his fellows. But it is of no less utility: I learned from him myself the essential thing for the real writer – that he must be prepared *to make his work the condition of his life.*


All this being obvious, why were the critics so mistaken about the quality of Trollope's work? Not all of them were equally wrong; but all of them underestimated its quality and its survival value. Why did the publication of the *Autobiography* have such a deleterious effect upon his reputation? Why did the Victorians dislike it so much? Why did Trollope so consistently write himself down in it? – for, of course, he gave his critics the excuse to take him at his own valuation, and place him even lower.

It has perhaps not been noticed that the *Autobiography* presents a curious psychological problem. Just as Trollope could never explain to himself his passion for hunting, so it is very hard to explain Trollope's passion for self-depreciation. It, in fact, misled people. There is not the slightest doubt that, the most honest and sincere of writers that ever lived, Trollope had no intention of doing so. He really did think that he was no genius; there he was wrong. He thought that he was not in the same class with Thackeray; but he was wrong. He regularly tells us where he thought novels of his were not good; *Ralph the Heir* was 'the worst' novel he ever wrote. He was surprised at the success of *Dr Thorne.* He had a poor opinion of *He Knew He Was Right*; Henry James knew better, thought highly of it, and compared the tragic ending with Balzac.

The psychological problem of the *Autobiography* is rather a subtle one. In the first place, as I have said, Victorians were unselfaware; and, though Trollope had a firm and wide understanding of human beings in general, he had the Victorian dislike of probing too far into himself. The whole realm of sex, for example, hardly makes an appearance. During his early years as a Post Office clerk living alone in London, frustrated and unfulfilled – though a fine upstanding figure of a man by then – he says, 'there was no house in which I could habitually see a lady's face and hear a lady's voice. No allurement to decent respectability came in my way. In such circumstances the temptations of loose life will almost certainly prevail with a young man.' And then he gives the only hint: 'the temptation at any rate prevailed with me'. And that is all he ever says. Of course Trollope was a gentleman, and a gentleman didn't write about that private side of his life.

The Victorian age was extraordinarily moralistic, censorious and inhibiting – middle-class standards largely prevailed, as against the upper-class standards of the eighteenth century. It is astonishing to our loose age to think what writers had to put up with: some of them were not merely inhibited but positively damaged by it – Dickens and Thackeray, notably. Trollope protested against the ludicrousness of some of the inhibitions imposed by religious humbug – the *Autobiography* gives us some examples; all the same, he suffered from his own inhibitions. He was deeply a moralist, regarded himself as a preacher preaching sermons, and he had been deeply wounded. (Out of the wound came the genius; the *Autobiography* kept the wound green, as genius does for its own occult purposes.)

I thing too that Trollope was overreacting against humbug. He hated the humbug of the age far more than anyone – much more than Dickens and Thackeray, George Eliot, Carlyle or Ruskin, who in part subscribed to it. Trollope had no illusions whatever – he told Millais one day that he was a pessimist at heart; and that is hard for people to take when it is revealed to them, as the *Autobiography* did in no uncertain terms.

The writing confraternity were insulted at having their mystery reduced to a trade. (George Eliot would have 'shuddered' at Trollope's view. For his part, Trollope, generous man, thought her 'a wonderful woman', far above himself. She wasn't.) Writing the *Autobiography* was a gesture like throwing a pot of ink at the artistic profession, and it reacted as might have been expected. Trollope wrote himself down, and the imperceptive took him literally. The real mystery remains – why did he so write himself down, as few have done?

It was partly defiance, I suspect, for that was in keeping with his nature. There may have been an element of inverted pride. For Trollope was very much a gentleman, and most of his rivals in the field were middle-class professionals. He wrote like one of the confraternity. One would hardly guess from the *Autobiography* that he came from an old upper-class family of Lincolnshire gentry: he just mentions that his grandfather was the fourth baronet, not that his cousin, the head of the family, was elevated to the peerage as Lord Kesteven, just a few years before the book was written. Trollope's father had married for love, but, socially speaking, he had married beneath him: his wife was a middle-class woman, and it is revealing that, in one of their quarrels, he described her as 'vulgar'.

It seems that the marriage had something to do with the devastating disappointment of the father's expectation of succeeding to the inheritance of his rich uncle, Adolphus Meetkerke. No one seems to have thought of the Dutch element in Trollope's complex make-up. Henry James speaks of his 'infinite love of detail' as a prime characteristic: isn't it just like a Dutch picture, interior or exterior, with the careful and veracious rendering of every detail, the sober realism in every line? And, when one looks at portraits of Trollope, he looks just like one of those faithful old men looking at one out of Rembrandt, or perhaps Ferdinand Bol.

With Trollope's long upper-class descent, and with a Dutch fortune in the immediate background, the humiliations of youth and adolescence must have been worse to bear than actual poverty and being out-at-elbows. Certainly Trollope's class background accounts for more than is realised – his desire to sit in Parliament, for example, his candidature for Beverley, to which he devotes a chapter. 'I have always thought that to sit in the British Parliament should be the highest object of ambition to every educated Englishman.' When he didn't succeed he got permission to sit in the House of Commons gallery and watch the proceedings.

Hence, too, Trollope's exceptionally firm and extensive grasp of the whole social structure: he saw it as a man of the upper classes would, from a vantage point such as his middle-class *confrères* did not have. Henry James, a great admirer, found the political novels 'dull'. Not so those highly intelligent politicians, Harold Macmillan and Douglas Jay – neither of them a man to suffer fools gladly – who find Trollope's political novels fascinating, precisely because he understood what politics was all about and how it worked. (Henry James did not: he missed out here.)

People have found it a mystery how Trollope knew so much about the Church, cathedral closes and their goings on, and why so many clergymen figure in his novels. There is no mystery in it: the family on both sides, both Trollopes and Miltons, was full of clergymen. Trollope's cousin Edward was a bishop, who wrote the family history (not all families have their history written), and was as prolific as an antiquarian as the rest of them with their pens. Perhaps it takes an historian to appreciate these things.

We come to a less obvious reason to account for the strange psychology of the *Autobiography* in one who, to all intents and purposes, was so normal a man. It is that, as with all men of genius, Trollope's youth was alive in him; so he recapitulates the view of himself when young: he was not a man of genius, unlike Thackeray or George Eliot, he was a tradesman; a good tradesman, true, who did not scamp his work. He had not scamped his work for the Post Office, he had been a hard-working public servant (to whom we owe pillar-boxes, among other things). He thought ill of anyone who took public money without giving a proper return – a very out of date view. Similarly with his writing: he had given of his best; it wouldn't have been any better if he had written less, or less quickly. And so on.

He realised that he would have been more highly thought of if he had not written so much – like those precious writers whose estimation goes up with every book they do *not* write (E. M. Forster's did, for example). But Henry James appreciated Trollope's 'abundance', and the exceptional width of experience that justified it – three separate careers, Post Office, writing, regular hunting; travels all over England, Ireland and America, twice around the globe, etc. Trollope himself was able to point to his exemplars, who wrote for money – William Shakespeare or Walter Scott. As for the slur against being prolific, were they not also prolific? Or what about Balzac, with the 130 volumes of the *Comédie humaine* to Trollope's sixty or seventy?

Here again Trollope misled people by his defiant stance, falling over backward with outrageous honesty, mistaken (not false) modesty. What impelled him – as with Balzac – was not really money, but the genius that possessed him and drove him on; the *Autobiography* provides evidence that he was really an artist, with an artistic conscience, *malgré lui*.


Since Trollope denied that he had genius, critics followed suit. Richard Garnett wrote that 'talent such as his almost amounts to genius, and yet Trollope was no genius; he never creates – he only depicts'. Today we see that it was silly to say that of a writer who created so many characters that live, when the characters of most of his contemporaries are forgotten; indeed, Trollope created a world, a parallel in fiction to the historian's mid-Victorian age. Even Trollope admitted that in Barsetshire he had 'added a new shire to the English counties. I had it all in my mind – its roads and railroads, its towns and parishes, its members of Parliament, and the different hunts which rode over it. I knew all the great lords and their castles, the squires and their parks, the rectors and their churches.' All this was so real not only to him but to his readers that another writer, with a touch of genius – Father Ronald Knox – was able to draw a map of Barsetshire and point out a few convincing inconsistencies. And Thomas Hardy copied Trollope with his Wessex.

The critics continued to be condescending to Trollope's 'talent', even when favourable – like Leslie Stephen, who thought he was 'a bit of a Philistine'. No doubt the *external* Trollope, the face he presented to the world, was – that is part of the paradox. Stephen, who knew him, describes 'the simple, masculine character' which 'revealed itself in every lineament and gesture'. But, as we have seen, Trollope was not so simple as even he himself fancied, and a Victorian gentleman was not one to bare his wound to the world; Dickens did – Trollope's was deeper and life-long, and he kept the revelation until after his death.

I have a poor opinion of the critics for their imperceptiveness in not reading the signs. Herbert Paul thought that 'Trollope was not only dead, but dead beyond all hopes of resurrection.' Critics reveal their stupidity in the absoluteness of their judgements, when these should be relative and comparative. The historian Frederic Harrison did better when he said that interest in

Trollope would revive when people wanted a faithful portrait of his age. It fell to other novelists of genius to see the point, notably two Americans: Nathaniel Hawthorne, so different a spirit, poetic and romantic, with whom Trollope was a favourite; and Henry James, who gives us the more sensitive and searching account of Trollope's spirit. James once crossed the Atlantic in company with his senior – if 'company' is the word, for Trollope shut himself up in his cabin and wrote the whole time. 'Trollope has been accused of being deficient in imagination . . . but the power to shut one's eyes, one's ears (to say nothing of another sense), upon the scenery of a pitching Cunarder and open them upon the loves and sorrows of Lily Dale or the conjugal embarrassments of Lady Glencora Palliser, is certainly a faculty which could take to itself wings.'

James points out different aspects of Trollope's well-rounded genius: not only the piercing, lucid observation of everything, but the *feeling* that always accompanied it, the tenderness, the sense of pathos, the special sympathy for people's perplexities; his marked turn for satire, which he did not much indulge, though he turned it to good purpose to create a masterpiece in *The Way We Live Now*. James notices his major concern with moral questions, and then 'it is a marvel by what homely arts' he excites the impression of life. It is partly due to his refusal to be abstracted from the close scrutiny of realistic detail – as with the Dutch masters. And James concludes that 'there is something masterly in the large-fisted grip with which Trollope handles his brush'.

Evidently we must come to terms with the term 'genius' itself. It has many connotations and applications, but it is always best to hold firm to the literal meaning: it means a spirit that obsesses one and drives a man to the limit of his powers (and sometimes beyond them). Trollope was such an obsessed person, for all his apparent normality: the *Autobiography* told me at once that his real life was the inner life of the imagination. But it tells one more. Genius, in artists, almost always arises from a state of tension, from conflicts in the personality that are resolved in – or at any rate, ejaculated into – their work. As to the objective work that comes out of it, the Oxford Dictionary bids us look out for 'extraordinary capacity for imaginative creation'.

We can only say of Trollope that all the signs and symptoms, the stigmata, are there in the *Autobiography*, and the objective imaginative creation in the world of his novels.

Henry James says that Trollope did not take himself seriously as an artist, but James was not taken in by that as the critics were. In the *Autobiography* Trollope was deliberately challenging the 'art for art's sake' school, which was coming to the fore and already displacing him when he wrote his book. Certainly he was no Flaubert, or George Eliot, to spend days unable to write a word; he was the kind of artist Balzac was, concerned above all with the veracity of the effect, the truth to life, and he had his own sense of form. Balzac's range, force and depth were even greater; but James points out that Trollope's range and knowledge of life were much wider than that of the French Naturalists, who were his contemporaries. That, from James, is a significant compliment.

Once again the *Autobiography* betrays the signs – Trollope was more of an artist than (perhaps) he thought. He modestly accepted the superiority of the poetic and the spiritual (was the portentous George Eliot so very much the superior he fancied?). In his own mind realism prevailed, not merely truth to fact, but truth to life. Every time he sat down to write he first of all read over what he had written at the previous sitting; what he was looking out for was the rhythm of the words and phrases, he tells us, to see whether they were exactly true to the character he had in mind. There is nothing more difficult in the art of the novelist than to catch the precise tones and rhythms and turns of speech of different characters. To be able to do it is in itself one of the signs of the true novelist. Quite a lot of contemporary novelists who are admired, and otherwise distinguished writers, are without it – in Lawrence Durrell's novels, for example, all the characters talk alike: they are all Durrell talking. Not so with Trollope or Hardy, or – for that matter – with Evelyn Waugh.

Trollope's sense told him that to heap horrors upon horrors was not only untrue to his sober view of life – in that he had the limitations of the civilised Victorian age, not the advantage of our own bestial time – but also detracted from the artistic effect. I think we may say, from the vantage-point of contemporary literature, that Trollope was right: the more the horrors are piled on, the less we react. But observe that the second half of that judgement was an artistic one.

As to form, Trollope gives his objection to serial publication – it distorted the ultimate form of the work. Many Victorian novels and novelists suffered from this; Trollope less so than others. If he went on too long for our taste it is largely due to his accumulation of detail, the passion for verisimilitude – though sometimes one catches him giving the plot an unnecessary twist to fill out a third volume. He did not regard himself as a good plotter; to him the interest of character was dominant, and the plot usually developed out of the characters. He held that nothing in the plot should be incompatible with, or untrue to, the characters; all was to be subordinated to the central conception. What was this but an artistic judgement, revealing of his own sense of form?

His idea of style was subjected to the same sober realism: the language should be clear, lucid, above all intelligible. He was said to be careless in composition, as his prose was in general prosaic – he disliked the mawkish sentimentalities of Dickens, hated the theatricalities of Disraeli, and had no respect (quite rightly) for the jargon of Carlyle. Actually, however, he cared about his own words; it made him irritable when editors or publishers interfered in any way with what he had written. It is a straw in the wind, a sign of the artist who cared.

As to criticism he was completely consistent, and what he has to say as a professional craftsman about his fellow practitioners is far more valuable than any opinion of a Herbert Paul (whom Stephen thought 'an excellent critic of Victorian novelists'!). Trollope thought most criticism mere 'chaff' and did not bother his head about it. But that he took personal criticisms to heart, and was not unamenable if it chimed with his own inner doubts, we know from his story of what happened at the Athenaeum one day. I can see him at the farther end of that famous drawing room, where Matthew Arnold used to write at a window at the other end. Trollope overheard a couple of club-bores discussing Mrs Proudie, saying that Trollope had gone on too long about her, they were tired of her appearances. Trollope interrupted to say that he would go home and kill her off. And did – with some regret, he says; and much to ours, for she is a wonderful character, of whom we can never have enough.

Trollope had an artistic conscience, and some inner dubiety, in spite of the alarming positiveness he showed on the surface. Henry James noticed the artistic tact, the moderation and 'temperance' with which Trollope stopped at just the right point in his portrayal of Archdeacon Grantly. If it had been Dickens the portrait would have become caricature, larger than life-size. This is what Trollope did not appreciate in Dickens, and, in the Victorian debate as to the respective claims of Dickens and Thackeray,

Trollope aligned himself with intellectual opinion, the highbrows – and was wrong. But his judgement was in accord with his own precepts and practice.

As with that other autobiography of particular interest to writers, Kipling's *Something of Myself*, Trollope's is paradoxical also for its reserves, for what it does not say. Intimately revealing as it is of himself, he sees himself from the outside, as he saw others. He says nothing about his wife and his own happy family life. It was the unhappiness that made the writer. Everybody who met him noticed the extraordinary brilliance of his eyes and the piercing look they gave; they took in everything at a glance – one sees the uncompromising expression, no illusions, no humbug, the 'pessimist at heart'. Then one notices the gleam of kindness in the gruff look.

Hawthorne's son noticed the paradox that bespoke the conflict out of which came the genius.

> Though his general contour and aspect were massive and sturdy, the lines of his features were delicately cut; his complexion was remarkably pure and fine, and his face was susceptible of very subtle and sensitive changes of expression. His organisation, though thoroughly healthy, was both complex and high-wrought. . . . Altogether, to a casual acquaintance, who knew nothing of his personal history, he was something of a paradox. There was some peculiarity in him – some element in his composition that made him different from other men; on the other hand, there was an ardent solicitude to annul or reconcile this difference, and to prove himself to be of absolutely the same cut and quality as all the rest of the world.

Here was the paradox; the difference was, of course, his genius.

# Trollope the Person

## N. JOHN HALL

What sort of person was Anthony Trollope? Who was the creator of the Barsetshire and Palliser novels and so many other memorable works of Victorian fiction? The question is as difficult to answer as the more important one – what makes Trollope so engaging a writer? But the first question remains intriguing, and for most of his readers one that will not go away. My investigation will concentrate on contemporary accounts and reminiscences. But these must be seen in the context of the autobiographical aspects of his own writings.

Of central importance is the *Autobiography*, published posthumously in 1883. Without it we would have little or no knowledge of Trollope's utterly miserable childhood and youth. Trollope begins by saying that 'it will not be so much my intention to speak of the details of my private life', adding only that 'the garrulity of old age' – he was sixty when he wrote the book – together with 'the aptitude of a man's mind to recur to the passages of his own life' may tempt him to 'say something' of himself.[1] These protestations are followed by the moving and convincing account of his wretched early years, the three chapters that are the most revealingly personal words he ever put to paper. The son of an eccentric and demanding father and a well-meaning but neglectful mother, a poor boy at rich boys' schools, Trollope was a social outcast – dirty, sullen, ineffectual. As a young man and junior clerk in the London General Post Office he was again a misfit, displeasing to his superiors and, worse still, apparently altogether unsatisfactory in his own eyes. He says of his first twenty-six years: 'In truth I was wretched, – sometimes almost unto death, and have often cursed the hour in which I was born. There had clung to me a feeling that I had been looked upon always as an evil, an encumbrance, a useless thing, – as a creature of whom those connected with him had to be ashamed.'[2] And although once Trollope gets to his career as writer the personal note is less intense, it is always there. The book details, for example, his obsessive writing habits, his inordinate passion for hunting; it even speaks pointedly if guardedly of his love for Kate Field. Throughout, the *Autobiography* is a record of his desire, as he says, 'to be something more than a clerk in the Post Office. To be known as somebody, – to be Anthony Trollope if it be no more, – is to me much.' In the final chapter he writes:

> It will not, I trust, be supposed by any reader that I have intended this so-called autobiography to give a record of my inner life. . . . If the rustle of a woman's petticoat has ever stirred my blood, if a cup of wine has been a joy to me; if I have thought tobacco at midnight in pleasant company to be one of the elements of an earthly Paradise; if now and again I have somewhat recklessly fluttered a £5 note over a card-table; – of what matter is that to any reader? . . . To enjoy the excitement of pleasure, but to be free from its vices and ill effects, – to have the sweet, and leave the bitter untasted, – that has been my study. The preachers tell us that this is impossible. It seems to me that hitherto I have succeeded fairly well. I will not say that I have never scorched a finger, – but I carry no ugly wounds.[3]

The book, despite its denials, is extraordinarily revealing and personal. Surely Trollope knew this, but his readers frequently miss his ironies.

Trollope's correspondence, some 1800 surviving letters, clarify, supplement and correct the crafted view of his life as given in the *Autobiography*. But deeply personal statements are infrequent in the letters. I offer excerpts from one, that written to G. W. Rusden in June 1876, shortly after he had completed the *Autobiography*:

> As to that leisure evening of life, I must say that I do not want it. I can conceive of no contentment of which toil is not to be the immediate parent. As the time for passing comes near me I have no fear as to the future – I am ready to go. I dread nothing but physical inability and that mental lethargy which is apt to accompany it. Since I saw you I have written a memoir of my own life; – not as regards its activity but solely in reference to its literary bearing, as to what I have done in literature and what I have thought about it, – and now I feel as though everything

were finished and I was ready to go. No man enjoys life more than I do, but no man dreads more than I do the time when life may not be enjoyable.

Then, provoked by Rusden's defence of what he considered religious cant in Macready's *Reminiscences* Trollope expresses his own religious sentiments:

> You tell me of his beautiful humility before God! I do not prize humility before God. I can understand that a man should be humble before his brother men the smallness of whose vision requires self-abasement in others; – but not that any one should be humble before God. To my God I can but be true, and if I think myself to have done well I cannot but say so. To you, if I speak of my own work, I must belittle myself. I must say that it is naught. But if I speak of it to my God, I say, 'Thou knowest that it is honest; – that I strove to do good; – that if ever there came to me the choice between success and truth, I stuck to truth'. And I own that I feel that it is impossible that the Lord should damn me, and how can I be humble before God when I tell him that I expect from him eternal bliss as the reward of my life here on earth.[4]

Aside from this unusual emphasis on religion, the letter, in its frankness and love of work, is quintessential Trollope; he even makes his oft-repeated comparison of the novelist and the shoemaker. But for the most part Trollope's letters, many of which are businesslike and perfunctory, reveal the inner man only indirectly. They show Trollope as honest, frank, blunt, crusty, gallant, playful, quick to take offence and quick to be reconciled, kind, self-depreciating but with a strong belief in his own worth and ability. Trollope is to be found in his letters, but one must work at it.

As for Trollope's novels and other books, direct autibiographical materials are few. We know of course that Charley Tudor in *The Three Clerks* and Johnny Eames in *The Small House at Allington* and *The Last Chronicle* are partly self-portraits. There is probably a bit of Trollope in Dr Wortle, in Mr Whittlestaff of *An Old Man's Love*, in Sir Thomas Underwood in *Ralph the Heir*. The novelist may even have provided some of the traits for Thady Macdermot, the blundering pathetic young man who is the centre of Trollope's first novel (even as Trollope's father may in some fashion have been the original for Thady's father, Larry Macdermot). But I believe the best source in Trollope's fiction of a knowledge of his person is to be found in the narrator. For this narrator is no 'persona', no created character or spokesman. The narrator is Anthony Trollope, 'the novelist', or, as he ironically calls himself many times, 'the poor fictionist'. His analyses and asides – seen as commonplace or as disruptive by some readers, and as sane, witty, broadly humane and sympathetic by others – display one side of Trollope's person. It is unacceptable to say that Trollope had a knack for writing readable stories, shored up by his remarkable ear for dialogue, but that at bottom he was a very commonplace person. He must be at least as subtle, perspicacious, ironic, and clever as the Trollopian narrator.[5] Chauncey Brewster Tinker, inquiring into the pleasure of reading Trollope even in 'painful' books such as *The Bertrams* and *Marion Fay*, asked: 'What is the explanation of that vivid warming of the heart that one feels from time to time as one reads on? Is it not due to the association with the author himself, a man worldly-wise, yet kindly and, above all, fair-minded?'[6] Yes; and Trollope must have produced that same feeling, and often, in his friends.

To come now to contemporary accounts and anecdotes of Trollope. These, if their flavour and nuance are to be accurately conveyed, must for the most part be quoted with some completeness. It may be well to begin with testimony about his career as a Post Office official. The very first such, from a provincial Irish newspaper, is unusual in that it reports his appearance in a court of law. Trollope, by this time in a position of some authority as a surveyor's clerk, was chief witness for the prosecution in a case tried at the 1849 summer assizes in Tralee. He had, by means of a marked sovereign, caught a young assistant postmistress stealing from the mails. The accused was young, pretty, and locally popular, and the services of the formidable Isaac Butt had been supplied for her defence. Trollope, who had an obsessive interest in the law and particularly in the liberties – he considered them abuses – permitted to cross-examiners, seems to have enjoyed this test of his ability to keep calm and unbefuddled. Trollope testified, for example, that 'the mark [on the sovereign] was made with a penknife under the neck on the head (loud laughter)':

Mr Butt – On the head under the neck!

Mr Trollope – I did not say that. You are making more mistakes than I am.

Mr Butt – I ask you was it on the head?

Mr Trollope – I marked it under the neck on the head (great laughter).

Mr Butt – You marked it under the neck on the head! You are acquainted with the English language, writing it occasionally?

Mr Trollope – Occasionally.

Mr Butt – And yet you cannot give an intelligible answer on this head.

Mr Trollope – You had better give it up.

Mr Butt – But – you marked it on – what was it?

Mr Trollope – I marked it under the neck on the head (renewed laughter).

Mr Butt – Be so kind as to tell his Lordship what part of the body that is?

Mr Trollope – I think you misunderstand me. I didn't say I marked the sovereign on the head under the neck, but I marked the neck under the head (great laughter).

To the Court – Means by the head, on the obverse.

Mr Butt – You would make it a head or harp?

Mr Trollope – I didn't mean a head and harp. I marked it under the neck on the head (laughter) – under the neck on the obverse part of the coin, that which has the Sovereign's head upon it. . . .

Mr Butt – What was the name of your Correspondent [the addressee of the letter from which the sovereign was taken]?

Mr Trollope – Miss Jemima Cotton.

Mr Butt – She had no existence except in your fine imagination?

Mr Trollope – It was a purely fictitious name.

Mr Butt – And Mr Payton?

Mr Trollope – Was equally a fictitious person.

Mr Butt – You seem to deal in fictitious characters?

Mr Trollope – In another way.

Mr Butt – Do you know 'The Macdermots of Ballycloran' (laughter).

Mr Trollope – I know a book of that name.

Mr Butt – Do you remember a barrister of the name of Allwind (laughter)?

Mr Trollope – I do.

Mr Butt – And another named O'Napper [? O'Laugher].

Mr Trollope – Yes.

Mr Butt – I believe in drawing that character, it was your intention to favour the world with the beau ideal of a good cross-examiner?

Mr Trollope – Yes. I dreamed of you (loud laughter).

Mr Butt – Do you remember the red moreen over the judge's head (laughter)?

Mr Trollope – Undoubtedly.

Mr Butt (reading from Mr Trollope's book) – You thought of that red moreen, if it could only speak, if it had a tongue to tell, what an indifferent account it could give of the conscience of judges, and the veracity of lawyers (loud laughter)? I hope you do not think that now (laughter)?

Mr Trollope – I'm rather strengthened in my opinion (tremendous laughter).

Mr Butt – 'He told them what he had to say should be very brief, and considering [that he was] a lawyer and a barrister, he kept his word with tolerable fidelity' (loud laughter). You pictured to yourself a model cross-examiner?

Mr Trollope – I dreamed of some one like you in cross-examination (laughter).

Mr Butt – Had you the mark of the money under the neck on the head when you dreamed of me?

Mr Trollope – Not *that* mark exactly.

Mr Butt – Fine imagination.

Mr Trollope – Admirable cross-examiner.[7]

An eyewitness, Justin MacCarthy, described the encounter as 'a duel in which neither combatant for a moment lost his temper or his self-control, and the spectators of the scene were filled with intense delight. . . . Butt himself felt, I think, that he had not had quite the better of it.'[8]

But the court-room circumstances were out of the ordinary. The accounts, from his fellow civil servants, of his more routine behaviour as Post Office official are remarkably consistent. Trollope was a demanding, no-nonsense superior. At worst he was a bully. That he was efficient and entirely devoted to his work no one disputed. Some of the earliest stories date from 1851–3, when Trollope was on special assignment overseeing the extension of

the rural post in the southwest of England. J. G. Uren, who met
Trollope at Falmouth, wrote:

> I remember his stalking into the office, booted and spurred,
> much to the consternation of the maiden lady in charge. He
> seemed to us then the very incarnation of a martinet, though I
> have since heard that he really was a kind-hearted man, and
> that this was the way he had of showing it. At any rate, he
> frightened the unfortunate rural messenger, whose walk he was
> about to test, almost out of his wits. The man had £1 of penny
> stamps . . . to take to the sub-office at Constantine and, flurried
> at the presence of so fierce looking a gentleman, he clapped
> them into his hat! The day was hot, and before they reached
> their journey's end the stamps had stuck so closely and firmly to
> poor old Pollard's head, that all the ingenuity they could muster
> could not detach them. Mr Trollope roared at the fun, and
> brought the man back, stamps and all, so that the aid of a
> barber might be invoked to release him from his predicament.[9]

Uren wrote that at Penzance Trollope 'met his match' in the
person of the postmistress, Miss Ellen Catherine Swain:

> When Mr Trollope bounced into the office and, with flaming
> eyes and distended nostrils, announced that he had come 'to
> survey the Land's End District', Miss Swain fired up like a
> tigress robbed of her young. . . . who was this interloper, a cross
> between a country farmer and a whipper-in, who without
> saying 'by your leave' had intruded on her privacy and shocked
> her sense of propriety? At any rate she would have none of him,
> and telling him, in no very complimentary terms, that he was
> 'no gentleman', she straightway ordered him out of the house.
> It should be recorded, however, that although Greek met Greek
> in this way, Mr Trollope made his peace with the peppery West
> Cornwall Postmistress, and they were afterwards capital
> friends.[10]

At the village of Mousehole, Cornwall, the sub-postmistress, Miss
Betsy Trembath, was recorded as having this conversation:

Mr Trollope: I am an Inspector from the General Post Office,
    and I wish to make some enquiries about the posts in this
    neighbourhood.

Miss Trembath: From the General Poast Office arta? I'm bra glad to see he sure 'nuf. Wusta ha' a dish o' tay?

Mr Trollope: I say I wish to make some enquiries. Can you tell me where –

Miss Trembath: Lor' bless the man. Doantee be in such a pore. I can't tellee noathin' if thee'st stand glazing at me like a chuked pig, as thee art now.

Mr Trollope (losing his temper): Don't thee and thou me my good woman, but answer my questions. I will report you.

Miss Trembath: Good woman am I? Report me wusta? And I be'n so civil toee, too. Thees't better report my tuppence-farden a day.[11]

Another postal employee reported:

I was attached to a country office in South Wales when he strode in one day, fresh from a tramp over the heather, just as Professor Wilson – Christopher North – was wont to do in surprising his students. No other description could well be applied to the gait of Trollope. About the first remark he made was, 'I have walked up from Cardiff' – a distance of 24 miles. 'Any hotels here; which is the best?' I directed him; and, as he marched out, still at a 6-mile-an-hour-stride, he said, 'back soon, going to have a raw beef steak'.

He left me pondering over his powerful build, his physical go, and his reference to the 'underdone'. . . . I was still pondering when the giant foot-fall was again heard. . . . One of the postmen of a neighbouring village had applied to the Department for increased pay, and now put in an appearance and stated his case. Unfortunately, he was not satisfied with putting his pleas forward in a manner seemly to a petitioner, but foolishly coupled them with the threat that if he couldn't get more money for the job he'd throw it up. I saw at once that this was not the way to obtain even a hearing, much less a favour. 'Look here, my man,' Trollope exclaimed, 'don't think that we cannot manage without you. Throw it up; there will be twenty after your place to-morrow', and then entered into facts and figures.

The postman was glad to beat a retreat, and lived not only to be placed on a better scale, in accordance with the increase asked for in his letter, but to attain a good old age in the service. To the last he never forgot energetic Mr Trollope.[12]

The rebuff followed by compliance with a request was probably part of Trollope's *modus operandi*. R. S. Smyth, who served under Trollope at Belfast in the 1850s and who found him 'brusque in manner, certainly, but [having] a kind heart', wrote that 'he was held out to the juniors in the service as a terror, and my early experience of him was not calculated to remove such an impression'. In 1857 Smyth had to record the time at which the postmen returned to the office from their deliveries, something he found difficult as there was no clock. Trollope on a visit of inspection told him he must buy a watch at once; when Smyth said he would prefer to wait till he could afford to pay cash for it, the only answer was a 'growl'. But after Trollope had completed his inspection he ordered that a clock should be provided. When Trollope came to Belfast in 1865 to report on a proposed revision of salaries and staff, Smyth took the opportunity of discussing his prospects in the service in light of a tempting offer of other employment, and wrote that Trollope 'entered into the matter in a very friendly, almost a fatherly way'.[13]

'R. W. J.', explaining how in the 1860s London was divided into postmasterships and placed under a surveyor, described Trollope at work at the Vere Street Office, headquarters under the new arrangement:

> I was detailed for duty there when the change took place, and I remember Anthony Trollope superintended the arrangements for constituting Postal London into so many separate towns. His method of attacking work was rather odd, and I have seen him slogging away at papers at a stand-up desk, with his handkerchief stuffed into his mouth, and his hair on end, as though he could barely contain himself. He struck me as being rather a fierce-looking man, and a remark which he made to a postmaster on one occasion did not appear to me to savour either of courtesy or kindness. This poor fellow, who had probably seen thirty years' service, and who was wedded to the old system of working the districts, was fretting terribly at the prospect of becoming a postmaster and of being left to his own resources, so to speak, when Trollope turned round on him with the remark: 'Why don't you pay an old woman sixpence a week to fret for you?'[14]

A somewhat more endearing glimpse of Trollope came from

Susan Gay, daughter of William Gay, who was a surveyor himself
and thus a colleague of Trollope:

> When any important alterations took place with regard to
> mails, a meeting of the Surveyors used to be convened ... a good
> deal of intricate work and calculation impossible by corres-
> pondence were carried out, enlivened by good dinners and an
> agreeable social time. . . . Among them at one time was Anthony
> Trollope, whom I remember at our house on occasions. . . . No
> more repose was left in the house when he awoke in the
> morning. Doors slammed, footsteps resounded, and a general
> whirlwind arose, as he came or returned from his bath, or
> walked out in the garden, and from that time until nightfall, he
> was as busy as a man could be. He had a scorn of everything in
> the way of pretensions – even of justice to time-honoured
> institutions – and slurred over his family history and belittled
> 'the service' right royally. 'Post Office' (he always omitted the
> 'General' or departmental style and title) – he would write with
> a little 'p' and a little 'o', as though it were a village sub-office,
> retailing stamps with tobacco and onions.[15]

Trollope in his *Autobiography* states how unequivocally he stood
in opposition to and relished 'delicious feuds' with Rowland Hill,
Secretary of the Post Office, 1854–64. Hill's daughter wrote:

> On one occasion [Trollope] was brought to our house, and a
> most entertaining and lively talker we found him to be. But
> somehow our rooms seemed too small for his large vigorous
> frame, and big, almost stentorian voice. Indeed, he reminded us
> of Dickens's Mr Boythorn, minus the canary, and gave us the
> impression that the one slightly-built chair on which he rashly
> seated himself during a great part of the interview, must infal-
> libly end in collapse, and sooner rather than later. After about a
> couple of hours of our society, he apparently found us uncon-
> genial company; and perhaps we did not take over kindly to
> him, however keen our enjoyment, then and afterwards, of his
> novels and his talk. He has left a record in print of the fact that
> he heartily detested the Hills, who have consoled themselves by
> remembering that when a man has spent many years in writing
> romance, the trying of his hand, late in life at history, is an
> exceedingly hazardous undertaking. In fact, Trollope's old

associates at the Post Office were in the habit of declaring that
his 'Autobiography' was one of the greatest, and certainly not
the least amusing, of his many works of fiction.[16]

And we have the testimony of Edmund Yates, a man who made
his way in the world of letters and journalism, but who also for
many years worked for the Post Office. Trollope and Yates had
been on good terms, but after the celebrated Dickens-Yates/
Thackeray affair at the Garrick Club (which resulted in Yates's
expulsion from the Club), Trollope in 1860 unwittingly exacerbated the feud. He supplied Yates with a story, which Yates,
retelling inaccurately, used to ridicule Thackeray and his publisher, George Smith.[17] Trollope, a partisan of Thackeray, was
thereafter at odds with Yates. Moreover the enmity flared up
again when in 1865 George Smith brought out his evening newspaper, the *Pall Mall Gazette*, in the early days of which Trollope
was for all practical purposes a staff writer. Yates, in his 'Flâneur'
column in the *Morning Star*, ridiculed the pretensions of the new
paper and took Trollope to task for sloppy writing and even for
misspelling. Eventually the *Pall Mall* came down hard in an
article called 'A New Type of Journalist': he 'is nobody in himself,
and can produce nothing. . . . He is a purveyor of gossip, a
collector of tittle-tattle, a disseminator of idle rumours.' He writes
under a fancy title, pretends to be a gentleman, gains entrance to a
club, writes up private conversation, and eventually this 'jolly
little Neddy Yapp' is kicked out of the club and his disgrace
written up by a rival journalist of the same kind.[18] Yates closed the
exchange by calling the attack a 'revival of an old scandal long
since repented and atoned for and [which] in its savage malignity
and utter blackguardism transcends anything in the annals of
modern journalism'. Yates will not pursue the discussion, for the
tone taken by the *Pall Mall* writer 'leaves the matter in dispute a
personal one between two men'.[19] This suggests that Yates
assumed the article had been written by Trollope, though the style
is hardly his. Yates's subsequent statements about Trollope were
no doubt coloured by this ill will, but with one exception they give
the appearance of fairness. Yates wrote that as one associated in
the Post Office with both Trollope and Hill he had ample
opportunity to watch their feuding. According to Yates, Hill
hated Trollope 'very cordially'. When brought into contact, the
two would treat the spectators to an amusing show:

Trollope would bluster and rave and roar, blowing and sputtering like a grampus; while the pale old gentleman opposite him, sitting back in his armchair and regarding his antagonist furtively under his spectacles, would remain perfectly quiet until he saw his chance, and then deliver himself of the most unpleasant speech he could frame in the hardest possible tone. . . .

It is scarcely possible to imagine a greater contrast to Rowland Hill than Anthony Trollope . . . one calm and freezing, the other bluff and boisterous; one cautious and calculating, weighing well every word before utterence . . . the other scarcely giving himself time to think, but spluttering and roaring out an instantly-formed opinion couched in the very strongest of terms. 'I differ from you entirely! What was it you said?' he roared out once to the speaker who preceded him at a discussion of Surveyors.

Yates said that Trollope

certainly was not popular among the subordinates of his district. He was a very kind-hearted man; but with persons in the position of clerks in small offices, letter-carriers, &c., manner has a great effect, and Trollope's manner was desperately against him. I do not believe any man of his time was more heartily, more thoroughly, more unselfishly charitable; and he not merely did not let his left hand know what his right hand did in such matters, but he would savagely rap the knuckles of any hand meddling in his affairs.[20]

But a few years later, Yates published in the *World* a paragraph responding to A. K. H. Boyd's remarks (quoted below) on Trollope's behaviour at a dinner given by John Blackwood. In this instance the old animosity surfaced:

A man with worse or more offensive manners than Trollope I have rarely met. He was coarse, boorish, rough, noisy, overbearing, insolent; he adopted the Johnsonian tactics of trying to outroar his adversary in argument; he spluttered and shouted, and glared through his spectacles, and waved his arms about, a sight for gods and men. . . . By the officials who were subordinate to him – I was not one – he was pretty generally hated for the particularly objectionable manner in which he treated them. By persons in general society he was regarded with perturbed wonder, as a specimen never before met with. By a few old whist-playing cronies at the Garrick, whose acquaintance he only made late in life, he was greatly liked. I have heard of several instances, and I know of one, to prove that he had a kind heart, and that his roaring bluster and offensive contradiction was 'only his manner'; but, as Mr Mantalini says of Ralph Nickleby, it was 'a demd uncomfortable private-madhouse kind of manner' all the same.[21]

Trollope's brother, when he read the above, remarked to Trollope's son that it was 'less venomous than those (now very few) who knew anything of the relations between your father and Mr Yates, might have expected'.[22]

Accounts of Trollope by social and literary acquaintances and friends abound. One of the earliest is given by George Augustus Sala in his description of the first of George Smith's celebrated *Cornhill* dinners, early in 1860. Thackeray was in the chair, and other guests included Sir Charles Taylor, Sir John Burgoyne, Richard Monckton Milnes, Frederick Leighton, John Everett Millais, G. H. Lewes, Robert Browning, Sir Edwin Landseer, Frederick Walker, and Matthew Higgins. For Trollope, who had spent most of his writing career in Ireland, the dinner marked his entrance into the literary and artistic life of London:

> Anthony Trollope was very much to the fore, contradicting everybody; afterwards saying kind things to everybody, and occasionally going to sleep on sofas or chairs; or leaning against sideboards, and even somnolent while standing erect on the hearthrug. I never knew a man who could take so many spells of 'forty winks' at unexpected moments, and then turn up quite wakeful, alert, and pugnacious, as the author of 'Barchester Towers', who had nothing of the bear but his skin, but whose ursine envelope was assuredly of the most grisly texture.[23]

(Sala inscribed the title page of his copy of Trollope's *Auto-biography*: 'Crusty, quarrelsome, wrong-headed, prejudiced, obstinate, kind-hearted and thoroughly honest old Tony Trollope. He would have made a capital Conservative County member of the Chaplin or Lowther type.' It is worth bearing in mind that Sala, an ally of Yates, was not close to Trollope.[24])

Lady Amberley recorded a Tuesday 'at home' of 9 April 1867:

> We had a little dinner of Huxley, Anthony Trollope[,] Lady Russell, and Mr Knatchbull Hugesson whom Amberley brought home from the H[ouse] of C[ommons]. Dinner very pleasant, Ly R enjoyed it very much and was pleased to make acquaintance with Trollope and Huxley. A and I thought Trollope's voice too loud, he rather drowned Huxley's pleasant quiet voice which was certainly better worth hearing.[25]

John Stuart Mill's disciple John Morley, editor of the *Pall Mall Gazette* and the *Fortnightly Review*, told the following anecdotes in a review of the *Autobiography*:

> Mr Mill once expressed a desire to make his acquaintance, and it was arranged that Trollope should go down to dine at Blackheath one Sunday afternoon. He came up from Essex for the express purpose, and said to a younger friend who was convoying him down, 'Stuart Mill is the only man in the whole world for the sake of seeing whom I would leave my own house on a Sunday.' The party was only a moderate success. The contrast was too violent between the modesty and courtesy of the host and the blustering fashions of Trollope. These came out worse when they figured in the same room with the gentle precision of Mill and the pleasant gravity of Cairnes. It was a relief to get the bull safely away from the china-shop. Trollope did not recognize the delicacy of Truth, but handled her as freely and as boldly as a slave-dealer might handle a beautiful Circassian. He once had an interview with a writer whom he wished to make the editor of a Review. 'Now, do you,' he asked, glaring as if in fury through his spectacles, and roaring like a bull of Bashan, 'do you believe in the divinity of our blessed Lord and Saviour Jesus Christ?' He had not a perfect sense of the shades and delicacies of things, nor had he exactly the spirit of urbanity.[26]

A close friend, Alfred Austin, said that Trollope, 'though a delightful companion and brimming over with active intelligence, was in no accurate sense of the word intellectual, and as unhelpful and impatient an arguer as I ever met'.[27]

Shirley Brooks, for whose widow Trollope was to work inde-
fatigably to raise money, recorded in January 1873:

> Anthony Trollope was one of the guests last night. He roars
> more than ever since Australia. He was exceedingly jolly and
> Billy Russell was opposite to him, so they fired away good
> stories. When they were at cards we heard Anthony's thunder,
> and then a wild Banshee cry from the Irishman, till we
> threatened them with the police. Then Anthony said we were
> conventional tyrants.[28]

Mark Twain in late years recalled another dinner – Trollope
dined out incessantly – given by Trollope in honour of Joaquin
Miller at the Garrick Club in 1873. Five guests, including Mark
Twain, Miller, Leveson Gower and Tom Hughes, were present.
According to Mark Twain:

> Trollope was voluble and animated, and was but vaguely aware
> that any other person was present excepting him of the noble
> blood, Levison-Gower [*sic*]. Trollope and Hughes addressed
> their talk almost altogether to Levison-Gower. . . . Joaquin
> Miller did his full share of the talking, but he was a discordant
> note. . . . He and Trollope talked all the time and both at the
> same time, Trollope pouring forth a smooth and limpid and
> sparkling stream of faultless English, and Joaquin discharging
> into it his muddy and tumultuous mountain torrent.[29]

In that same year, 1873, an unidentified 'personal friend' wrote of
Trollope:

> I remember a man hitting off a very good description of
> Trollope's manner, by remarking that 'he came in at the door
> like a frantic windmill'. The bell would peal, the knocker begin
> thundering, the door be burst open, and the next minute the
> house be filled with the big resonant voice inquiring who was at
> home. I should say he had naturally a sweet voice, which
> through eagerness he had spoilt by halloing. He was a big man,
> and the most noticeable thing about his dress was a black
> handkerchief which he wore tied *twice* round his neck. A trick of
> his was to put the end of a silk pocket-handkerchief in his mouth
> and to keep gnawing at it – often biting it into holes in the excess

of his energy; and a favourite attitude was to stand with his thumbs tucked into the armholes of his waistcoat. He was a full-coloured man, and joking and playful when at his ease. Unless with his intimates, he rarely laughed, but he had a funny way of putting things, and was usually voted good company. . . . His manner was bluff, hearty, and genial, and he possessed to the full the great charm of giving his undivided attention to the matter in hand. He was always enthusiastic and energetic in whatever he did. He was of an eager disposition, and doing nothing was a pain to him. . . . Either subject [hunting or books], however, and for the matter of that I might add *any* subject, was attacked by him with equal energy. . . . While he talked to me, I and my interests might have been the only things for which he cared; and any passing topic of conversation was, for the moment, the one and absorbing topic in the world.[30]

The 'frantic windmill' image recalls Wilkie Collins's words, written to a friend shortly after Trollope's death:

His immeasurable energies had a bewildering effect on my invalid constitution. To me, he was an incarnate gale of wind. He blew off my hat; he turned my umbrella inside out. Joking apart, as good and staunch a friend as ever lived.[31]

Joseph Langford, London manager of Blackwood's, wrote to John Blackwood in March 1877: 'There was a great scene between Trollope and [Sir Henry] James [a close friend of Trollope]. Trollope raging and roaring with immense vehemence against the system of cross-examination as practised, and James defending it with charming calmness and good nature.'[32] In the same year John Bright, whom Trollope had rather unfairly caricatured in the character of Turnbull in the *Phineas* novels, dined with Trollope and recorded that the novelist was 'rather loud and boisterous in his manner of speaking'.[33] James Bryce wrote:

Personally, Anthony Trollope was a bluff, genial, hearty, vigorous man, typically English in his face, his talk, his ideas, his tastes. His large eyes, which looked larger behind his large spectacles, were full of good-humoured life and force; and though he was neither witty nor brilliant in conversation, he was what is called very good company, having travelled widely, known all sorts of people, and formed views, usually positive views, on all the subjects of the day, views which he was prompt to declare and maintain. There was not much novelty in them – you were disappointed not to find so clever a writer more original – but they were worth listening to for their solid common-sense, tending rather to commonplace sense, and you enjoyed the ardour with which he threw himself into a discussion. Though boisterous and insistent in his talk, he was free from assumption or conceit, and gave the impression of liking the world he lived in, and being satisfied with his own place in it.[34]

Frederick Locker-Lampson gave this reading of Trollope's manner and character:

Anthony Trollope . . . was boisterous, but goodnaturedly so. He was abrupt in manners and speech; he was ebullient, and therefore he sometimes offended people. I suppose he was a wilful man, and we know that such men are always in the right; but he was a good fellow.

Some of Trollope's acquaintance used to wonder how so commonplace a person could have written such excellent novels; but I maintain that so honourable and interesting a man could not be commonplace.

Hirsute and taurine of aspect, he would glare at you from behind fierce spectacles. His ordinary tones had the penetrative capacity of two people quarrelling, and his voice would ring through and through you, and shake the windows in their frames, while all the time he was most amiably disposed towards you under his waistcoat. To me his *viso sciolto* and bluff geniality were very attractive, and so were his gusty denunciations, but most attractive of all was his unselfish nature. Literary men might make him their exemplar, as I make him my theme; for he may quite well have been the most generous man of letters, of mark, since Walter Scott. . . . Trollope had a furious hatred of shams and toadyism, and he sometimes recognised and resented these weaknesses where they would hardly have been detected by an ordinary observer. He could not be said to be quarrelsome, but he was crotchety. . . . Not the worst part of a distinguished man's reputation is the esteem in which he is held by his friends, and in this Trollope was rich. He indulged in no professional jealousies; indeed he had none to indulge in. He only had much nobility of nature.[35]

Locker-Lampson touched upon the vexed issue of the apparent difference between the man and the books, the loud extrovert and the relaxed, delicate novels. The contrast was especially surprising, even disillusioning, to those who knew him but slightly. In 1866 Lady Rose Fane, staying at Lord Houghton's estate, Fryston, where Trollope was also a house-guest, wrote to her mother: 'I wish I had never seen Mr Trolloppe [*sic*]. I think he is detestable – vulgar, noisy & domineering – a mixture of Dickens vulgarity & Mr Burton's selfsufficiency – as unlike his books as possible.'[36] But even those who knew him fairly well bring up the contrast between the author and his works. Charles Lever, whom Trollope in his *Autobiography* was to speak of as 'my dear old friend', wrote (privately, of course) to John Blackwood in 1868:

I don't think Trollope *pleasant*, though he has a certain hard common-sense about him and coarse shrewdness that prevents him being dull or tiresome. His books are not of a high order, but still I am always surprised that he could write them. He is a good fellow, I believe, *au fond*, and has few jealousies and no rancours; and for a writer, is not that saying much?[37]

W. P. Frith wrote:

It would be impossible to imagine anything less like his novels than the author of them. The books, full of gentleness, grace, and refinement; the writer of them, bluff, loud, stormy, and contentious; neither a brilliant talker nor a good speaker; but a kinder-hearted man and a truer friend never lived.[38]

James Bryce, already quoted, took up the question, giving Browning as an extreme instance of someone very unlike his work, at least until one had had 'a long *tête à tête*' with him:

Trollope at first caused a similar though less marked suprise. This bluff burly man did not seem the kind of person who would trace with a delicate touch the sunlight sparkling on, or a gust of temper ruffling, the surface of a youthful soul in love. Upon further knowledge one perceived that the features of Trollope's talent, facile invention, quick observation, and a strong commonsense view of things, with little originality or intensity, were really the dominant features of his character as expressed in talk. Still, though the man was more of a piece with his books than he had seemed, one could never quite recognise in him the delineator of Lily Dale.[39]

Another who discussed this issue was T. H. S. Escott. As a young man Escott in the early 1870s interviewed Trollope for a journal. Escott took notes about Trollope's personal life and said that Trollope later urged him to be sure to 'take care' of these notes, which eventually formed the basis of his 1913 biography. Trollope befriended Escott, and, as their surviving correspondence shows, was to some extent a mentor of the younger man. In 1882 Trollope was partly responsible for Escott's succeeding John Morley as editor of the *Fortnightly Review*. In 1879 Escott published an article about Trollope in *Time* (a journal edited by Edmund Yates; Trollope declined to be included in the 'Celebrities at Home' series in the *World*, also edited by Yates). Escott wrote:

If the identity between the Mr Anthony Trollope of private life and the Mr Anthony Trollope [the novelist] . . . is not immediately perceived, it can only be because the observer is destitute of the faculty of perception. 'The syle is the man'; the popular and successful author is the straightforward unreserved friend; the courageous, candid, plain-speaking companion. As it is with the dialogue of Mr Trollope's literary heroes and heroines, so is it with the conversation of Mr Trollope himself. In each there is the same definiteness and directness; the same Anglo-Saxon simplicity which can only not be called studied, because in all things it is Mr Trollope's characteristic to be spontaneous. As a writer – I do not of course speak of the elaboration of his plots – Mr Trollope is precisely what he is as a talker, and what he is, or used to be, as a rider across country. He sees the exact place at which he wants to arrive. He makes for it; and he determines to reach it as directly as possible. There may be obstacles, but he surmounts them. Sometimes, indeed, they prove for the moment serious impediments. Perhaps they actually place him *hors de combat*, like a post and rails that cannot be negotiated, or a ditch of impracticable dimensions. It does not matter. He picks himself up, pulls himself together, and presses on as before. The sympathy which is the invariable accompaniment of a broad and manly imagination, Mr Trollope has in abundance. But an opinion rapidly crystalises with him into a conviction, and a conviction is, in his estimation, a thing for which to live or die. He does not exclude from his consideration all that conflicts with this view, but he has for it only a theoretical toleration.

Escott then discussed Trollope's recently published *Thackeray* and found Trollope so enthusiastic about his subject that the book amounted to 'hero-worship with a vengeance'. Had Trollope looked upon a similar work by a different hand on a different subject, he would have criticised the portraiture as too 'angelically perfect'. Escott continued, in his inflated prose, to dissect Trollope's 'intensity of enthusiasm':

> Mr Trollope, enthusiast and castle-builder though he is and has always been [a phrase predating the *Autobiography*, and evidence of Trollope's having given Escott biographical information], is practical as well. He may have his fantasies and chimeras and crotchets and hobbies; yet for all this the world in which he lives is no visionary one, but one in which close attention to facts and details is a paramount necessity. Enthusiasm – it may be impetuosity – is only one of the accidental modes of development assumed by Mr Trollope's imagination. It has become a species of necessary condition of his thought; and just as great athletes find it desirable frequently to exercise their muscles and sinews by wielding dumb-bells, brandishing Indian clubs, and other feats of strength, so does Mr Trollope keep his mental elasticity fresh and vigorous by tilting against windmills and by defending paradoxes. This is part of the charm of the man, or at least of the secret of his charm. As with his writings, so with his social converse. In Mr Trollope's nature extremes may be said to balance extremes. The most enthusiastic of men, he is of all men also the most practical.[40]

(Trollope, in a comment typical of him, wrote to Escott: 'Many thanks for the excessive kindness of your remarks. Agree with you about myself of course I cannot! or if I did I should not dare to say so.'[41]) Escott's analysis, arising partly from shrewd observation and partly from the same kind of ardent discipleship he marked in

Trollope for Thackeray, helps bridge the seeming gap between the man and the books, though not altogether satisfactorily.

I believe that one must try to sort out from these contemporary accounts just how much of Trollope's 'bow wow' manner was a deliberate tactic, a stance he assumed. His basic shyness and insecurity, the legacy of his wretched childhood when he was always the outsider, never left him. The scorched-earth conversational manner provided a kind of safety. His commonplaces, his apparently simplistic and absolute opinions, expounded so boisterously and definitively – did he always subscribe to them? Or did he love to lead people on? Frank O'Connor said that Trollope's favourite device in his fiction was 'to lead his reader very gently up the garden path of his own conventions and prejudices' and then chime in with a phrase like, 'With such censures I cannot profess that I completely agree.'[42] The ironies in his talk and manner were not sufficiently recognised, even as the subtleties of his fiction have to this day eluded so many who believe him an 'easy' writer whose work surrenders all it has to say immediately and completely. Trollope in company was a humourist and ironist who did not insist that people catch his drift; rather, he delighted in allowing others to think they understood him when they did not. There is the well-known instance of the dinner with Lowell, Holmes, Emerson and Hawthorne. Lowell wrote:

> I dined the other day with Anthony Trollope, a big, red-faced, rather underbred Englishman of the bald-with-spectacles type. A good roaring positive fellow who deafened me (sitting on his right) till I thought of Dante's Cerberus. He says he goes to work on a novel 'just like a shoemaker on a shoe, only taking care to make honest stitches'. Gets up at 5 every day, does all his writing before breakfast, and always writes just so many pages a day. He and Dr Holmes were very entertaining. The Autocrat started one or two hobbies, and charged, paradox in rest – but it was pelting a rhinoceros with seed-pearl.
>
> *Dr.* You don't know what Madeira is in England?
> *T.* I'm not so sure it's worth knowing.
> *Dr.* Connoisseurship in it with us is a fine art. There are men who will tell you a dozen kinds, as Dr Waagen would know a Carlo Dolci from a Guido.
> *T.* They might be better employed!

*Dr.* Whatever is worth doing is worth doing well.

*T.* Ay, but that's begging the whole question. I don't admit it's *worse* doing at all. If they earn their bread by it, it may be *worse* doing (roaring).

*Dr.* But you may be assured –

*T.* No, but I may n't be asshŏrred. I *won't* be asshored. I don't intend to be asshŏred (roaring louder)!

And so they went it. It was very funny. Trollope would n't give him any chance. Meanwhile, Emerson and I, who sat between them, crouched down out of range and had some very good talk, with the shot hurtling overhead. I had one little passage at arms with T. *apropos* of English peaches. T. ended by roaring that England was the only country where such a thing as a peach or a grape was known. . . . I rather liked Trollope.[43]

That Trollope was pulling the legs of his hearers should have been clear to all – but it wasn't. Clara Kellogg, the American soprano, met Trollope in Boston at about the same time (autumn 1861), Trollope having come to the United States to write his book on North America:

Mr Trollope knew nothing of America, and did not seem to want to know anything. Certainly, English people when they are not thoroughbred can be very common! Trollope was full of himself and wrote only for what he could get out of it. I never, before or since, met a literary person who was so frankly 'on the make'. The discussion that afternoon was about the recompense of authors, and Trollope said that he had reduced his literary efforts to a working basis and wrote so many words to a page and so many pages to a chapter. He refrained from using the actual word 'money' – the English shrink from the word 'money' – but he managed to convey to his hearers the fact that a considerable consideration was the main incentive to his literary labour, and put the matter more specifically later, to my mother, by telling her that he always *chose the words that would fill up the pages quickest.*[44]

Sometimes even the most transparent of his ironies went undetected.

Mrs W. F. Pollock, a good friend of Trollope's, wrote to Henry Taylor about Taylor's knighthood:

A. Trollope is pleased about your colonial order, and his plain understanding cannot conceive the fastidiousness which thinks a form of distinction not worth having because it is sometimes ill bestowed. 'Let the man of high desert be satisfied that his desert is acknowledged,' he says, 'and not be scrupulous in weighing the exact degrees. Things cannot be so finely balanced in a rough world.'

He is a man of direct sympathies, strong in a straightforward direction, but to whom many devious, delicate turns and subtle ways of thought and feeling are not intelligible.[45]

Yet the very wording of Trollope's advice, with its 'scrupulous' and 'finely balanced', reveals his awareness of Taylor's 'fastidiousness' – a quality he valued in his friend's personality and writings. And no alert reader of Trollope's fiction would say that devious, delicate turns and subtle ways of thought were unintelligible to Trollope. But many of his contemporaries invariably took what he said at face value. After Trollope had written *The Fixed Period*, that odd book about euthanasia, he is reported to have told an intimate friend: 'It's all true – I *mean* every word of it.'[46] Meant what? That he thought every man of sixty-eight ought to be put to death? After all, the scheme for mandatory euthanasia in Britannula fails.

James Payn wrote:

Trollope was the least literary man of letters I ever met; indeed, had I not known him for the large-hearted and natural man he was, I should have suspected him of some affectation in this respect. Though he certainly took pleasure in writing novels, I doubt whether he took any in reading them; and from his conversation, quite as much as from his own remarks on the subject in his autobiography, I should judge he had not read a dozen, even of Dickens's, in his life. His manners were rough and, so to speak, tumultuous, but he had a tender heart and a strong sense of duty.[47]

In fact, Trollope, who read widely and voraciously – almost combatively – knew the contemporary English novel thoroughly. He was a most literary man of letters who liked to play the role of an innocent who did not realise his own excellences, much less those of others. One can imagine the delight he took in misleading acquaintances about the extent of his reading, even as he continued to belittle his own writings, calling them unimaginative, saying they were products of a process very like that of shoe-making. Well might he be suspected of 'some affectation in this respect'.

A. K. H. Boyd told of a large party convened to meet Trollope in August 1868 at John Blackwood's home near the St Andrews golf course:

> Filled with the enthusiasm of one who had very rarely met a popular author, I entered Strathtyrum that day. The sight of the great novelist was a blow. He was singularly unkempt, and his clothes were very wrinkled and ill-made. His manner was a further blow. We listened for the melodious accents which were due from those lips: but they did not come. Indeed, he was the only man I had heard swear in decent society for uncounted years. The swearing, which was repeated, was the most disagreeable of all: the actual asseverating, by the Holiest Name, of some trumpery statement. How could that man have written the well-remembered sentences which had charmed one through these years? Then, by way of making himself pleasant in a gathering of Scotsmen, he proceeded (the ladies being gone and we all gathered to hear him) to vilipend our beloved Sir Walter. One was much interested in hearing what one of the most popular of recent novelists thought of the founder of the modern school of fiction. Mr Trollope said that if any of Sir Walter's novels were offered to any London publisher of the present day, it would be at once rejected. We listened, humbly. Then it was asked whether this was because time had gone on and Sir Walter grown old-fashioned. 'Not a bit: it is just because they are so dull.' He went on to say that the only heroine in the Waverley series with whom one could really sympathise, was Jeanie Deans. The tone was most depreciatory, all through. Possibly it was wilfulness on the part of the critic, or a desire to give his auditors a slap in the face; for I have in after time read a page of Trollope's on which Scott was praised highly. It is sometimes very difficult to know what is a man's real and abiding opinion.[48]

Yes it is. Both privately and publicly, while lamenting some dull stretches in Scott, Trollope was a staunch admirer. He was having some fun with these people and giving them no hint that he was doing so. As for the swearing, this may have been deliberately intended to disturb his Scots hearers' religiosity. Yates, in the *World* article quoted above, declared: 'I do not remember ever having heard Trollope swear. He may have [used the word *damned*] but he certainly was not an habitual swearer.'[49] But evidence on this point is contradictory. Arthur Waugh, for example, recorded E. F. Gibbons, who worked for Chapman & Hall for more than half a century, as saying that Trollope was a 'terror to the staff, among whom he splashed around like a Triton in a shoal of minnows'. Trollope 'used to tramp into the office, as soon as the doors were open, clad in his pink coat, with a sheaf of proofs in his great side pocket . . . he would bang on the table with his hunting crop, and swear like a sergeant-major because there was no one in authority yet arrived to receive his hectic instructions.'[50]

John Blackwood's daughter told of other dinners in Trollope's honour at her father's house, occasions on which the auditors were aware of Trollope's play:

> Mr Trollope's big voice drowned every one else, as he chaffed my father down the length of the dinner-table. He had jested over golf, what would he not do next? He used to make daring assaults upon the most cherished articles of the Blackwood faith. Blind unswerving devotion to the Sovereign was one of his favourite points of attack. 'Now, Blackwood, how could the death of the Sovereign possibly affect *you*?' he would say. 'If you heard of it to-morrow morning you know perfectly well you would eat just as good a breakfast – you would not even deny yourself that second kidney.' It was in vain to protest that in face of such a calamity the very thought of broiled kidneys was distasteful. Mr Trollope bore everything before him, and prepared for another attack. The Conservative party and Dizzy was a tempting subject for a tilt. 'You *know*, Blackwood, you think exactly about Dizzy as I do; you *know* you would be very glad to hear he had been had up for – for shoplifting.' *Tableau!* all holding up their hands, and Mr Trollope delighted with the sensation he had produced.[51]

Michael Sadleir, without giving his source, recorded this anecdote:

The children at a house where he would often dine can still recall hanging over the banisters as the guests came to the big drawing-room and seeing Trollope – all rosy cheeks and bushy whiskers – pause for a moment at a mirror by the door, ruffle his hair and plunge into the room with a huge roar of greeting.[52]

It was in fact the house of George Smith, and the story came from his daughter, Mrs Reginald Smith.[53] Trollope deliberately ruffled his hair before making his stage entrance (Trollope's entrances are often commented upon). His social manner was largely an act. To some extent the same may be said of everyone, but in Trollope's case the assertion is more literally true. To be sure, it was an act that suited well his temperament; moreover, his increasing deafness doubtless exacerbated his loudness. But his manner served chiefly to shield the shy and insecure man who was the product of those miserable years at Harrow and Winchester and who – rather against the odds – had succeeded in becoming a respected official of the Post Office, and later a famous author of novels. In time the act or stance became habitual, exuberated so to speak into a 'persona' all but inseparable from the 'real' Trollope. Still, his behaviour at social functions (especially those of notables) had about it an unusual degree of 'performance'.

In private conversation Trollope was more gentle, more 'well mannered', though very forthright. Young Walter Pollock, a neighbour at Montagu Square and the son of Trollope's friends Sir Frederick and Lady Pollock, wrote in a memorial essay:

To younger men his ways and manner had the special charm that, without for a moment losing dignity, he put them on an equality with himself. He happened to be older, and therefore more experienced, than they were – I do not think it ever occurred to him that he was more clever or more gifted – and whatever help might come to them from his greater experience was at their service as between comrade and comrade. It was impossible for the shyest young man to be with him without feeling at ease. Once a young writer who was admitted to his friendship went to him and said, 'A book of yours has been sent to me for review, and I don't think I ought to review it, but I have come to ask you.' He leaned back in his chair and looked hard through his spectacles, as was his wont, and said, 'No, my boy, I don't think you ought to review a book of mine, any more than I ought to review a book of yours.'

Pollock went on to speak of the atmosphere of 'cheerfulness, of good humour, of light-heartedness' that prevailed at visits to his study: 'He loved fun; he loved laughing; he loved his kind. There was not a scrap of sentimentality about him, but there was plenty of sensibility, as well as sense.'[54]

With women Trollope was more tactful, less abrupt (his susceptibility to feminine charms was considerable). Cecilia Meetkerke, a distant relative whom Trollope assisted in having her poems published, wrote that during the Montagu Square years, 1873–80, 'any intimate friend' was welcome to Trollope's 'midday breakfast' – eaten after the novelist had worked at his writing for three hours. 'And those who came for counsel, or sympathy, might count on both, and solid information and assistance too, which might always be had for asking.' Moreover:

> A not too hurried interview might be obtained in the quaint and quiet book-room. . . . and after a search upon the chimneypiece amongst a whole army of spectacles for the exact pair which should enable him to read the face of his guest, he would take his own arm-chair: not however occupying it for long, but jumping up violently, and taking up his usual position on the hearthrug, too impetuous even for the appearance of ease.

Cecilia Meetkerke bristled at 'offhand ignorant criticism' such as Morley's account of the visit to Mill; such impressions ought to be balanced by testimony of friends and relations:

> It should be told that he was a perfect gentleman in every fibre of his nature, that he was astoundingly chivalrous, and that his manner, however vehement, was never ungentle. . . . A fear of hurting anybody's feelings was one of his strongest character-istics, and though he dearly liked a 'delicious feud', however violent his words might be, his sentiments were always soft.

She asserted that after Trollope had been told he had angina pectoris (a diagnosis disputed by a specialist who said his heart was 'weak' and that 'hard work had made an old man of him'), he was 'impressively' warned to avoid over-work and exertion:

The injunction was perfectly vain. He was extraordinarily impatient and reckless of his own condition; would still dash out of railway-carriages before the stopping of the train, would hurry in and out of cabs, and give way in all things to his usual impetuosity.[55]

From other friends and relatives come a few recollections of Trollope at play. Mary Porter, John Blackwood's daughter, wrote of his visits to her father's house, remembered from her girlhood days:

> The echo of Mr Trollope's laugh seems to come back to me as I strive to recall his genial presence, and the incidents of his visits: the walks, the games of golf he insisted on playing on the Ladies' Links, pretending to faint when he made a bad shot, his immense weight causing a sort of earthquake on the sandy ground.[56]

Mrs M. Evangeline Bradhurst, granddaughter of Trollope's friend Lady Wood, recalled Trollope as a house guest:

> On a hunting morning Trollope used to be in the best of spirits, and as he dressed it was his habit to wander into the rooms of his men friends while getting ready, chatting and laughing, for, he declared, it was such waste of boon companionship not to make the most of every minute available.
>
> It was a great amusement to those in the house to listen to him when wandering back to his room; he talked to his garments, his poor sight making it hard for him to lay his hands on the various parts of his hunting kit, such as, 'Oh, Mrs Sock, where have you got to? Not under there? No. Perhaps the chest of drawers. Why, I do declare, there you are hiding near the curtain. I've got you, ha! ha! ha!' 'Now, Mr Top Boot, where is your twin? Can't go hunting alone, you know. A fine thing to run away on a hunting morning.' Then snatches of song in a gutteral [*sic*] voice, always horribly out of tune – 'A hunting we will go, ho! ho!' with a delighted bellow on the final 'ho!' Then down to breakfast, where the children of the house were wildly impatient to be on their ponies . . . and their young riders inclined to scamp their foods, being reminded 'no-one-can't-go-hunting who don't eat a good breakfast'.[57]

One of Trollope's nephews, probably a son of John Tilley, recorded that

> the children's parties at Waltham [i.e., during the 1860s] were so like those at Noningsby in *Orley Farm* – with blind-man's buff and snap-dragon by candlelight at Christmas time, and 'Commerce' on any and every occasion – that he has only to re-read that novel to live again those childhood days. Trollope would join in all the games, contriving with great ingenuity that at 'Commerce' the children got the winning cards.[58]

In which connection it is worth noting how Morley and Mrs Ward closed their somewhat lukewarm review, quoted above, of the *Autobiography*: 'He was a staunch friend, and children delighted in him.'

Reactions to Trollope, then, were mixed, in keeping with the sensitivity of the observer and the degree of intimacy and frequency of contact. Those who met him only in public and briefly were sometimes dismayed at his aggressiveness. (Sometimes the aggressive manner went beyond conversational sparring. Mrs Ward wrote: 'One day we were driving through Lord Cowper's fine estate of Panshanger, when we saw to our intense amusement Anthony Trollope about to have a fight with a broad-shouldered rubicund tradesman. Anthony had divested himself of his coat and was shaking his fists in his opponent's face, as he danced around him. Though we never heard which gladiator won, the betting was all on Anthony, who had gained a reputation for never risking defeat when he made a challenge.'[59]) On the other hand, those who had frequent contact with Trollope and who were discriminating saw and marked the contrast between the outer and inner man: Sala, Bryce, Frith and Payn were among these. Others said essentially the same thing. Percy Fitzgerald: 'Trollope had an outspoken manner, but was good-natured and friendly.' (Fitzgerald quoted with approval Richard Garnett's article in the *Dictionary of National Biography* – 'His vociferous roughness repelled many, but was the disguise of real tenderness' – and his apt reference to Trollope's 'aggressive cordiality'. [60]) Walter Sichel: 'He struck me as outwardly a curmudgeon, inwardly the soul of good fellowship.'[61] Rider Haggard: 'Mr Trollope was a man who concealed a kind heart under a somewhat rough manner.'[62]

Two writers undertook a more extended analysis of Trollope's character. Escott's biography, *Anthony Trollope: His Work, Associates and Literary Originals*, published in 1913, is notorious for its inaccuracies in dates, identifications and other factual matters. But there is no reason to doubt the honesty or accuracy of his observations about Trollope's personality. Escott not only knew Trollope fairly well, but years had given him some distance from his subject and also freed him from the constraints of his 1879 *Time* article, written while Trollope was still living. Hence the book is not an uncritical panegyric. He says, for example, that Trollope was 'morbidly sensitive', that 'throughout life it was Trollope's tendency to ponder a petty vexation or trivial crossing of his own will till it became a grievance', that Trollope inherited from his father 'an irritable intolerance of fools and bores'. Escott draws a picture of Trollope at the height of his ascendancy: a popular writer, a person in authority at the Post Office, a man of excellent health, with easy access to his beloved hunting, more than ample income and increasing savings, a thriving club and social life – all that he could have asked for:

> And yet Trollope's life was chronically saddened by recurrent moods of indefinable dejection and gloom. A sardonic melancholy he had himself imputed to Thackeray. In his own case the sardonic element was wanting, but the melancholy was habitually there, darkening his outlook alike upon the present and the future. 'It is, I suppose,' he said, addressing the friend to whom, more than to any other, he unbosomed himself, Sir J. E. Millais, 'some weakness of temperament that makes me, without intelligible cause, such a pessimist at heart'.

Escott continues:

> His manner, habitually abrupt and sometimes imperious, concealed an almost feminine sensibility to the opinions of others, a self-consciousness altogether abnormal in a seasoned and practical man of the world, as well as a strong love of approbation, whether from stranger or friend. The inevitable disappointment of these instincts and desires at once pained and ruffled him beyond his power to conceal, and so produced what his physician and friend, Sir Richard Quain, once happily called 'Trollope's genial air of grievance against the world in

general, and those who personally valued him in particular.'[63]

Escott's appraisal of Trollope's character seems corroborated by the evidence. But perhaps that by Julian Hawthorne – remarkable in that it was formed from much slighter acquaintance – is even more telling. Hawthorne met Trollope at a gathering of literary men in the rooms of a publisher in 1879. He wrote that Trollope

seemed to be in a state of some excitement; he spoke volubly and almost boisterously, and his voice was full-toned and powerful, though pleasant to the ear. He turned himself, as he spoke, with a burly briskness, from one side to another, addressing himself first to this auditor and then to that, his words bursting forth from beneath his white moustache with such an impetus of hearty breath that it seemed as if all opposing arguments must be blown quite away. Meanwhile he flourished in the air an ebony walking-stick, with much vigor of gesticulation, and narrowly missing, as it appeared, the pates of listeners. He was clad in evening dress, though the rest of the company was, for the most part, in mufti; and he was an exceedingly fine-looking old gentleman. At the first glance, you would have taken him to be some civilized and modernized Squire Western, nourished with beef and ale, and roughly hewn out of the most robust and least refined variety of human clay. Looking at him more narrowly, however, you would have reconsidered this judgment. Though his general contour and aspect were massive and sturdy, the lines of his features were delicately cut; his complexion was remarkably pure and fine, and his face was susceptible of very subtle and sensitive changes of expression. Here was a man of abundant physical strength and vigor, no doubt, but carrying within him a nature more than commonly alert and impressible. His organization, though thoroughly healthy, was both complex and high-wrought; his character was simple and straightforward to a fault, but he was abnormally conscientious, and keenly alive to others' opinion concerning him. It might be thought that he was overburdened with self-esteem, and unduly opinionated; but, in fact, he was but over-anxious to secure the goodwill and agreement of all with whom he came in contact. There was some peculiarity in him – some element or bias in his composition that made him different from other men; but, on the other hand, there was an ardent solicitude to annul or reconcile this difference, and to prove himself to be, in fact, of absolutely the same cut and quality as all the rest of the world. Hence when he was in a demonstrative, expository or argumentative mood, he could not sit quiet in the face of a divergence between himself and his associates; he was incorrigibly strenuous to obliterate or harmonize the irreconcilable points between him and others; and since these points remained irreconcilable, he remained in a constant state of storm and stress on the subject.

It was impossible to help liking such a man at first sight; and I believe that no man in London society was more generally liked than Anthony Trollope. There was something pathetic in his attitude as above indicated; and a fresh and boyish quality always invested him. His artlessness was boyish, and so were his acuteness and his transparent but somewhat belated good-sense. He was one of those rare persons who not only have no reserves, but who can afford to dispense with them. After he had shown you all he had in him, you would have seen nothing that was not gentlemanly, honest and clean. He was a quick-tempered man, and the ardor and hurry of his temperament made him seem more so than he really was; but he was never more angry than he was forgiving and generous. He was hurt by little things, and little things pleased him; he was suspicious and perverse, but in a manner that rather endeared him to you than otherwise. Altogether, to a casual acquaintance, who knew nothing of his personal history, he was something of a paradox – an entertaining contradiction.[64]

One thing comes through all the accounts quite consistently: Trollope, more than most men, prepared a face to meet the faces that he met. He assumed a role, put on a mask, acted out a part. It was a strategy to keep people, friendly or otherwise, at arm's length, to camouflage the insecurities and fears that lay so close to the surface. It was his way of coming to terms with his early years, which wretched circumstances together with his acute sensitivity to mental pain had made a horror. When he came to wield authority in Ireland – among people who knew nothing of his failures and frustrations, among people worse off than himself – he apparently resolved to put the past aside. At first the effort must have been difficult. But he was good at his work; he was forceful;

his physical and mental energies were tireless. With time his deliberate behaviour became as it were an acquired characteristic of his personality. The blustering, loud, affirmative, preemptory manner of the postal surveyor brought success in the service – why not carry this style over among his broadening circle of social and literary friends? It is not enough to say that the rough exterior cloaked a tender interior. This is true of many extroverted people. Trollope's special peculiarity lay in the depth of that inner shyness and insecurity and in the lengths to which he went to cover his fears. Of course, like all writers, he was 'different' from his books; they came from the inner man whom Trollope generally managed to keep private, layered over with boisterous distractions, and hidden even from relatively close friends. He differed from most people in that he more deliberately, more consciously, kept the world from his hypersensitive, somewhat melancholy self. The loudness, the apparent insistence on the commonplace, the shouting, the violent gesticulation, the belittling of his own accomplishment, the loud joking, the bullying, the forthright, almost physical attack he made upon all chores of work and play, the passionate hunting (in spite of unsuitably heavy weight and poor eyesight), the *insistent* manner in which he did everything – these kept the world at bay. Whatever some may have found objectionable in his *modus vivendi*, his manner of meeting the world, the most remarkable thing about this act, or stance, or strategy, or whatever we choose to call it, is that it worked, and worked well. It enabled him to keep his balance, to prosper; it enabled him to write his novels.

## NOTES

1  *An Autobiography*, ed. Frederick Page (London: Oxford University Press, 1950) p. 1.
2  Ibid., p. 60.
3  Ibid., pp. 365–6.
4  Letter of 8 June 1876, quoted with permission of Trinity College, University of Melbourne.
5  Ruth apRoberts writes similarly of Trollope and his characters: 'I think we ought to make a declaration that an author cannot be more naïve than his characters. Trollope must be at least as capable of subtle rhetoric as his dazzling lawyer Mr Chaffanbrass, or the wily Prime Minister Mr Daubeny; he must have at least the terrible acquaintance with the human demonic that oppresses Josiah Crawley; he must have at least the wit of Glencora Palliser, and at least her rueful understanding and love for that very trying

and very admirable man her husband.' See *The Moral Trollope* (Athens, Ohio: Ohio University Press, 1971) p. 35.

6 C. B. Tinker, 'Trollope', *Yale Review*, n.s. XXXVI (Mar. 1947) 432.

7 *Kerry Evening Post*, 28 July 1849.

8 Justin MacCarthy, *Reminiscences* (New York: Harper, 1900) p. 372.

9 J. G. Uren, 'My Early Recollections of the Post Office in the West of England', *Blackfriars*, IX (July–Dec. 1889) 157–8.

10 Ibid., p. 158.

11 Ibid., pp. 158–9. Trollope gave a bit of this speech to Mrs Crump, postmistress in *The Small House at Allington*.

12 Anonymous, 'Anthony Trollope as a Post Office Surveyor', *St Martin's-le-Grand*, XIV (Oct. 1904) 453–4. I am grateful to Coral Lansbury for bringing to my attention this article and that by J. G. Uren.

13 R. S. Smyth, 'The Provincial Service Fifty Years Ago', *St Martin's-le-Grand*, XII (Oct. 1903) 375–6. Trollope followed up the conversation with a letter of 21 June 1865, printed by Smyth, which closed: 'I think you should endeavour, if you remain where you are, to teach yourself not to regard the service with dissatisfaction.'

14 'R. W. J.', 'Early Post Office Days', *St Martin's-le-Grand*, VI (July 1896) 295.

15 Susan E. Gay, *Old Falmouth* (London: Headley Bros, 1903) p. 216.

16 *Sir Rowland Hill: The Story of a Great Reform*, Told by His Daughter (London: T. Fisher Unwin, 1907) pp. 277–8.

17 The story of the Cornhill dinner at which Thackeray asked Smith if Dr Johnson were getting his dinner behind the screen; Trollope cancelled in manuscript his account of the incident, but it is included as Appendix I in the Page edition of the *Autobiography*, pp. 369–7.

18 *Pall Mall Gazette*, 18 Feb. 1865.

19 *Morning Star*, 27 Feb. 1865.

20 *Edmund Yates: His Recollections and Experiences* (London: Bentley, 1884) II.223, 228–9.

21 *The World*, 24 Feb. 1892, p. 19.

22 N. John Hall, 'Letters of Thomas Adolphus Trollope to Henry Merivale Trollope, 1882–92', *University of Pennsylvania Library Chronicle*, XXXIX (Spring 1973) 116.

23 George Augustus Sala, *Things I Have Seen and People I Have Known* (London: Cassell, 1894) I.30–1.

24 Title page reproduced in Frederick Page edition of *An Autobiography* (1950). Henry Chaplin, 1st Viscount Chaplin (1840–1923), was a Conservative MP who had a passion for hunting; James Lowther (1840–1904) was a Conservative MP and a sportsman who trained racehorses. Sala's *Echoes of the Year 1883* (1884), which reprinted his columns in the *Illustrated London News*, questioned the poverty of Trollope's youth as set forth in *An Autobiography* by claiming that his mother's income from her writing would have been more than sufficient to offset his father's embarrassed circumstances; but this ignorantly or maliciously misreads the chronology (pp. 17–18). Yates began his antagonistic column in the *World* (quoted above) on the pretext of Sala's request that Yates 'say something in mitigation of the sweeping condemnation of the tone and manners of the deceased novelist which has lately been published by Dr Boyd'.

25  *The Amberley Papers*, ed. Bertrand and Patricia Russell (London: Hogarth Press, 1938) II.27.
26  *Macmillan's Magazine*, XLIX (Nov. 1883) 55–6. The review was written with Mrs Humphry Ward.
27  *The Autobiography of Alfred Austin* (London: Macmillan, 1911) I.166.
28  Letter quoted in George Somes Layard, *A Great 'Punch' Editor: Being the Life, Letters, and Diaries of Shirley Brooks* (London: Isaac Pitman, 1907) p. 526.
29  *Mark Twain in Eruption*, ed. Bernard DeVoto (New York: Harpers, 1940) pp. 332–3.
30  *Word Portraits of Famous Writers*, ed. Mabel E. Wotton (London: Bentley, 1887) pp. 313–16.
31  Letter quoted in Robert Ashley, *Wilkie Collins* (New York: Roy, 1952) p. 105.
32  Letter quoted in F. D. Tredrey, *The House of Blackwood, 1804–1954* (Edinburgh: Blackwood, 1954) p. 261.
33  *The Diaries of John Bright*, ed. Philip Bright (London: Cassell, 1930) p. 391.
34  James Bryce, *Studies in Contemporary Biography* (New York: Macmillan, 1903) pp. 118–19.
35  Frederick Locker-Lampson, *My Confidences* (London: Smith, Elder, 1896) pp. 331–3, 336.
36  Letter of 17 Jan. 1866, Weigall MSS, Kent County Archives.
37  Edmund Downey, *Charles Lever: His Life in His Letters* (Edinburgh: Blackwood, 1906) II.227.
38  W. P. Frith, *My Autobiography and Reminiscences* (New York: Harpers, 1888) p. 496.
39  James Bryce, *Studies in Contemporary Biography*, pp. 126–7.
40  T. H. S. Escott, 'A Novelist of the Day', *Time* I (Aug. 1879) 627–9.
41  Letter of 31 July 1879; quoted by permission of the British Library.
42  Frank O'Connor, *The Mirror in the Roadway: A Study of the Modern Novel* (New York: Knopf, 1956) pp. 167–8.
43  Letter of 20 Sep. 1861, quoted in Horace Elisha Scudder, *James Russell Lowell: A Biography* (Boston, Mass.: Houghton Mifflin, 1901) II.82–4.
44  Clara Louise Kellogg, *Memoirs of an American Prima Donna* (New York: Putnam, 1913) p. 48.
45  *Correspondence of Henry Taylor*, ed. Edward Dowden (London: Longmans, 1888) p. 296.
46  [W. Lucas Collins] Review of *An Autobiography*, *Blackwood's Magazine*, CXXXIV (Nov.1883) 594.
47  James Payn, *Some Literary Recollections* (New York: Harpers, 1884) p. 167.
48  A. K. H. Boyd, *Twenty-five Years of St Andrews* (London: Longmans, 1892) I.100–1.
49  *World*, 24 Feb. 1892, p. 19.
50  Arthur Waugh, *A Hundred Years of Publishing* (London: Chapman & Hall, 1930) p. 87.
51  Mrs Gerald Porter, *John Blackwood: Annals of a Publishing House* (Edinburgh: Blackwood, 1898) pp. 197–8.
52  Michael Sadleir, *Trollope: A Commentary*, 3rd edn (London: Oxford University Press, 1961) p. 333.
53  Mrs Smith told the story in precisely these words to Gordon Ray.

54   Walter Herries Pollock, 'Anthony Trollope', *Harper's New Monthly Magazine*, LXVI (May 1883) 912.
55   'Last Reminiscences of Anthony Trollope', *Temple Bar*, LXX (Jan.1884) 130–4 (this article has been mistakenly attributed to Alfred Austin). Cecilia Meetkerke quotes from a letter Trollope wrote to her in regard to his conversational manner with women: 'I own I like a good contradictory conversation in which for the moment the usual subserviency of coat and trousers to bodies [bodices?], skirts, and petticoats, may be – well – not forgotten – but for the moment put on one side.'
56   Porter, *Blackwood*, p. 197.
57   M. Evangeline Bradhurst, 'Anthony Trollope – The Hunting Man', *Essex Review*, XXXVIII (1928) 187.
58   Sadleir, *Commentary*, p.202.
59   Mrs E. M. Ward, *Memories of Ninety Years*, ed. Isabel G. McAlister (London: Hutchinson, 1924) p. 147.
60   Percy Fitzgerald, *The Garrick Club* (London: Stock, 1904) p. 78.
61   Walter Sichel, *The Sands of Time: Recollections and Reflections* (London: Hutchinson, 1923) p. 217.
62   Sir H. Rider Haggard, *The Days of My Life*, ed. C. J. Longman (London: Longmans, 1926) I.137.
63   T. H. S. Escott, *Anthony Trollope: His Work, Associates and Literary Originals* (London: John Lane, 1913) pp. 25, 248, 170–1.
64   Julian Hawthorne, *Confessions and Criticisms* (Boston, Mass.: Ticknor, 1887) pp. 140–3.

# Index

*Note* Titles of books and other publications, other than those by Trollope himself, are followed either by the author's name or by a description, such as 'periodical', placed in brackets. In sub-entries throughout the index, 'Trollope' has been abbreviated to 'T'.

Albury, Lady, 75–6
*All the Year Round* (periodical)
  serialisation of *The Duke's Children*, 121
  serialisation of *Mr Scarborough's Family*, 129
'The Alpine Club Man', 48n
  *see also Travelling Sketches*
Amberley, Lady, 159
Amedroz, Clara, 84, 120–1
*The American Senator*, 27
  on the pursuits of gentlemen, 93
  Taylor's collation of MS with first edition, 110
Arabin, Francis, 106
Austen, Jane, xiv, 71–2, 76
  on social distinctions, 86
Austin, Alfred, 159
Australia, T's trip to, 27
*Australia and New Zealand*, 24, 25
  comments on expeditions, 28
  criticism, 25
*Autobiography*, xiii, 134–45
  bitterness of early years, 146
  catalogue of early humiliations, 134–6
  comments on *The West Indies*; *North America*; *Australia and New Zealand*; and *South Africa*, 24
  criticism, 141
  evidences of genius, 142–3
  exaggerations, 8, 67n
  gives fuel to critics, 137
  hints of intimate life, 138
  importance in tracing personality, 146
  on arrival in Dublin, 53–4
  on classical education, 1, 2
  on dialogue, 95
  on father's acquisition of land, 70
  on feuds with Rowland Hill, 155
  on method of revision of writings, 111
  on role of 'gentlemen' in society, 86
  on roots of impulse to write, 109–10
  on *The Small House at Allington*, 119
  on 'trade' of writing, 109, 111
  on use of classics to produce 'harmonious' prose style, 6
  Oxford Trollope edition, 110
  personal reserve evident, 145
  review containing anecdotes of T's personality, 159
  scorn for education received, 7
  supplemented by letters, 147
*Ayala's Angel*
  host-guest relationship, 82
  matchmaking ability of hostess, 75–6
  superstitions related to particular places, 81–2
Aylmer, Captain, 73, 120–1

Ballandine, Lord, 61–2
Balzac, Honoré de, compared with T, 138, 140–1, 143
Banagher, Co. Offaly, 54
*Barchester Towers*, xii